The Budget and Economic Outlook: Fiscal Years 2008 to 2018

January 2008

The Congress of the United States ■ Congressional Budget Office

Notes

Unless otherwise indicated, all of the years referred to in describing the economic outlook are calendar years; other years referred to in this report are federal fiscal years (which run from October 1 to September 30).

Numbers in the text and tables may not add up to totals because of rounding.

Figures on the cover and in Chapters 2 and 4 use shaded vertical bars to indicate periods of recession as well as dashed vertical lines to separate actual from projected data. (A recession extends from the peak of a business cycle to its trough.)

Supplemental data for this analysis are available on the home page of the Congressional Budget Office's Web site (www.cbo.gov) under "Budget Projections" and "Economic Projections."

For sale by the Superintendent of Documents, U.S. Government Printing Office
Internet: bookstore.gpo.gov Phone: toll free (866) 512-1800; DC area (202) 512-1800
Fax: (202) 512-2104 Mail: Stop IDCC, Washington, DC 20402-0001

ISBN 978-0-16-079932-7

Preface

This volume is one of a series of reports on the state of the budget and the economy that the Congressional Budget Office (CBO) issues each year. It satisfies the requirement of section 202(e) of the Congressional Budget Act of 1974 for CBO to submit to the Committees on the Budget periodic reports about fiscal policy and to furnish baseline projections of the federal budget. In accordance with CBO's mandate to provide impartial analysis, the report makes no recommendations.

The baseline spending projections were prepared by the staff of CBO's Budget Analysis Division under the supervision of Peter Fontaine, Keith Fontenot, Theresa Gullo, Janet Airis, Tom Bradley, Kim Cawley, Jeffrey Holland, Sarah Jennings, Leo Lex, and Sam Papenfuss. The revenue estimates were prepared by the staff of the Tax Analysis Division under the supervision of Thomas Woodward, Frank Sammartino, Mark Booth, and David Weiner, with assistance from the Joint Committee on Taxation. (A detailed list of contributors to the revenue and spending projections appears in Appendix G.)

The economic outlook presented in Chapter 2 was prepared by CBO's Macroeconomic Analysis Division under the direction of Robert Dennis, Kim Kowalewski, and John Peterson. Robert Arnold and Christopher Williams produced the economic forecast and projections. David Brauer, Ufuk Demiroglu, Naomi Griffin, Douglas Hamilton, Juann Hung, Mark Lasky, Angelo Mascaro, Benjamin Page, Frank Russek, David Torregrosa, and Steven Weinberg contributed to the analysis. Adam Weber and Eric Miller provided research assistance.

An early version of CBO's economic forecast was discussed at a meeting of the agency's Panel of Economic Advisers. At that time, members of the panel were Martin Baily, Richard Berner, Jared Bernstein, Martin Feldstein, Robert J. Gordon, Robert E. Hall, Lawrence Katz, Allan H. Meltzer, Laurence H. Meyer, William D. Nordhaus, Rudolph G. Penner, Adam S. Posen, James Poterba, Alice Rivlin, Nouriel Roubini, Diane C. Swonk, and Stephen P. Zeldes. Luci Ellis and Mark Zandi attended the panel's meeting as guests. Although CBO's outside advisers provided considerable assistance, they are not responsible for the contents of this report.

Jeffrey Holland wrote the summary. Christina Hawley Anthony, with assistance from Eric Schatten, wrote Chapter 1 (David Newman authored Box 1-1). Naomi Griffin wrote Chapter 2, with assistance from Kim Kowalewski, Angelo Mascaro, John Peterson, and David Torregrosa. Barry Blom wrote Chapter 3, with assistance from Eric Schatten (Shinobu Suzuki wrote Box 3-2; Gregory Hitz and Dave Hull wrote Box 3-3). Mark Booth wrote Chapter 4, with assistance from Barbara Edwards, Zachary Epstein, Pamela Greene, and Andrew Langan. Amber Marcellino wrote Appendix A, with assistance from Pamela Greene. Eric Schatten wrote Appendix B. Luis Serna wrote Appendix C (Frank Russek wrote Box C-1). Frank Russek also wrote Appendix D, for which Luis Serna compiled the tables. Adam Weber and Eric Miller compiled Appendix E. Amber Marcellino compiled Appendix F. Mark Hadley and Eric Schatten produced the glossary.

Christine Bogusz, Kate Kelly, Loretta Lettner, Leah Mazade, and John Skeen edited the report. Denise Jordan-Williams and Linda Lewis Harris assisted in its preparation. Maureen Costantino designed the cover and prepared the report for publication. Lenny Skutnik printed the initial copies, Linda Schimmel handled the print distribution, and Annette Kalicki and Simone Thomas prepared the electronic version for CBO's Web site (www.cbo.gov).

Peter R. Orszag
Director

January 2008

Contents

Tables

Tables (Continued)

Tables (Continued)

Figures

Figures (Continued)

Boxes

Summary

The Congressional Budget Office (CBO) projects that after three years of declining budget deficits, a slowing economy this year will contribute to an increase in the deficit. Under an assumption that current laws and policies do not change, CBO projects that the budget deficit will rise to 1.5 percent of gross domestic product (GDP) in 2008 from 1.2 percent in 2007 (see Summary Table 1). Enactment of legislation to provide economic stimulus or additional funding for military operations in Iraq and Afghanistan could further increase the deficit for this year.

The state of the economy is particularly uncertain at the moment. The pace of economic growth slowed in 2007, and there are strong indications that it will slacken further in 2008. In CBO's view, the ongoing problems in the housing and financial markets and the high price of oil will curb spending by households and businesses this year and trim the growth of GDP. Although recent data suggest that the probability of a recession in 2008 has increased, CBO does not expect the slowdown in economic growth to be large enough to register as a recession.[1] Economic performance worse than that suggested in CBO's forecast could significantly decrease projected revenues and increase projected spending. Furthermore, policy changes intended to mitigate the economic slowdown would, by design, tend to increase the budget deficit in the short term.[2]

CBO expects the economy to rebound after 2008, as the negative effects of the turmoil in the housing and financial markets fade. Under the assumptions that govern CBO's baseline, the budget deficit will amount to 1.5 percent of GDP or less each year from 2009 to 2011. Subsequently, the budget will show a small surplus of 0.5 percent of GDP in 2012 and remain near that level each year through 2018 (the end of the current 10-year projection period).

The relatively sanguine outlook suggested by the 10-year baseline projections should not be interpreted as implying that the nation's underlying fiscal condition is sound, both because the United States continues to face severe long-term budgetary challenges and because many observers expect policy changes that would deviate from the current-law baseline over the next decade. Ongoing increases in health care costs, along with the aging of the population, are expected to put substantial pressure on the budget in coming decades; those trends are already evident in the current projection period. Economic growth alone will be insufficient to alleviate that pressure, as Medicare and Medicaid and, to a lesser extent, Social Security require ever greater resources under current law. A substantial reduction in the growth of spending, a significant increase in tax revenues relative to the size of the economy, or some combination of the two will be necessary to maintain the nation's long-term fiscal stability.[3]

CBO's baseline budget projections for the next 10 years are not a forecast of future outcomes; rather, they are based on the assumption that current laws and policies remain the same. The projections stem from long-standing procedures that were, until recently, specified in law, and they serve as a benchmark that lawmakers and

---

1. The National Bureau of Economic Research, which by convention is responsible for dating the peaks and troughs of the business cycle, defines a recession as "a significant decline in economic activity spread across the economy, lasting more than a few months, normally visible in real [inflation-adjusted] GDP, real income, employment, industrial production, and wholesale-retail sales."

2. See Congressional Budget Office, *Options for Responding to Short-Term Economic Weakness* (January 2008).

3. For a detailed discussion of the long-term pressures facing the federal budget, see Congressional Budget Office, *The Long-Term Budget Outlook* (December 2007).

Summary Table 1.

CBO's Baseline Budget Outlook

	Actual 2007	2008	2009	2010	2011	2012	2013	2014	2015	2016	2017	2018	Total, 2009- 2013	Total, 2009- 2018
	In Billions of Dollars													
Total Revenues	2,568	2,654	2,817	2,907	3,182	3,442	3,585	3,763	3,941	4,131	4,334	4,548	15,933	36,649
Total Outlays	2,731	2,873	3,015	3,148	3,299	3,355	3,524	3,666	3,824	4,037	4,183	4,325	16,341	36,376
Total Deficit (-) or Surplus	**-163**	**-219**	**-198**	**-241**	**-117**	**87**	**61**	**96**	**117**	**95**	**151**	**223**	**-408**	**274**
On-budget	-344	-414	-396	-450	-343	-151	-184	-154	-136	-160	-102	-27	-1,525	-2,104
Off-budget[a]	181	195	198	210	226	238	244	251	254	254	253	249	1,117	2,378
Debt Held by the Public at the End of the Year	5,035	5,232	5,443	5,698	5,827	5,751	5,701	5,613	5,503	5,414	5,269	5,050	n.a.	n.a.
	As a Percentage of Gross Domestic Product													
Total Revenues	18.8	18.7	19.0	18.6	19.3	19.9	19.9	20.0	20.0	20.1	20.2	20.3	19.4	19.8
Total Outlays	20.0	20.2	20.4	20.2	20.1	19.4	19.5	19.4	19.4	19.7	19.5	19.3	19.9	19.7
Total Deficit (-) or Surplus	**-1.2**	**-1.5**	**-1.3**	**-1.5**	**-0.7**	**0.5**	**0.3**	**0.5**	**0.6**	**0.5**	**0.7**	**1.0**	**-0.5**	**0.1**
Debt Held by the Public at the End of the Year	36.8	36.8	36.7	36.5	35.4	33.3	31.6	29.8	28.0	26.4	24.6	22.6	n.a.	n.a.
Memorandum: Gross Domestic Product (Billions of dollars)	13,670	14,201	14,812	15,600	16,445	17,256	18,043	18,856	19,685	20,540	21,426	22,355	82,156	185,018

Source: Congressional Budget Office.

Note: n.a. = not applicable.

a.   Off-budget surpluses comprise surpluses in the Social Security trust funds as well as the net cash flow of the Postal Service.

others can use to assess the potential impact of future policy decisions.[4] Following those procedures generates deficits and surpluses in the baseline that are predicated on two key projections:

■ That revenues will rise from 18.7 percent of GDP this year to almost 20 percent of GDP in 2012 and then remain near that historically high level through 2018. Much of the projected increase in revenues results from the growing impact of the alternative minimum tax (AMT) and, even more significantly, the expiration at the end of 2010 of various provisions originally enacted in the Economic Growth and Tax Relief Reconciliation Act of 2001 (EGTRRA) and the Jobs

and Growth Tax Relief Reconciliation Act of 2003 (JGTRRA).

■ That outlays for discretionary programs (those whose spending levels are set anew each year through appropriation acts) will decline from 7.6 percent of GDP last year to 6.1 percent by 2018—a lower percentage than any recorded in the past 40 years. Such a projection derives mainly from the assumption in the baseline that discretionary funding will grow at the rate of inflation, which is lower than the growth rate that CBO projects for nominal GDP. Implicit in the projection for discretionary spending is an assumption that no additional funding is provided for military operations in Iraq and Afghanistan in 2008 and that future appropriations for activities related to the war on terrorism remain equivalent, in real (inflation-adjusted) terms, to the $88 billion appropriated so far this year.

---

4.   The Balanced Budget and Emergency Deficit Control Act of 1985, which established rules that have governed the calculation of CBO's baseline, expired on September 30, 2006. Nevertheless, CBO continues to prepare baselines according to the methodology prescribed in that law.

Summary Figure 1.

Projected Growth of the U.S. Economy and Federal Spending for Major Mandatory Programs

(Cumulative nominal percentage growth from 2007 level)

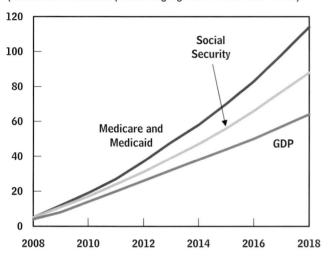

Source: Congressional Budget Office.

Policy choices that differ from the assumptions in the baseline would produce different budgetary outcomes. For example, if lawmakers continued to provide relief from the AMT (as they have done on a short-term basis for the past several years) and if the provisions of EGTRRA and JGTRRA that are scheduled to expire were instead extended, total revenues would be $3.6 trillion lower over the next 10 years than CBO now projects. Similarly, if discretionary spending (other than that for military operations in Iraq and Afghanistan and other spending labeled as emergency) grew at the rate of nominal GDP over the next 10 years, total discretionary outlays during that period would be about $1.4 trillion higher than in the baseline. Combined, those policy changes—and associated debt-service costs—would produce a deficit of $402 billion (2.3 percent of GDP) in 2012 and a cumulative deficit of $5.7 trillion (3.1 percent of GDP) over the 2009–2018 period.

The Budget Outlook

CBO estimates that if today's laws and policies did not change, federal spending would total $2.9 trillion in 2008 and revenues would total $2.7 trillion, resulting in a budget deficit of $219 billion. That deficit could increase

significantly if legislation is enacted to provide economic stimulus—as is currently under consideration. Furthermore, additional funding that is likely to be needed to finance military operations in Iraq and Afghanistan could add $30 billion to outlays this year.

Baseline Projections for the 2009–2018 Period

According to CBO's projections, under current laws and policies the deficit will drop slightly in 2009, to $198 billion. That decrease results primarily from two factors. On the revenue side of the budget, receipts from the AMT are estimated to increase by about $75 billion next year, largely because of the scheduled expiration of the relief provided through tax year 2007. On the spending side of the budget, outlays for military operations in Iraq and Afghanistan are about $10 billion lower in 2009 than in 2008 under the assumptions of the baseline.

The deficit is projected to rise modestly in 2010, as outlays grow by about 4.4 percent and revenues increase by about 3.2 percent. That projected growth rate for revenues is lower than in recent years, mainly because of a projected slowdown in corporate tax receipts (to a level that is more consistent with their historical relationship to GDP).

After 2010, spending related to the aging of the baby-boom generation will begin to raise the growth rate of total outlays. The baby boomers will start becoming eligible for Social Security retirement benefits in 2008, when the first members of that generation turn 62. As a result, the annual growth of Social Security spending is expected to accelerate from about 5.1 percent in 2008 to 6.4 percent by 2018.

More important, because the cost of health care is likely to continue rising rapidly, spending for Medicare and Medicaid is anticipated to grow even faster—generally in the range of 7 percent to 8 percent annually. Total outlays for those two health care programs are projected to more than double during the baseline period, increasing by 114 percent, while GDP is projected to grow somewhat more than half as fast, by 64 percent (see Summary Figure 1). Under the assumptions underlying CBO's baseline, spending for Medicare and Medicaid will rise to 5.9 percent of GDP in 2018, compared with about 4.6 percent this year, and spending for Social Security will rise to 4.9 percent of GDP from 4.3 percent this year.

Summary Figure 2.

Total Revenues and Outlays as a Percentage of Gross Domestic Product

(Percent)

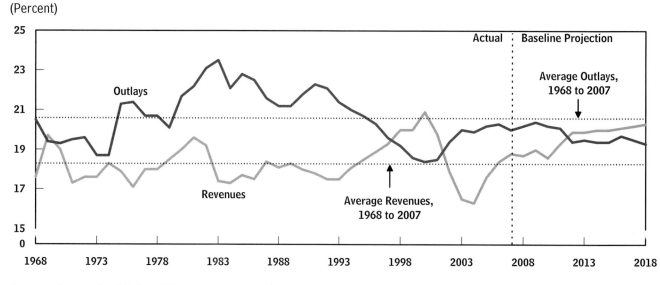

Source: Congressional Budget Office.

Revenues are projected to increase sharply after 2010 under the assumption that various tax provisions expire as scheduled. In the baseline, total revenues grow by 9.4 percent in 2011 and by 8.2 percent in 2012, thereby bringing the budget into surplus. Beyond 2012, revenues are projected to grow at roughly the same pace as outlays (between 4 percent and 5 percent a year), keeping the budget in the black through 2018.

Outlays over the 2009–2018 period are projected to range between 19.3 percent and 20.4 percent of GDP under the assumptions of the baseline—somewhat lower than the 20.6 percent average of the past 40 years (see Summary Figure 2). Mandatory spending (funding determined by laws other than annual appropriation acts) is projected to grow by nearly 6 percent a year over that period, which is faster than the economy as a whole. By contrast, discretionary appropriations are assumed simply to keep pace with inflation and, to a lesser extent, with the growth of wages. Thus, discretionary outlays are projected to increase by about 2.2 percent a year, on average, or less than half as fast as nominal GDP.

In CBO's projections, revenues average 18.8 percent of GDP in 2009 and 2010 (close to the 18.7 percent level expected for this year) before the sharp jump in 2011 and

2012 with the expiration of tax provisions originally enacted in EGTRRA and JGTRRA. After that, revenues continue growing faster than the overall economy for three reasons: increases in total real income combined with the progressive structure of the tax code, the increasing reach of the AMT, and taxable withdrawals of retirement savings as the population ages. Under the assumptions used for the baseline, CBO projects that revenues will equal 20.3 percent of GDP by 2018—a level reached only once since World War II.

Federal government debt that is held by the public (mainly in the form of Treasury securities sold directly in the capital markets) is expected to equal about 37 percent of GDP at the end of this year. Thereafter, the baseline's projections of short-term deficits followed by emerging surpluses diminish the government's need for additional borrowing, causing debt held by the public to shrink to 22.6 percent of GDP by 2018.

Changes in the Baseline Budget Outlook Since August

The budget outlook for 2008 has deteriorated somewhat since CBO issued its previous projections in August, but the pattern of deficits and surpluses in the outlook for the

Summary Table 2.

CBO's Economic Projections for Calendar Years 2008 to 2018

(Percentage change)

	Estimated 2007	Forecast		Projected Annual Average	
		2008	2009	2010-2013	2014-2018
Nominal GDP					
Billions of dollars	13,828	14,330	14,997	18,243 [a]	22,593 [b]
Percentage change	4.8	3.6	4.7	5.0	4.4
Real GDP	2.2	1.7	2.8	3.1	2.5
GDP Price Index	2.5	1.9	1.8	1.9	1.9
PCE Price Index[c]	2.5	2.6	1.8	1.9	1.9
Core PCE Price Index[d]	2.1	1.9	1.9	1.9	1.9
Consumer Price Index[e]	2.8	2.9	2.3	2.2	2.2
Core Consumer Price Index[f]	2.3	2.2	2.2	2.2	2.2
Unemployment Rate (Percent)	4.6	5.1	5.4	4.9	4.8
Interest Rates (Percent)					
Three-month Treasury bills	4.4	3.2	4.2	4.6	4.7
Ten-year Treasury notes	4.6	4.2	4.9	5.2	5.2

Sources: Congressional Budget Office; Department of Commerce, Bureau of Economic Analysis; Department of Labor, Bureau of Labor Statistics; Federal Reserve Board.

Notes: GDP = gross domestic product; PCE = personal consumption expenditure.

Percentage changes are measured from one year to the next.

Year-by-year economic projections for 2008 to 2018 appear in Appendix E.

a. Level in 2013.

b. Level in 2018.

c. The personal consumption expenditure chained price index.

d. The personal consumption expenditure chained price index excluding prices for food and energy.

e. The consumer price index for all urban consumers.

f. The consumer price index for all urban consumers excluding prices for food and energy.

following 10 years is about the same.[5] At $219 billion, the deficit projected for 2008 is $64 billion higher than what CBO estimated in August. Because the August projections already reflected some expected slowing of the economy in 2008, most of that difference stems from legislation that extended relief to individuals from the AMT for one year.

For the 2009–2017 period, the baseline's bottom line has improved slightly, compared with CBO's projections in August. In the current baseline, projected revenues are

lower, mostly as a result of lower estimates of corporate profits. Projected outlays are also lower, primarily because of the use of partial-year funding for military operations in Iraq and Afghanistan; this baseline extrapolates the $88 billion appropriated thus far for 2008, whereas the August baseline extended the entire funding provided for 2007 (about $170 billion). With the effect of partial-year funding excluded, the current baseline would show an increase in the cumulative deficit for 2008 through 2017 of more than $850 billion (0.5 percent of GDP).

The Economic Outlook

Underlying CBO's baseline projections is a forecast that U.S. economic growth will slow in calendar year 2008

---

5. Those projections were published in Congressional Budget Office, *The Budget and Economic Outlook: An Update* (August 2007).

but pick up in 2009. Specifically, CBO anticipates that GDP will grow by 1.7 percent in real terms for 2008 as a whole, about half a percentage point less than the growth recorded last year. For 2009, CBO forecasts that GDP growth will rebound to 2.8 percent (see Summary Table 2).

Problems in the housing and financial markets, along with high oil prices, triggered much of the recent slowdown. Between mid-2006 and the end of 2007, residential investment (which includes the construction of new housing units, improvements to existing units, and brokers' commissions) declined, but the drop was largely offset by growth in both consumer spending and business fixed investment (businesses' spending on structures, equipment, and software). Those two sectors are unlikely to provide as much support to economic growth this year. Residential investment is expected to continue to decline through much of 2008; in addition, the growth of consumer spending, sustained thus far by solid growth in people's real income as well as by their borrowing and use of savings, is likely to fall off, curtailed by a drop in housing wealth (home equity), increased costs for borrowing, the high price of oil, and slower growth of real income. The resulting weak domestic demand for goods and services in turn is expected to slow the growth of business fixed investment, which is likely to further diminish the pace of overall economic growth this year.

In contrast, the relative economic strength of the United States' major trading partners—in particular, developing countries with emerging market economies—when combined with the dollar's decline will partially offset the sluggishness in domestic demand expected in 2008 and support U.S. economic growth by stimulating exports. Emerging economies have become increasingly less dependent on demand in the United States to fuel their expansions and, as a result, have become less vulnerable to slowdowns in U.S. economic growth. Moreover, the pace of the decline begun in 2002 in the value of the dollar relative to the currencies of major trading partners—which helps make U.S. exports less expensive—has quickened. Those developments, accompanied by less domestic demand for imports, are likely to reduce the U.S. current-account deficit (broadly, the summary measure of the United States' trade with the rest of the world).

Inflation (as measured by the year-to-year change in the price index for personal consumption expenditures) is likely to be about the same this year as last year; in 2009, CBO forecasts, the rate will fall, to 1.8 percent, as inflation in energy and food prices eases. The unemployment rate, which was 4.6 percent last year, will average 5.1 percent in 2008 and reach 5.3 percent by the end of the year, CBO estimates. Interest rates on Treasury securities are expected to remain low this year and to increase in 2009 as the economy works through and emerges from its current difficulties. In CBO's forecast, the rate on 3-month Treasury bills averages 3.2 percent in 2008 and moves higher, to 4.2 percent, in 2009. Similarly, the rate on 10-year Treasury notes moves from an average of 4.2 percent in 2008 to 4.9 percent in 2009.

For 2010 to 2018, CBO projects that real growth will average 2.7 percent and the personal consumption expenditure price index, 1.9 percent. CBO also projects that in the latter years of the projection period, the unemployment rate will average 4.8 percent and that the interest rates on 3-month Treasury bills and 10-year Treasury notes will average 4.7 percent and 5.2 percent, respectively.

The Budget Outlook

The Congressional Budget Office (CBO) projects that if current laws and policies remained unchanged, the federal budget would show a deficit of $219 billion for 2008 (see Table 1-1). That deficit would amount to 1.5 percent of gross domestic product (GDP), slightly larger than the shortfall of 1.2 percent of GDP ($163 billion) posted in 2007.

That increase in the deficit in 2008 would come after three consecutive years of declining deficits. Without changes in law, revenues would increase by only 3.4 percent, but outlays would grow by 5.2 percent. Those estimates—along with the other projections that make up the agency's budget baseline—reflect an assumption that no further legislation affecting the budget will be enacted. Accordingly, the current deficit projection excludes the effects of potential policy changes to spending or revenues, including any steps lawmakers may take to bolster a weakening economy through fiscal stimulus.[1]

In addition, so far this year funding has been provided for only a portion of the anticipated costs for operations in Iraq and Afghanistan and the war on terrorism.[2] Supplemental appropriations for such purposes could increase outlays by about $30 billion this year.

Beyond 2008, deficits under baseline projections continue each year until 2012, when they yield to modest surpluses through 2018. Under the assumptions that govern those projections, the deficit falls from $219 billion in 2008 (1.5 percent of GDP) to $198 billion in 2009 (1.3 percent of GDP) and $117 billion (0.7 percent of

GDP) in 2011 and then changes to small surpluses in 2012 and later years (see Figure 1-1). By 2018, the surplus reaches 1.0 percent of GDP.

CBO's budget baseline, however, is not intended as a forecast of future outcomes, but rather as a benchmark that encompasses current laws and policies. It is predicated on two key projections that stem from long-standing statutory procedures, one affecting revenues and one affecting discretionary outlays.

■ Under current law, revenues will increase from 18.7 percent of GDP in 2008 to almost 20 percent of GDP in 2012 and remain near that historically high level through 2018. Much of that increase results from two factors: the growing impact of the alternative minimum tax (AMT) and, even more significant, the scheduled expiration in December 2010 of provisions originally enacted in the Economic Growth and Tax Relief Reconciliation Act of 2001 (EGTRRA) and the Jobs and Growth Tax Relief Reconciliation Act of 2003 (JGTRRA).

■ Discretionary outlays, measured relative to the economy, will decline from 7.6 percent in 2007 to 6.1 percent by 2018, a ratio lower than any recorded in the past 40 years. That projection results primarily from the assumption that discretionary funding grows at the rate of inflation, a pace slower than the estimated rate of growth of GDP.

It is likely that appropriations will differ from those assumed in the baseline and that lawmakers will enact changes in spending and tax policies. Although CBO's baseline projections do not incorporate such potential changes in policy, this chapter shows the implications that some alternative policy assumptions would have for the budget over the next 10 years. For example, CBO has constructed two possible scenarios for future spending

---

1. See Congressional Budget Office, *Options for Responding to Short-Term Economic Weakness* (January 2008).

2. In addition to the $88 billion in funding already provided this year, the Administration has requested $105 billion for military operations in Iraq and Afghanistan and other activities associated with the war on terrorism.

Table 1-1.

Projected Deficits and Surpluses in CBO's Baseline

(Billions of dollars)

	Actual 2007	2008	2009	2010	2011	2012	2013	2014	2015	2016	2017	2018	Total, 2009-2013	Total, 2009-2018
On-Budget Deficit	-344	-414	-396	-450	-343	-151	-184	-154	-136	-160	-102	-27	-1,525	-2,104
Off-Budget Surplus[a]	181	195	198	210	226	238	244	251	254	254	253	249	1,117	2,378
Total Deficit (-) or Surplus	**-163**	**-219**	**-198**	**-241**	**-117**	**87**	**61**	**96**	**117**	**95**	**151**	**223**	**-408**	**274**
Memorandum:														
Social Security Surplus	187	197	199	210	226	238	244	250	253	254	253	249	1,118	2,378
Postal Service Outlays	5	2	2	1	*	*	*	*	*	*	*	*	2	*
Total Deficit (-) or Surplus as a Percentage of GDP	-1.2	-1.5	-1.3	-1.5	-0.7	0.5	0.3	0.5	0.6	0.5	0.7	1.0	-0.5	0.1
Debt Held by the Public as a Percentage of GDP[b]	36.8	36.8	36.7	36.5	35.4	33.3	31.6	29.8	28.0	26.4	24.6	22.6	n.a.	n.a.
Probability of a Budget Deficit (Percent)	n.a.	97	83	79	62	42	45	c	c	c	c	c	n.a.	n.a.

Source: Congressional Budget Office.

Note: GDP = gross domestic product; n.a. = not applicable; * = between -$500 million and zero.

a.   Off-budget surpluses comprise surpluses in the Social Security trust funds as well as the net cash flow of the Postal Service.

b.   Debt held at the end of the year.

c.   Probabilities for years after 2013 cannot be calculated because of an insufficient history of past comparisons between projections and outcomes.

related to military operations in Iraq and Afghanistan and other activities associated with the war on terrorism. Those scenarios incorporate different assumptions about how rapidly troop levels might be reduced over the next several years—and have different effects on the path of spending projections.

Alternative assumptions about tax policy also would change CBO's projections. If all of the tax provisions that are set to expire over the next 10 years were extended and the AMT was indexed for inflation, the budget outlook for 2018 would change from a surplus of $223 billion to a deficit of $617 billion. In addition, debt held by the public at the end of 2018 would nearly double from 22.6 percent of GDP to 44.4 percent, and the 10-year, or cumulative, bottom line would change from a surplus of $0.3 trillion to a deficit of $4.6 trillion.

Over the long term, the nation faces substantial fiscal difficulties, which are already becoming apparent in CBO's baseline. Throughout the coming decade, spending for the government's health care programs and spending on the nation's elderly population will increasingly strain the federal budget. In CBO's projections, outlays for Medicare grow at an average rate of almost 7 percent per year between 2010 and 2018. Projected federal spending for Medicaid increases even more rapidly. Also, beginning this year, the first baby boomers become eligible for Social Security retirement benefits, and increasing numbers of beneficiaries will help boost the annual rate of growth of spending for Social Security from about 5.1 percent this year to 6.4 percent in 2018.

Beyond 2018, those trends will accelerate. Health care costs are likely to continue growing faster than GDP—as they have for the past 40 years. Indeed, the rate at which

Figure 1-1.

The Total Deficit or Surplus as a Share of Gross Domestic Product, 1968 to 2018

(Percent)

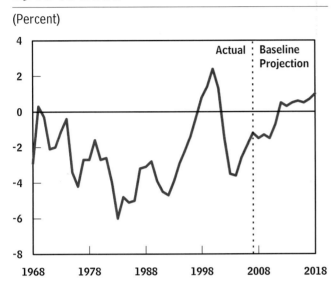

Sources: Congressional Budget Office.

health care costs grow relative to national income will be the most important determinant of future federal spending. In addition, as the percentage of the population age 65 or older continues to increase, spending for Medicare, Medicaid, and Social Security will, under current law, exert such pressure on the federal budget as to make the current path of fiscal policy unsustainable.[3] Substantial changes in federal spending and tax policies will be necessary to maintain fiscal stability.

A Review of 2007

The budget deficit fell in 2007 for the third year in a row, dropping from $318 billion in 2005 to $248 billion in 2006 and to $163 billion in 2007. As a percentage of GDP, the deficit declined from 2.6 percent in 2005 to 1.2 percent in 2007.

Revenues

Revenues in 2007 totaled $2.6 trillion (or 18.8 percent of GDP), an increase of 6.7 percent from the amount the previous year. They were buoyed by a rise of 11.5 percent ($120 billion) in individual income tax receipts (see

Table 1-2). In contrast, such tax receipts grew by 4.7 percent annually from 1997 to 2006. Revenues from other sources grew more slowly than they have in recent years.

Corporate income tax receipts grew by 4.6 percent ($16 billion) last year, compared with 7.5 percent annually over the preceding decade (which included a particularly rapid average annual growth rate of nearly 40 percent between 2003 and 2006). Social insurance tax revenues (including payroll tax receipts for Social Security and Medicare) grew by 3.8 percent ($32 billion) in 2007, lower than the 5.1 percent average annual growth over the 1997–2006 period.

Revenues from all other sources, including excise, estate, and gift taxes as well as customs duties, dropped by 4.2 percent ($7 billion) in 2007, in part as a result of the abolition of certain telephone tax payments and the refund of some previous payments of those taxes. Those revenues had increased at an average rate of 4 percent per year in the previous 10 years.

Outlays

Outlays totaled $2.7 trillion in 2007, or 20.0 percent of GDP. Federal spending grew modestly last year, by 2.9 percent (if adjusted for shifts in the timing of certain payments, the rate of increase was slightly less—2.6 percent). In recent years, the growth of spending was much higher, averaging 5.5 percent from 1997 to 2006. Both mandatory and discretionary spending grew more slowly in 2007 than they did over the past 10 years.

Mandatory spending rose by 2.7 percent (to $1.45 trillion) in 2007, compared with 6.0 percent average annual growth from 1997 to 2006.[4] Growth in Medicare spending, which rose by 16.7 percent in 2007, was well above the average annual rate for that program of 6.9 percent over the previous 10 years. That percentage difference from 2006 outlays, however, overstates the growth in Medicare spending because it reflects shifts in the timing of certain payments. After adjusting for payments that were shifted from 2006 to 2007, CBO estimates that outlays for Medicare grew by 12.8 percent in 2007 and by 7.1 percent, on average, from 1997 to 2006. That substantial increase in 2007 occurred in part because 2007

---

3. See Congressional Budget Office, *The Long-Term Budget Outlook* (December 2007).

4. After adjusting for shifts in the timing of some payments, CBO estimates that mandatory spending grew by 2.0 percent in 2007 and that growth from 1997 to 2006 averaged 6.1 percent.

Table 1-2.

Average Annual Growth Rates of Revenues and Outlays Since 1997 and in CBO's Baseline

(Percent)

	Actual		Estimated	Projected[a]	
	1997-2006	**2007**	**2008**	**2009**	**2010-2018**
Revenues					
Individual Income Taxes	4.7	11.5	4.1	10.6	6.9
Corporate Income Taxes	7.5	4.6	-1.7	-2.2	1.0
Social Insurance Taxes	5.1	3.8	4.6	4.1	4.5
Other[b]	4.0	-4.2	3.1	3.0	6.6
Total Revenues	**5.2**	**6.7**	**3.4**	**6.1**	**5.5**
Outlays					
Mandatory	6.0	2.7	6.9	6.7	5.6
Discretionary	6.7	2.6	4.5	2.9	2.2
Net Interest	-0.6	5.0	-1.6	3.1	0.8
Total Outlays	**5.5**	**2.9**	**5.2**	**4.9**	**4.1**
Memorandum:					
Consumer Price Index	2.6	2.3	3.2	2.3	2.2
Nominal GDP	5.4	4.6	3.9	4.3	4.7

Source: Congressional Budget Office.

Note: The growth rates in this table do not account for shifts in the timing of certain payments or receipts.

a.   CBO's baseline budget projections. CBO uses the employment cost index for wages and salaries to inflate discretionary spending related to federal personnel and the gross domestic product price index to adjust other discretionary spending when constructing its baseline.

b.   Includes excise, estate, and gift taxes as well as customs duties.

was the first full fiscal year in which the new prescription drug program (Part D of Medicare) was in effect and because of rapid growth in the Medicare Advantage component of the program (under which beneficiaries may enroll in private health insurance plans).

Outlays for Social Security grew at a faster pace than in recent history—6.9 percent in 2007 versus 4.6 percent, on average, over the past decade. (Outlays for Social Security were held down in 2006 because the Treasury adjusted both Social Security outlays and revenues down by $6.2 billion to correct for previous accounting errors related to taxes withheld from Social Security benefits. With that accounting change excluded, the growth rate was 6.0 percent in 2007, and the adjusted rate over the 1997–2006 period was 4.7 percent.) Growth in Medicaid was below average, with outlays 5.5 percent above the 2006 level, compared with average annual growth of about 7 percent over the preceding decade. (See

Chapter 3 for a more detailed discussion of these and other spending programs.)

All other mandatory spending experienced a sharp drop in growth compared with that in the past 10 years, returning to more typical levels. In recent years, this component of mandatory spending (with Medicare, Medicaid, and Social Security excluded) had increased markedly because of a variety of factors, including increases in the amounts and refundable portions of the earned income tax credit (EITC) and child tax credit, higher spending on agricultural subsidies, and large outlays for flood insurance payments following Hurricane Katrina.

Discretionary spending also grew more slowly than it had in the past—by 2.6 percent in 2007 (reaching $1.0 trillion), compared with 6.7 percent, on average, over the previous 10 years. That slower growth happened in part because, in 2007, many federal agencies were operating under a continuing resolution, which stipulated funding levels at or below the amounts they received in 2006. Within the category of discretionary spending, outlays for defense increased by 5.5 percent, whereas nondefense spending contracted slightly, dropping by 0.6 percent in 2007.[5] In contrast, from 1997 through 2006, defense spending grew by 6.9 percent annually, and nondefense spending increased by 6.4 percent.

Funding for U.S. operations in Iraq and Afghanistan and other activities in the war on terrorism expanded significantly in 2007. Budget authority for those purposes totaled $171 billion in that year, compared with $120 billion in 2006. (Funding for those operations and activities is discussed in greater detail in Box 1-1.) CBO estimates that outlays for those purposes totaled about $120 billion in 2007.

Outlays for net interest rose by 5.0 percent in 2007 after a decade in which they declined, on average, by 0.6 percent per year. That increase in net interest payments reflects an uptick in short-term interest rates and a larger amount of federal debt. In 2007, short-term interest rates were nearly 30 basis points higher than in 2006, and the debt increased by about $200 billion.[6]

The Concept Behind CBO's Baseline Projections

The projections that make up CBO's baseline are not intended to be predictions of future budgetary outcomes—rather, they represent CBO's best judgment of how the economy and other factors would affect federal spending and revenues if current laws and policies remained in place. CBO constructs its baseline in accordance with provisions set forth in the Balanced Budget and Emergency Deficit Control Act of 1985 and the Congressional Budget and Impoundment Control Act of 1974. (Although the relevant provisions in the Deficit Control Act expired at the end of September 2006, CBO continues to follow that law's specifications in preparing its projections.) In general, those provisions spell out how the agency should project federal spending and revenues under current laws and policies. The resulting baseline can then be used as a benchmark against which to

measure the effects of proposed changes in spending and tax laws and policies.

For discretionary spending, the Deficit Control Act specified that the baseline should be derived by assuming that the most recent year's budget authority, including any supplemental appropriations, is provided in each future year, with adjustments to reflect projected inflation (as measured in specified indexes) and certain other factors (such as the annual cost-of-living adjustments to federal benefits).

For revenues and mandatory spending, the Deficit Control Act required that baseline projections assume that present laws continue unchanged.[7] In many cases, the laws that govern revenues and mandatory spending are permanent. Thus, CBO's baseline projections for those programs reflect anticipated changes in the economy, demographics, and other relevant factors that affect the implementation of those laws.

CBO's Baseline Projections for 2008 to 2018

Under CBO's assumptions for its baseline, the federal budget will show a deficit in 2008 of around 1.5 percent of GDP—though that figure could be higher if economic stimulus is provided or if additional appropriations are made for operations in Iraq and Afghanistan. In the baseline, deficits of about the same magnitude remain through 2011, at which point they give way to surpluses as a result of the rise in projected revenues when certain tax provisions expire. By 2018, the surplus equals about 1.0 percent of GDP (see Table 1-3).

Outlays
Even without additional legislation that might increase outlays, federal spending is expected to pick up in 2008. Spending will rise by 5.2 percent from 2007 levels, CBO

---

5. After adjusting for the effects of shifts in the timing of payments, defense spending in 2007 grew by 6.0 percent.

6. A basis point is one one-hundredth of a percentage point.

7. The Deficit Control Act provided some exceptions. For example, it directed that spending programs whose authorizations are set to expire be assumed to continue if they have outlays of more than $50 million in the current year and were established on or before the enactment of the Balanced Budget Act of 1997. Programs established after that law was enacted are not automatically assumed to continue. The Deficit Control Act also required CBO to assume that expiring excise taxes dedicated to trust funds will be extended at their current rates. The law did not provide for the extension of other expiring tax provisions, even if they had been extended routinely in the past.

Box 1-1.

Funding for Activities in Iraq and Afghanistan and for the War on Terrorism

Since September 2001, the Congress and the President have provided a total of $691 billion in budget authority for military and diplomatic operations in Iraq, Afghanistan, and other regions in support of the war on terrorism and for related veterans' benefits and services (see the table). Appropriations specifically designated for those activities, which averaged about $93 billion a year from 2003 through 2005, rose to $120 billion in 2006 and $171 billion in 2007. The Administration has requested $193 billion for war-related purposes in 2008, of which $88 billion has been appropriated thus far.

Funding to date for military operations and other defense activities related to the war totals $618 billion, most of which has gone to the Department of Defense (DoD). Lawmakers also provided $33 billion to train and equip indigenous security forces in Iraq and Afghanistan.[1] A total of $651 billion has thus been appropriated since September 2001 for defense operations in Iraq and Afghanistan and for the war on terrorism.

In addition, $40 billion has been provided for diplomatic operations and foreign aid to Iraq, Afghanistan, and other countries that are assisting the United States in the war on terrorism. Of that amount, $16 billion was appropriated for the Iraq Relief and Reconstruction Fund.

DoD reports that it obligated an average of about $11 billion per month in 2007 for operations in Iraq

---

1.   The $33 billion includes $5 billion provided for Iraqi security forces in 2004 in an appropriation for the Department of State's Iraq Relief and Reconstruction Fund.

and Afghanistan and for other activities related to the war on terrorism—an increase of about $3 billion compared with average monthly obligations in 2006. Operation Iraqi Freedom accounted for approximately 85 percent of all reported obligations; Operation Enduring Freedom (which refers mainly to operations in and around Afghanistan) accounted for another 15 percent. Additional security missions that have taken place in the United States since the terrorist attacks of September 11, 2001—such as combat air patrols over Washington, D.C., and New York City (known as Operation Noble Eagle)—accounted for less than 1 percent.

Because most appropriations for operations in Iraq and Afghanistan and for other activities related to the war on terrorism appear in the same budget accounts that record appropriations for DoD's other functions, determining how much has actually been spent for those activities is difficult. However, CBO estimates that appropriations for defense operations in Iraq and Afghanistan and for the war on terrorism resulted in outlays of about $430 billion through fiscal year 2007 (with about $115 billion occurring in 2007). Of the funds appropriated for international affairs related to the war, about $30 billion was spent through 2007, CBO estimates. In total, by the agency's estimate, outlays for operations in Iraq and Afghanistan amounted to about $120 billion last year. The President has requested another $105 billion for the war in 2008, in addition to the $88 billion that has been appropriated for that year. If that amount is provided, outlays in 2008 (which also include outlays from prior years' appropriations) would total about $145 billion, CBO estimates.

Box 1-1.

Continued

Estimated Appropriations Provided for Activities in Iraq and Afghanistan and for the War on Terrorism, 2001 to 2008
(Billions of dollars)

	2001	2002	2003	2004	2005	2006	2007	2008	Total, 2001-2008
Military Operations and Other Defense Activities									
Iraq[a]	0	0	46	68	53	89	113	71	440
Other[b]	14	18	34	21	18	22	39	13	178
Subtotal	14	18	80	88	70	111	152	84	618
Indigenous Security Forces[c]									
Iraq	0	0	0	5	6	3	6	2	21
Afghanistan	0	0	0	0	1	2	7	1	12
Subtotal	0	0	0	5	7	5	13	3	33
Diplomatic Operations and Foreign Aid									
Iraq	0	0	3	15	1	3	3	1	26
Other	*	2	5	2	2	1	2	1	15
Subtotal	*	2	8	17	3	4	5	1	40
Veterans' Benefits and Services[d]									
Iraq	0	0	0	0	0	0	1	0	1
Other	0	0	0	0	0	0	*	0	*
Subtotal	0	0	0	0	0	0	1	0	1
Total[e]	**14**	**19**	**88**	**111**	**81**	**120**	**171**	**88**	**691**

Source: Congressional Budget Office.

Note: * = between zero and $500 million.

a. CBO estimated how much money has been provided for Operation Iraqi Freedom by allocating funds on the basis of obligations reported by the Department of Defense (DoD). For more information about funding for that operation, see Congressional Budget Office, *Estimated Costs of U.S. Operations in Iraq Under Two Specified Scenarios* (July 13, 2006).

b. Includes Operation Enduring Freedom (in and around Afghanistan), Operation Noble Eagle (homeland security missions, such as combat air patrols, in the United States), the restructuring of Army and Marine Corps units, classified activities other than those funded by appropriations for the Iraq Freedom Fund, and other operations. (For 2005 through 2008, funding for Operation Noble Eagle has been intermingled with regular appropriations for the Department of Defense. That funding is not included in this table because it cannot be separately identified.)

c. Funding for indigenous security forces—which went to accounts for diplomatic operations and foreign aid (budget function 150) in 2004 and, since 2005, has gone to defense accounts (budget function 050)—is used to train and equip local military and police units in Iraq and Afghanistan.

d. Excludes almost $2 billion in spending for medical care, disability compensation, and survivors' benefits for veterans of operations in Iraq and Afghanistan and the war on terrorism. Those amounts are based on CBO's estimates of spending from regular appropriations for the Department of Veterans Affairs and were not explicitly appropriated for war-related expenses.

e. At the current rate of military operations, the funding provided to date for 2008 will not be sufficient to pay for all of the costs that will be incurred this year.

Table 1-3.

CBO's Baseline Budget Projections

	Actual 2007	2008	2009	2010	2011	2012	2013	2014	2015	2016	2017	2018	Total, 2009-2013	Total, 2009-2018
							In Billions of Dollars							
Revenues														
Individual income taxes	1,163	1,211	1,340	1,399	1,611	1,753	1,863	1,962	2,070	2,184	2,307	2,438	7,966	18,928
Corporate income taxes	370	364	356	334	333	357	327	342	350	361	374	388	1,707	3,522
Social insurance taxes	870	910	947	997	1,049	1,101	1,149	1,199	1,249	1,301	1,355	1,411	5,244	11,758
Other	164	169	174	177	188	231	245	260	272	285	298	311	1,016	2,441
Total	**2,568**	**2,654**	**2,817**	**2,907**	**3,182**	**3,442**	**3,585**	**3,763**	**3,941**	**4,131**	**4,334**	**4,548**	**15,933**	**36,649**
On-budget	1,933	1,990	2,123	2,177	2,414	2,636	2,743	2,883	3,024	3,175	3,337	3,509	12,093	28,020
Off-budget	635	665	694	730	768	806	842	880	918	957	997	1,039	3,839	8,629
Outlays														
Mandatory spending	1,450	1,550	1,654	1,737	1,846	1,884	2,022	2,138	2,270	2,451	2,578	2,706	9,142	21,285
Discretionary spending	1,042	1,089	1,121	1,145	1,170	1,186	1,216	1,243	1,272	1,307	1,335	1,360	5,838	12,356
Net interest	238	234	241	266	283	286	285	285	282	278	271	259	1,360	2,735
Total	**2,731**	**2,873**	**3,015**	**3,148**	**3,299**	**3,355**	**3,524**	**3,666**	**3,824**	**4,037**	**4,183**	**4,325**	**16,341**	**36,376**
On-budget	2,277	2,404	2,519	2,628	2,757	2,788	2,926	3,037	3,160	3,334	3,439	3,536	13,618	30,124
Off-budget	454	469	496	520	541	568	597	629	664	702	744	789	2,723	6,251
Deficit (-) or Surplus	**-163**	**-219**	**-198**	**-241**	**-117**	**87**	**61**	**96**	**117**	**95**	**151**	**223**	**-408**	**274**
On-budget	-344	-414	-396	-450	-343	-151	-184	-154	-136	-160	-102	-27	-1,525	-2,104
Off-budget	181	195	198	210	226	238	244	251	254	254	253	249	1,117	2,378
Debt Held by the Public	5,035	5,232	5,443	5,698	5,827	5,751	5,701	5,613	5,503	5,414	5,269	5,050	n.a.	n.a.
Memorandum:														
Gross Domestic Product	13,670	14,201	14,812	15,600	16,445	17,256	18,043	18,856	19,685	20,540	21,426	22,355	82,156	185,018
							As a Percentage of Gross Domestic Product							
Revenues														
Individual income taxes	8.5	8.5	9.0	9.0	9.8	10.2	10.3	10.4	10.5	10.6	10.8	10.9	9.7	10.2
Corporate income taxes	2.7	2.6	2.4	2.1	2.0	2.1	1.8	1.8	1.8	1.8	1.7	1.7	2.1	1.9
Social insurance taxes	6.4	6.4	6.4	6.4	6.4	6.4	6.4	6.4	6.3	6.3	6.3	6.3	6.4	6.4
Other	1.2	1.2	1.2	1.1	1.1	1.3	1.4	1.4	1.4	1.4	1.4	1.4	1.2	1.3
Total	**18.8**	**18.7**	**19.0**	**18.6**	**19.3**	**19.9**	**19.9**	**20.0**	**20.0**	**20.1**	**20.2**	**20.3**	**19.4**	**19.8**
On-budget	14.1	14.0	14.3	14.0	14.7	15.3	15.2	15.3	15.4	15.5	15.6	15.7	14.7	15.1
Off-budget	4.6	4.7	4.7	4.7	4.7	4.7	4.7	4.7	4.7	4.7	4.7	4.6	4.7	4.7
Outlays														
Mandatory spending	10.6	10.9	11.2	11.1	11.2	10.9	11.2	11.3	11.5	11.9	12.0	12.1	11.1	11.5
Discretionary spending	7.6	7.7	7.6	7.3	7.1	6.9	6.7	6.6	6.5	6.4	6.2	6.1	7.1	6.7
Net interest	1.7	1.6	1.6	1.7	1.7	1.7	1.6	1.5	1.4	1.4	1.3	1.2	1.7	1.5
Total	**20.0**	**20.2**	**20.4**	**20.2**	**20.1**	**19.4**	**19.5**	**19.4**	**19.4**	**19.7**	**19.5**	**19.3**	**19.9**	**19.7**
On-budget	16.7	16.9	17.0	16.8	16.8	16.2	16.2	16.1	16.1	16.2	16.1	15.8	16.6	16.3
Off-budget	3.3	3.3	3.3	3.3	3.3	3.3	3.3	3.3	3.4	3.4	3.5	3.5	3.3	3.4
Deficit (-) or Surplus	**-1.2**	**-1.5**	**-1.3**	**-1.5**	**-0.7**	**0.5**	**0.3**	**0.5**	**0.6**	**0.5**	**0.7**	**1.0**	**-0.5**	**0.1**
On-budget	-2.5	-2.9	-2.7	-2.9	-2.1	-0.9	-1.0	-0.8	-0.7	-0.8	-0.5	-0.1	-1.9	-1.1
Off-budget	1.3	1.4	1.3	1.3	1.4	1.4	1.4	1.3	1.3	1.2	1.2	1.1	1.4	1.3
Debt Held by the Public	36.8	36.8	36.7	36.5	35.4	33.3	31.6	29.8	28.0	26.4	24.6	22.6	n.a.	n.a.

Source: Congressional Budget Office.

Note: n.a. = not applicable.

estimates, reaching nearly $2.9 trillion this year (or 20.2 percent of GDP, compared with 20.0 percent of GDP for 2007). In CBO's baseline, spending relative to GDP falls slightly over the coming years—to 19.3 percent by 2018. Baseline projections of trends for mandatory and discretionary spending move in opposite directions relative to GDP: Growth in mandatory spending outstrips growth in the economy, while projected discretionary spending loses ground relative to GDP.

Mandatory spending, which currently constitutes over half of all federal spending, is projected to grow at rates approaching 7 percent per year in 2008 and 2009. In later years, the growth of mandatory spending slows somewhat, averaging around 5.6 percent from 2010 to 2018. CBO estimates that under current laws and policies, outlays for such spending will reach 12.1 percent of GDP by 2018, 1.5 percentage points above their level in 2007.

In contrast, discretionary spending is assumed simply to keep pace with inflation and is therefore estimated to grow at a rate of 2.2 percent per year after 2009—less than half as fast as the projected rate of growth of nominal GDP (4.7 percent). Projected growth in discretionary spending is also less than one-third the rate of increase in such spending over the past 10 years: From 1997 to 2006, discretionary spending grew by about 6.7 percent annually.

Revenues

Revenues in the baseline average less than 19 percent of GDP until 2011, when they start to rise; in 2012 and years thereafter, revenues continue to grow relative to the size economy and reach 20.3 percent of GDP by 2018. That increase in revenues follows the baseline's underlying assumptions regarding laws that affect individual income taxes. In particular, the projections assume the expiration of various tax provisions originally enacted in EGTRRA and JGTRRA.

The baseline also does not assume any further legislation to provide relief from the alternative minimum tax. Such legislation has been in effect to varying degrees since 2001 but expired on December 31, 2007. As a result, the number of taxpayers who pay the AMT in the baseline projection jumps markedly in tax year 2008, and revenues jump most significantly a year later, in 2009. The share of total revenues attributable to the AMT is projected to rise through 2010.[8] Consequently, the impact

on revenues and on the budget from modifying the tax so that it does not apply to a broad array of taxpayers (which was not the intent when it was originally enacted) becomes greater over time. The Joint Committee on Taxation estimates that the relief provided for the 2007 tax year (in Public Law 110-166) will reduce revenues by a total of slightly more than $50 billion; similar changes in subsequent years would have a bigger effect.

Debt Held by the Public

In CBO's baseline, accumulated federal debt held by the public (mainly in the form of Treasury securities sold directly in the capital markets) equals 36.8 percent of GDP at the end of 2008—the same level as in 2007. Under baseline projections, debt held by the public as a percentage of GDP falls each year of the 2009–2018 period as deficits decline and surpluses emerge, thus diminishing the government's anticipated borrowing needs. In the projections, in 2018, public debt drops to 22.6 percent of GDP (see Figure 1-2). Alternative assumptions about spending and tax policies, however, could produce a substantially different debt-to-GDP ratio in that year.

Changes in CBO's Baseline Since August 2007

CBO's estimate of the deficit for 2008 is higher than the one that it published in its previous *Budget and Economic Outlook,* in August 2007, primarily because revenues are expected to be lower than previously estimated.[9] In December, the Congress and the President enacted the Tax Increase Prevention Act of 2007 (P.L. 110-166), which provided some relief from the AMT for the tax year that ended on December 31, 2007. That law, along with other legislation with much smaller effects, boosted the projected deficit for 2008 by $59 billion (see Table 1-4). Changes due to economic and other factors increased the projected deficit for 2008 by another $5 billion.

---

8. Like the rate structure of the regular income tax, the AMT extracts a greater proportion of overall income as real income rises. But unlike the regular income tax, the AMT is not indexed for inflation. So as income rises each year with the overall level of prices, a larger number of taxpayers find themselves subject to the AMT. Chapter 4 discusses the increased role of the tax in CBO's projections.

9. See Congressional Budget Office, *The Budget and Economic Outlook: An Update* (August 2007).

Figure 1-2.

Debt Held by the Public as a Share of Gross Domestic Product, 1940 to 2018

(Percent)

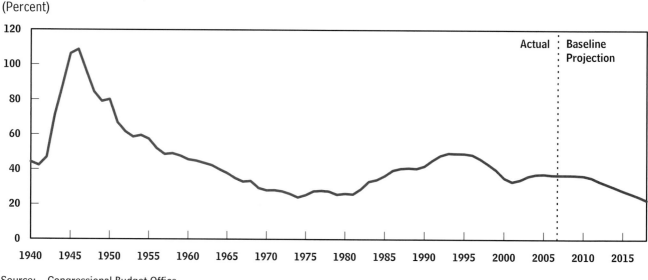

Source: Congressional Budget Office.

For the years after 2008, CBO's baseline projections show slightly lower deficits and higher surpluses than they did in August. (Changes to the baseline projections are discussed in detail in Appendix A.) Much of the improvement in the baseline's bottom line is related to the timing of appropriations for operations in Iraq and Afghanistan and other activities related to the war on terrorism, rather than to changes in the underlying budgetary and economic environment.

Because baseline projections are derived from the most recent appropriations, CBO based its August projections on appropriations for 2007, which included about $170 billion in funding for military and diplomatic operations in Iraq and Afghanistan and other activities in the war on terrorism.

In contrast, the basis for CBO's most recent baseline is the level of funding enacted for 2008, which includes only partial-year funding for those purposes.[10] To date, $88 billion has been provided in 2008 for operations in Iraq and Afghanistan and other activities related to the war on terrorism. The effect of extending that smaller

amount of enacted appropriations throughout the projection period is partially offset by increases in spending in other areas, resulting in a net reduction of $546 billion in outlays between 2008 and 2017.

Other changes, in the aggregate, worsen the projected budget outlook by a total of $371 billion over the 2008–2017 period. Most of that difference results from a deteriorating economic outlook. CBO's projections incorporate a slowdown in economic growth in the final quarter of 2007 and in 2008 and a slight reduction in the economy's potential rate of growth during the next 10 years. (Chapter 2 discusses the details of CBO's economic projections.) Over the entire 10-year projection period, the net result of changes in the economic outlook is a reduction of $479 billion in revenues, most of which stems from lower projections of corporate income tax receipts. Economic changes affecting projections of outlays offset $8 billion of that reduction.

The remaining revisions to CBO's baseline result from technical factors—those not directly related to changes in legislation or the economic outlook. Such revisions since August have generally raised projections of revenues and lowered estimates of outlays from 2008 to 2017, thereby reducing this year's estimated deficit by $12 billion and the 10-year cumulative deficit by $159 billion.

---

10. Appropriations for 2008 were provided in the Department of Defense Appropriations Act, 2008 (P.L. 110-116), in the Consolidated Appropriations Act, 2008 (P.L. 110-161), and in a joint resolution making continuing appropriations for fiscal year 2008 (P.L. 110-92).

Table 1-4.

Changes in CBO's Baseline Projections of the Deficit Since August 2007

(Billions of dollars)

	2008	2009	2010	2011	2012	2013	2014	2015	2016	2017	Total, 2008-2012	Total, 2008-2017
Total Deficit as Projected in August 2007	-155	-215	-255	-134	62	36	65	85	58	109	-696	-343
Changes												
Legislative												
Revenues	-69	20	*	1	3	-1	1	1	*	*	-46	-44
Outlays[a]	-10	-29	-45	-54	-56	-58	-66	-71	-77	-81	-194	-546
Subtotal, legislative	-59	49	45	54	59	57	67	71	77	81	148	502
Economic												
Revenues	-33	-60	-63	-55	-45	-44	-44	-45	-45	-45	-256	-479
Outlays[a]	-16	-14	-5	-2	*	3	8	10	11	13	-37	8
Subtotal, economic	-17	-46	-58	-52	-45	-47	-52	-55	-56	-58	-218	-486
Technical												
Revenues	-14	2	19	10	7	10	7	4	2	1	25	51
Outlays[a]	-26	-12	-7	-4	-4	-5	-9	-11	-13	-17	-53	-108
Subtotal, technical	12	15	26	15	11	15	16	16	16	18	79	159
Total Effect on the Deficit[b]	**-64**	**17**	**14**	**17**	**25**	**25**	**32**	**32**	**36**	**42**	**8**	**175**
Total Deficit (-) or Surplus as Projected in January 2008	-219	-198	-241	-117	87	61	96	117	95	151	-688	-168

Source: Congressional Budget Office.

Notes: * = between -$500 million and $500 million.

See Appendix A for more details on changes in CBO's projections since August 2007.

a. Includes net interest payments.

b. Negative numbers represent an increase in the deficit.

Uncertainty and Budget Projections

Actual budgetary outcomes are almost certain to differ from CBO's baseline projections because of future legislative actions, unanticipated changes in conditions affecting the economy, and many other factors that affect federal spending and revenues.

Uncertainty of Future Legislative Actions

To illustrate how different fiscal policies might affect the baseline, CBO estimated the budgetary impact of some alternative policy actions (see Table 1-5). The discussion below focuses on their direct effects on revenues and out-lays. Such changes would also affect projected debt-service costs (shown separately in Table 1-5).

Activities Related to Iraq and Afghanistan and the War on Terrorism. CBO's baseline includes outlays that arise from the $88 billion in appropriations already provided for 2008 for operations in Iraq and Afghanistan and for other activities related to the war on terrorism and from the resulting $979 billion in budget authority for those purposes that is projected over the 2009–2018 period (as well as outlays from funding provided in 2007 and prior years). However, the funding for 2008 represents only a

Table 1-5.

The Budgetary Effects of Selected Policy Alternatives Not Included in CBO's Baseline

(Billions of dollars)

	2008	2009	2010	2011	2012	2013	2014	2015	2016	2017	2018	Total, 2009-2013	Total, 2009-2018
					Policy Alternatives That Affect Discretionary Spending								
Reduce the Number of Troops Deployed for Military Operations in Iraq and Afghanistan and Other Activities Related to the War on Terrorism to 30,000 by 2010[a]													
Effect on the deficit or surplus[b]	-30	-43	-14	22	45	55	60	63	65	68	70	65	390
Debt service	*	-2	-4	-4	-2	0	3	6	9	13	17	-12	35
Reduce the Number of Troops Deployed for Military Operations in Iraq and Afghanistan and Other Activities Related to the War on Terrorism to 75,000 by 2013[c]													
Effect on the deficit or surplus[b]	-30	-58	-59	-51	-29	-13	4	17	21	24	25	-210	-120
Debt service	*	-2	-5	-9	-11	-13	-13	-14	-13	-13	-12	-40	-106
Increase Regular Discretionary Appropriations at the Rate of Growth of Nominal GDP[d]													
Effect on the deficit or surplus[b]	0	-9	-33	-64	-95	-125	-154	-184	-214	-246	-280	-324	-1,403
Debt service	0	*	-1	-4	-8	-13	-21	-30	-41	-55	-70	-26	-243
Freeze Total Discretionary Appropriations at the Level Provided for 2008													
Effect on the deficit or surplus[b]	0	17	38	62	87	114	142	171	202	232	263	316	1,326
Debt service	0	*	2	4	8	13	20	29	39	52	67	28	235
					Policy Alternatives That Affect the Tax Code[e]								
Extend EGTRRA and JGTRRA[f]													
Effect on the deficit or surplus[b]	*	-3	-6	-147	-254	-281	-292	-304	-316	-329	-344	-692	-2,277
Debt service	*	*	*	-4	-14	-28	-43	-60	-78	-98	-119	-46	-444
Extend Other Expiring Tax Provisions													
Effect on the deficit or surplus[b]	-6	-14	-22	-31	-38	-44	-49	-53	-58	-63	-67	-149	-438
Debt service	0	-1	-1	-3	-5	-7	-10	-12	-16	-20	-24	-16	-97
Index the AMT for Inflation[g]													
Effect on the deficit or surplus[b]	-6	-75	-76	-71	-42	-49	-58	-68	-80	-94	-110	-313	-724
Debt service	0	-2	-5	-9	-13	-16	-19	-23	-28	-34	-40	-45	-189

Continued

Table 1-5.

Continued

(Billions of dollars)

	2008	2009	2010	2011	2012	2013	2014	2015	2016	2017	2018	Total, 2009-2013	Total, 2009-2018
Memorandum:													
Interactive Effect of Extending EGTRRA and JGTRRA and Indexing the AMT[e]													
Effect on the deficit or surplus[b]	0	0	0	-18	-61	-69	-76	-83	-90	-97	-105	-148	-598
Debt service	0	0	0	*	-2	-6	-9	-14	-19	-24	-30	-9	-105
Total Discretionary Outlays in CBO's Baseline	1,089	1,121	1,145	1,170	1,186	1,216	1,243	1,272	1,307	1,335	1,360	5,838	12,356
Total Outlays for Operations in Iraq and Afghanistan in CBO's Baseline	115	103	96	93	93	95	97	98	100	102	104	480	981
Total Deficit (-) or Surplus in CBO's Baseline	-219	-198	-241	-117	87	61	96	117	95	151	223	-408	274

Sources: Congressional Budget Office; Joint Committee on Taxation.

Notes: GDP = gross domestic product; EGTRRA = Economic Growth and Tax Relief Reconciliation Act of 2001; JGTRRA = Jobs and Growth Tax Relief Reconciliation Act of 2003; AMT = alternative minimum tax; * = between -$500 million and $500 million.

a. This alternative does not extrapolate the $88 billion in funding for military operations and associated costs in Iraq and Afghanistan provided for 2008. However, it incorporates the assumption that an additional $105 billion in budget authority will be provided in 2008 to carry out operations in those countries. Future funding for operations in Iraq, Afghanistan, or elsewhere would total $118 billion in 2009, $50 billion in 2010, and then about $34 billion a year from 2011 on—for a total of $440 billion over the 2009–2018 period.

b. Excluding debt service.

c. This alternative does not extrapolate the $88 billion in funding for military operations and associated costs in Iraq and Afghanistan pro-vided for 2008. However, it incorporates the assumption that an additional $105 billion in budget authority will be provided in 2008 to carry out operations in those countries. Future funding for operations in Iraq, Afghanistan, or elsewhere would total $161 billion in 2009, $147 billion in 2010, $128 billion in 2011, $101 billion in 2012, $79 billion in 2013, and then about $77 billion a year from 2014 on—for a total of $1 trillion over the 2009–2018 period.

d. Under this alternative, appropriations for 2008 for operations in Iraq and Afghanistan (as well as other emergency appropriations) are extrapolated according to rules for the baseline.

e. The Joint Committee on Taxation's estimates for the tax policy alternatives are preliminary and will be updated later.

f. These estimates do not include the effects of extending the increased exemption amount or the treatment of personal credits for the AMT that expired at the end of 2007. The effects of that alternative are shown separately.

g. This alternative incorporates the assumption that the exemption amount for the AMT (which was increased through 2007 in the Tax Increase Prevention Act of 2007) is extended at its higher level and, together with the AMT tax brackets, is indexed for inflation after 2007. In addition, the treatment of personal credits against the AMT (which was also extended through the end of 2007 in that act) is assumed to be continued. If this alternative was enacted jointly with the extension of the expiring tax provisions, an interactive effect after 2010 would make the combined revenue loss over the 2011–2018 period greater than the sum of the two separate estimates (see the memorandum).

portion of what will be needed for those operations throughout this year.

In subsequent years, the annual funding required for military operations in Iraq and Afghanistan or in other locations may eventually be less than the amounts in the baseline if the number of troops and pace of operations diminish over time. Because of considerable uncertainty about those future operations, CBO has formulated two scenarios. Under both, the number of active-duty, Reserve, and National Guard personnel would average 205,000 in fiscal year 2008, after which those force levels would decline at different rates and to different sustained levels. Many other budgetary outcomes—some costing more, some less—are also possible for the operations described in these scenarios.

■ Under the first scenario, troop levels would be rapidly reduced, with deployed forces declining until 30,000 military personnel were stationed overseas in support of the war on terrorism at the beginning of 2010 and in each year over the 2011–2018 period, although not necessarily in Iraq and Afghanistan. Under such a scenario, discretionary outlays for 2008 would be about $30 billion higher than the amount in the baseline, but annual outlays would be lower beginning in 2011. In total, over the 2008–2018 period, discretionary outlays would be close to $360 billion less than the amount in the current baseline.

■ Under the second scenario, the number of troops would decline more gradually, dropping to about 175,000 in 2009 and continuing to fall steadily in subsequent years, until 75,000 remained overseas in 2013 and each year thereafter. Under such a scenario, discretionary outlays for 2008 would increase by about $30 billion compared with the amount in the current baseline, but annual outlays would be less than the projection beginning in 2014. During the 2008–2018 period, total outlays for military activities related to Iraq, Afghanistan, and the war on terrorism would be greater than the amount in the baseline by about $150 billion.

Other Discretionary Spending. Many alternative assumptions about the future growth of discretionary spending are possible. For example, if appropriations (other than those for activities in Iraq and Afghanistan and other funding declared as an emergency requirement) were assumed to grow through 2018 at the same rate as nomi-

nal GDP instead of at the rate of inflation, total projected discretionary spending would be $1.4 trillion higher than the amount in the current baseline. In contrast, if lawmakers did not increase appropriations after 2008 to account for inflation, cumulative discretionary outlays would be $1.3 trillion lower. Under that latter scenario (sometimes referred to as a freeze in appropriations), total discretionary spending would fall from 7.6 percent of GDP in 2007 to 4.9 percent in 2018.

Revenues. The baseline assumes that major provisions of EGTRRA and JGTRRA—such as the introduction of the 10 percent tax bracket, increases in the child tax credit, repeal of the estate tax, and lower rates for capital gains and dividends—will expire as scheduled at the end of 2010. On balance, the tax provisions that are set to expire during the 2009–2018 period reduce revenues; thus, under a scenario in which they all were extended, projected revenues would be lower than the amount in the current baseline. For example, if all expiring tax provisions (except those related to the exemption amount for the AMT) were extended, total revenues over the 2009–2018 period would be about $2.7 trillion lower than the current baseline projection.[11] That estimate reflects the fact that the effect of lowering the amount of taxpayers' liabilities would be partially offset by an increase in the number of taxpayers subject to the AMT.

Another change in policy that could affect revenues involves the modification of the AMT, which many observers believe cannot be maintained in its current form. Because the AMT's exemption amount and brackets are not adjusted for inflation, the impact of the tax will grow in coming years as more taxpayers become subject to it. If the AMT was indexed for inflation after 2007 and no other changes were made to the tax code, federal revenues over the next 10 years would be $724 billion lower than the amount in the baseline, according to CBO and the Joint Committee on Taxation's estimate.

Because the number of taxpayers who are subject to the AMT will depend on whether the tax provisions originally enacted in EGTRRA and JGTRRA are still in effect, the combination of indexing the AMT for inflation and extending the expiring provisions would reduce

---

11. That estimate does not include any macroeconomic effects—unlike CBO's baseline projections, which incorporate the effects that the tax provisions' expiration would have on the economy as a whole. However, such effects are likely to be small relative to GDP.

revenues by more than indexing alone. The effect of that interaction would lower revenues by an additional $598 billion between 2011 and 2018.

Other Sources of Uncertainty

In addition to being affected by future legislative actions, the federal budget is sensitive to economic and technical factors that are difficult to forecast. In constructing its baseline, CBO must make assumptions about such economic variables as interest rates, inflation, and the growth of GDP. (CBO's economic assumptions are explained in detail in Chapter 2.) Discrepancies between those assumptions and actual economic conditions can significantly affect the extent to which budgetary outcomes differ from baseline projections. For instance, CBO's baseline reflects an assumption that real GDP grows by 1.7 percent in calendar year 2008, by 2.8 percent in 2009, and by an average of 2.7 percent annually from 2010 to 2018. If the actual rate was 0.1 percentage point higher or lower each year, the effect on the projection of the cumulative surplus for the 2009–2018 period would be about $300 billion. (For further discussion of the effect of economic assumptions on budget projections, see Appendix C.)

Uncertainty also surrounds technical factors that affect CBO's baseline budget projections. For example, the rate of spending per enrollee for Medicare and Medicaid, which has generally grown faster than GDP, is difficult to forecast, but it will have a large impact on the costs of those programs in coming years. CBO's projections of spending for those programs also depend on assumptions about the growth of their enrollment and, indirectly, general inflation. For example, if per capita costs or enrollment in the next 10 years grew 1 percentage point faster or slower than CBO has projected, the impact on Medicare and Medicaid outlays would be $625 billion over that period.

Other projections also are vulnerable to technical uncertainty. For example, CBO must estimate prices for various agricultural commodities as well as crop yields, all of which are volatile and strongly affect how much the government will pay farmers under price- and income-support programs. Assumptions about revenues are particularly sensitive to technical uncertainty. Although CBO uses its economic projections to estimate overall income from current production, it must make technical assumptions about the amount of revenues to expect from a given amount of such income. Differences

between the expectations and actual revenues can lead to significant deviations from CBO's baseline projections.

To help illustrate the uncertainty surrounding CBO's baseline projections, Figure 1-3 displays the range of possible outcomes for the total deficit or surplus under current law (that is, excluding the possible impact of future legislation). The current baseline projection of the deficit falls in the middle of the highest-probability area, as shown in the darkest part of the figure. The probabilities of other projections are based in part on the differences between CBO's past baselines and actual budgetary results. The other paths in that dark portion of the figure have nearly the same probability of occurring as CBO's current projections. Projections that are increasingly different from the baseline are shown in the lighter areas, but they have a significant likelihood of coming to pass. For example, CBO projects a baseline deficit of 1.3 percent of GDP for 2009, but even with no changes in policy, there is a roughly 25 percent chance that the deficit that year will be higher by 1.0 percent of GDP and a roughly 20 percent chance that the budget in that year will be in balance.

The uncertainty surrounding CBO's baseline compounds over time. By 2013, when CBO projects a baseline surplus of about 0.3 percent of GDP, there is a 25 percent likelihood that the federal government will post a deficit in that year of about 1.8 percent of GDP. However, there is also a 25 percent chance that the surplus will be higher by about 2 percent of GDP (under an assumption that current laws and policies do not change).

Federal Debt Held by the Public

Debt held by the public comprises debt that the Department of the Treasury issues to raise cash to fund the operations and pay off the maturing liabilities of the federal government. (Other measures of debt are discussed in Appendix B.) When the federal government runs a deficit, the Treasury borrows money from the public by selling securities in the capital markets. That debt is purchased by various domestic buyers, such as mutual funds, state and local governments, Federal Reserve banks, commercial banks, insurance companies, and individuals, as well as by private foreign entities and central banks. Of the $5.0 trillion in outstanding public debt at the end of 2007, domestic investors owned 55 percent ($2.8 trillion) and foreign investors held 45 percent ($2.2 trillion).

Figure 1-3.

Uncertainty of CBO's Projections of the Budget Deficit or Surplus Under Current Policies

(Percent)

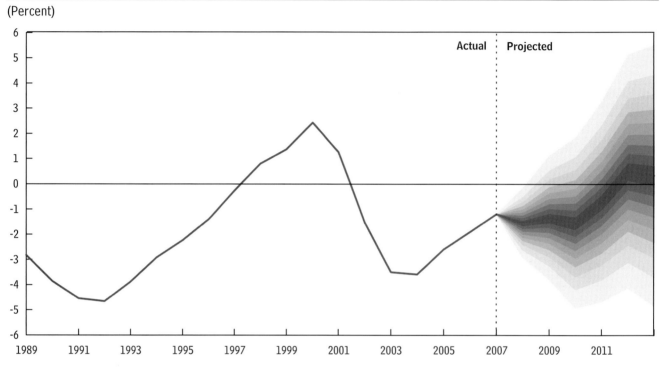

Source: Congressional Budget Office.

Notes: This figure, calculated on the basis of CBO's track record in forecasting, shows the estimated likelihood of alternative projections of the budget deficit or surplus under current policies. The baseline projections described in this chapter fall in the middle of the darkest area of the figure. Under the assumption that tax and spending policies do not change, the probability is 10 percent that actual deficits or surpluses will fall in the darkest area and 90 percent that they will fall within the whole shaded area.

Actual deficits or surpluses will be affected by legislation enacted in future years, including decisions about discretionary spending. The effects of future legislation are not reflected in this figure.

For an explanation of how CBO calculates the probability distribution underlying this figure, see Congressional Budget Office, *The Uncertainty of Budget Projections: A Discussion of Data and Methods* (March 2007). An updated version of that publication is forthcoming.

Among investors from other nations, those in Japan, China, and the United Kingdom have the biggest holdings of Treasury securities.[12] The central banks and private entities in those countries hold about $1.2 trillion of such debt—roughly 25 percent of the total. In 2007, for-

eign investors added about $220 billion in Treasury securities—or about $15 billion more than the amount of money that the Treasury borrowed from the public last year. In the past five years, investors from abroad have added more than $1 trillion in securities, or roughly 70 percent of the total increase in public debt during that time. Investors in China have increased their holdings by $292 billion of such debt in the past five years, and investors in Japan and the United Kingdom have added $208 billion and $189 billion, respectively, to their holdings.

---

12. See Department of the Treasury, "Major Foreign Holders of Treasury Securities" (December 17, 2007), available at www.ustreas.gov/tic/mfh.txt. That information should be viewed as approximate, because in many cases, it is impossible to accurately determine the home country of foreign holders of U.S. securities, as intermediaries may be involved in the custody, management, purchase, or sale of the securities.

Table 1-6.

CBO's Baseline Projections of Federal Debt

(Billions of dollars)

	Actual 2007	2008	2009	2010	2011	2012	2013	2014	2015	2016	2017	2018
Debt Held by the Public at the Beginning of the Year	4,829	5,035	5,232	5,443	5,698	5,827	5,751	5,701	5,613	5,503	5,414	5,269
Changes to Debt Held by the Public												
Deficit or surplus (-)	163	219	198	241	117	-87	-61	-96	-117	-95	-151	-223
Other means of financing	43	-22	13	14	12	11	10	9	7	6	5	4
Total	**206**	**197**	**211**	**255**	**129**	**-76**	**-51**	**-87**	**-111**	**-88**	**-146**	**-219**
Debt Held by the Public at the End of the Year	5,035	5,232	5,443	5,698	5,827	5,751	5,701	5,613	5,503	5,414	5,269	5,050
Memorandum:												
Debt Held by the Public at the End of the Year as a Percentage of GDP	36.8	36.8	36.7	36.5	35.4	33.3	31.6	29.8	28.0	26.4	24.6	22.6

Source: Congressional Budget Office.

Among domestic investors, Federal Reserve banks, state and local governments, and mutual funds are the largest investors in Treasury securities, holding around $775 billion, $511 billion, and $266 billion, respectively, of debt sold to the public.[13]

Debt held by the public fluctuates according to changes in the government's borrowing needs. In 1993, it equaled nearly 50 percent of GDP, but by 2001, it measured 33 percent (see Figure 1-2 on page 10). Since then, debt held by the public has risen to 37 percent of GDP. Under assumptions in the baseline (in particular, that discretionary spending grows at the rate of inflation and that tax provisions expire as scheduled), debt held by the public remains at 37 percent of GDP until 2010 and then falls to 35 percent in 2011 (the average debt-to-GDP ratio during the past 40 years). After 2011, it falls more rapidly, dropping to 23 percent of GDP by 2018 (see Table 1-6). At that time, debt held by the public totals $5.0 trillion in CBO's baseline, or roughly the same amount that it is currently.

Changes in policy, however (such as those shown in Table 1-5 on page 12), would lead to a different amount of public debt. For example, if the number of troops involved in military operations in Iraq, Afghanistan, and elsewhere in support of the war on terrorism declined to 30,000 by the beginning of 2010 and all other policies were consistent with those assumed in the baseline, debt held by the public in 2018 would fall by $426 billion relative to the amount in the baseline, bringing the total to $4.6 trillion, or 20.7 percent of GDP. By contrast, if the provisions in EGTRRA and JGTRRA set to expire in 2010 were extended through 2018, debt held by the public in 2018 would rise by $2.7 trillion relative to the baseline amount, bringing the total to $7.8 trillion, or 34.8 percent of GDP.

The Composition of Debt Held by the Public. About 88 percent of publicly held debt consists of marketable securities—Treasury bills, notes, bonds, and inflation-indexed issues (called TIPS). The remaining 12 percent comprises nonmarketable securities, such as savings bonds and securities in the state and local government series, which are nonnegotiable, nontransferable debt instruments issued to specific investors.[14]

---

13. Department of the Treasury, Financial Management Service, *Treasury Bulletin* (December 2007).

14. State and local government securities are time deposits that the Treasury sells to the issuers of state and local government tax-exempt debt to help them comply with the provisions of the Internal Revenue Code prohibiting arbitrage.

The Treasury sells marketable securities to brokers in regularly scheduled auctions, whose size varies with changes in the government's cash flow. (Periodically, the Treasury also sells cash-management bills to cover shortfalls in cash balances.) In May 2007, the Treasury stopped issuing three-year notes. CBO projects that, under the assumptions incorporated in its baseline, the elimination of those issues will cause a modest decline in the amount of notes outstanding as a percentage of total marketable debt. That percentage is projected to fall from 55 percent at the end of 2007 to 49 percent by 2011. In contrast, the share of marketable debt accounted for by bills and inflation-protected securities is expected to expand over the next five years: The share for bills is projected to grow from 22 percent to 27 percent and for inflation-protected securities from 10 percent to 12 percent of the total. Finally, bonds are expected to drop from their current level of 13 percent to 12 percent of total marketable debt.

Why Changes in Debt Held by the Public Do Not Equal Surpluses and Deficits. In most years, the amount of debt that the Treasury borrows or redeems roughly equals the annual budget deficit or surplus. However, a number of factors—which are broadly labeled "other means of financing"—also affect the government's need to borrow money from the public. For 2008, CBO's projection of debt held by the public shows borrowing to be $22 billion less than the amount of the deficit because CBO estimates that the Treasury will reduce its cash balance from its level at the end of 2007. Debt held by the public will grow by more than the cumulative deficit over the 2009–2018 period, CBO projects, because changes in other means of financing will increase the Treasury's borrowing needs.

Among such means of financing, the capitalization of financing accounts used for federal credit programs usually has the biggest effect on the government's borrowing. Direct student loans, rural housing programs, loans made by the Small Business Administration, and other credit programs require the government to disburse money up front in anticipation of repayment at a later date. Those initial disbursements are not counted in the budget, which reflects only the programs' estimated costs for subsidies, defaults, and other items. Each year from 2009 to 2018, the amount of loans disbursed will typically be larger than the amount of repayments and interest collected. Thus, the government's annual borrowing needs will, on average, be $9 billion greater than the annual budget deficit or surplus might indicate.

The Long-Term Budget Outlook

Although the baseline projections show budget surpluses in the later years of the 10-year projection period, the nation faces substantial fiscal challenges over the long term. Growth in spending—particularly for Medicare and Medicaid—is likely to exceed growth in federal revenues as well as in the economy. Attaining fiscal stability in the coming decades almost certainly will require some combination of reductions in the growth of spending and increases in taxes as a share of the economy.

The future rates of growth for the government's major health care programs—Medicare and Medicaid—will be the primary determinant of the nation's long-term fiscal balance. Over the past four decades, per-beneficiary costs in the programs have increased about 2.5 percentage points faster per year than has per capita GDP. If current laws and policies remained in place, federal spending on those two programs alone would rise from 4.6 percent of GDP in 2007 to about 12 percent by 2050 and 19 percent by 2082.[15] That percentage represents about the same share of the economy that the entire federal budget does today (see Figure 1-4).

The aging of the nation's population also will affect the federal budget over time. CBO projects that under current law, Social Security spending will rise from its current level of 4.3 percent of GDP in 2007 to around 6 percent in 25 years (and roughly stabilize at that rate), in part because of that demographic shift.

If tax revenues as a share of GDP remain at current levels (roughly 19 percent of GDP), additional spending for Medicare, Medicaid, and Social Security will eventually cause future budget deficits to become unsustainable. Even if revenues follow the path projected under current law and rise to about 24 percent of GDP by 2050, budgetary pressures will increase significantly. As a result, substantial reductions in the projected growth of spending, a sizable increase in taxes as a percentage of the economy, or some combination of changes in policies for spending and revenues is likely to be necessary to achieve fiscal stability. Such policy changes would certainly have some effect on the economy, but those effects would probably be less than the costs of allowing deficits to grow to unsustainable levels.

---

15. For more details, see Congressional Budget Office, *The Long-Term Budget Outlook* (December 2007).

Figure 1-4.

Projected Federal Spending Over the Long Term

(Percentage of gross domestic product)

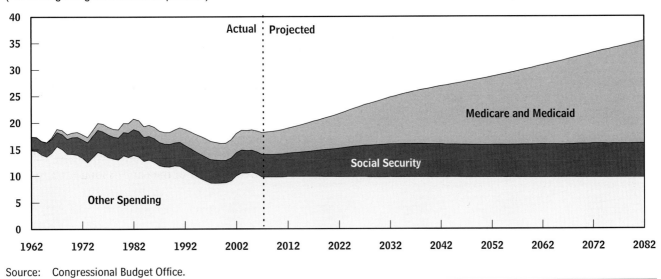

Source: Congressional Budget Office.

CHAPTER
2

The Economic Outlook

The economy has been buffeted recently by several interlinked shocks, and the risk of recession is significantly elevated compared with what it is during normal economic conditions. The pace of economic growth slowed in 2007, and there are strong indications that it will slacken further in 2008. In the Congressional Budget Office's view, the ongoing problems in the financial and housing markets and the high price of oil will curb spending by households and businesses this year and trim the growth of gross domestic product. In contrast, the relative economic strength of the United States' major trading partners—in particular, the robustness of emerging economies—when combined with the dollar's decline will stimulate net exports, thus partially offsetting the sluggishness in domestic demand anticipated this year. Although recent data suggest that a recession in 2008 has become more likely, CBO does not expect the slowdown in economic growth to be large enough to register as a recession.[1] For 2009, CBO forecasts that the economy will rebound, as the negative effects of the turmoil in the housing and financial markets fade.

Specifically, CBO forecasts that GDP will increase in 2008 by 1.7 percent in real terms (after an adjustment for inflation) and rebound in 2009 to 2.8 percent (see Table 2-1). Given the prospect of weak domestic demand this year, CBO expects inflation to be contained over the next two years. Employment growth, which slowed during 2007, is likely to slow further in 2008, and unemployment, in CBO's estimation, will average 5.1 percent

this year. Interest rates on Treasury securities will remain low in 2008 and increase in 2009, CBO forecasts, as the economy works through and emerges from its current difficulties.

The economic outlook this year is particularly vulnerable to uncertainty about the degree to which the problems in the housing and financial markets will spill over to affect other sectors of the economy. Growth in 2008 could be weaker than CBO expects if the turmoil in the financial markets leads to a more severe economywide curtailment of lending than CBO anticipates. Growth could also be slower if crude oil prices, which jumped sharply late last year, rise even higher and further undercut spending by consumers and businesses.

Alternatively, growth in 2008 could be stronger than CBO is currently forecasting. In particular, financial institutions may be able to absorb mortgage-related losses without triggering significant repercussions in the broader economy. Also, unrelated sectors of the economy (that is, nonhousing and nonfinancial sectors) may continue to support the growth in employment and income necessary to sustain consumer spending.

For the medium-term period (2010 through 2018), CBO projects that real growth will average 2.7 percent and inflation will average 2.2 percent. Those estimates rest on CBO's assumption that the economy will grow at a pace faster than its potential rate of 2.5 percent during the years after 2009 to close the projected gap between GDP and potential GDP at the end of 2009. (Potential GDP is a level of output that corresponds to a high level of resource—labor and capital—use.) CBO also projects that the unemployment rate will average 4.8 percent and interest rates on 3-month Treasury bills and 10-year Treasury notes will average 4.7 percent and 5.2 percent, respectively, during the latter years of the period.

---

1. The National Bureau of Economic Research is by convention responsible for dating the peaks and troughs of the business cycle. According to its Business Cycle Dating Committee, a recession is "a significant decline in economic activity spread across the economy, lasting more than a few months, normally visible in real [inflation-adjusted] GDP, real income, employment, industrial production, and wholesale-retail sales." For further discussion, see www.nber.org/cycles/jan08bcdc_memo.html.

Table 2-1.

CBO's Economic Projections for Calendar Years 2008 to 2018

	Estimated 2007	Forecast 2008	Forecast 2009	Projected Annual Average 2010 to 2013	Projected Annual Average 2014 to 2018
		Year to Year (Percentage change)			
Nominal GDP (Billions of dollars)	13,828	14,330	14,997	18,243 [a]	22,593 [b]
Nominal GDP	4.8	3.6	4.7	5.0	4.4
Real GDP	2.2	1.7	2.8	3.1	2.5
GDP Price Index	2.5	1.9	1.8	1.9	1.9
PCE Price Index[c]	2.5	2.6	1.8	1.9	1.9
Core PCE Price Index[d]	2.1	1.9	1.9	1.9	1.9
Consumer Price Index[e]	2.8	2.9	2.3	2.2	2.2
Core Consumer Price Index[f]	2.3	2.2	2.2	2.2	2.2
		Calendar Year Average (Percent)			
Unemployment Rate	4.6	5.1	5.4	4.9	4.8
Three-Month Treasury Bill Rate	4.4	3.2	4.2	4.6	4.7
Ten-Year Treasury Note Rate	4.6	4.2	4.9	5.2	5.2
Tax Bases (Billions of dollars)					
Economic profits	1,599	1,620	1,649	1,842 [a]	2,320 [b]
Wages and salaries	6,368	6,615	6,913	8,401 [a]	10,354 [b]
Tax Bases (Percentage of GDP)					
Economic profits	11.6	11.3	11.0	10.3	10.1
Wages and salaries	46.0	46.2	46.1	46.1	45.9
		Fourth Quarter to Fourth Quarter (Percentage change)			
Nominal GDP	4.7	3.7	5.1	5.0	4.4
Real GDP	2.5	1.5	3.3	3.0	2.4
GDP Price Index	2.2	2.1	1.8	1.9	1.9
PCE Price Index[c]	3.2	2.1	1.9	1.9	1.9
Core PCE Price Index[d]	2.0	1.9	1.9	1.9	1.9
Consumer Price Index[e]	3.8	2.5	2.2	2.2	2.2
Core Consumer Price Index[f]	2.2	2.2	2.2	2.2	2.2

Sources: Congressional Budget Office; Department of Commerce, Bureau of Economic Analysis; Department of Labor, Bureau of Labor Statistics; Federal Reserve Board.

Notes: GDP = gross domestic product; PCE = personal consumption expenditure.

Economic projections for each year from 2008 to 2018 appear in Appendix E.

a. Level in 2013.

b. Level in 2018.

c. The personal consumption expenditure chained price index.

d. The personal consumption expenditure chained price index excluding prices for food and energy.

e. The consumer price index for all urban consumers.

f. The consumer price index for all urban consumers excluding prices for food and energy.

Compared with its August 2007 estimates, CBO's current forecast for the near term—that is, the next two years—indicates much slower growth, significantly higher inflation in 2008, lower interest rates, and a smaller share of GDP attributable to firms' profits. The weakness in the housing sector, the turbulence in the financial markets, and the rise in energy prices now appear to be undercutting the growth of GDP to a greater degree than CBO envisioned last summer. The less expansive outlook for the near term also results in lower interest rates on Treasury securities in 2008 than CBO had expected in August. Inflation as measured by the consumer price index for all urban consumers (CPI-U) during the last few months of 2007 was much higher than anticipated—prices for motor fuel shot up unexpectedly—and that growth has boosted the year-over-year rise in prices that CBO expects in 2008. However, the measure of inflation that excludes food and energy—core inflation—grew only slightly more than CBO anticipated last August, and consequently, the outlook for core inflation is essentially unchanged.

The Threat to the Economy From the Turmoil in the Financial Markets

The nation's financial markets have been buffeted by events stemming from the downturn in the housing sector and the losses associated with subprime mortgage loans—that is, loans extended to borrowers who have low credit ratings and a high risk of default. The ultimate magnitude of the subprime-related losses is highly uncertain, in part because it depends on how the economy evolves over the next few years and how far house prices fall. However, rough estimates by some financial analysts suggest that the losses are in the range of $200 billion to $500 billion.[2] Moreover, because most subprime loans have been pooled into mortgage-backed securities, rather than held by their originators, and those securities have subsequently been restructured as parts of other complex investment securities, who will actually bear those losses is unclear. The uncertainty among investors about their exposure to subprime-related losses has led many of them to reassess the creditworthiness of a wide variety of financial instruments.

Increased aversion to risk in the nation's financial markets, which marks a shift from an unusually high level of tolerance for risk taking in recent years, could threaten to slow economic activity above and beyond the direct effects of the subprime losses. The availability of credit has become severely restricted for some borrowers, especially those seeking money for risky mortgages and businesses. In addition, borrowing costs have increased not only for subprime residential mortgages but also for some consumer and business loans. The troubles in the U.S. subprime mortgage market have also affected financial markets in other industrialized countries, threatening to slow economic growth there as well. Consequently, policymakers in the United States and abroad have worked to reduce the turmoil in the markets.

CBO does not expect that turmoil to balloon into a severe, economywide credit crunch. The pullback from risk in the financial markets, though, is likely to contribute to the continued tightness of credit, especially for housing and the riskier ventures among businesses' investments. If a severe credit crunch did occur, it would drive the economy into recession by significantly curbing financial activity and consumer spending. However, CBO assumes in its forecast that the Federal Reserve will implement policies to prevent such a crunch and that the financial sector is capable of absorbing most of the losses it faces. In fact, despite their current financial stresses, some banks that have suffered large losses from their subprime-related investments have thus far survived those setbacks and are now successfully raising needed capital. Moreover, most prime borrowers—those whose credit ratings are solid—are unlikely to encounter major difficulties in funding their investments.

Problems in Subprime Mortgage Markets

The recent turbulence in the financial markets originated with subprime mortgage lending, especially on subprime adjustable-rate mortgages, or ARMs.[3] The number of

---

2. The Organisation for Economic Co-operation and Development (OECD) suggests that the ultimate cumulative losses will be in the range of $200 billion to $300 billion (see Adrian Blundell-Wignall, *Structured Products: Implications for Financial Markets*, Paris, OECD, 2007). Wall Street investment firms project larger losses: Goldman Sachs estimates total losses of around $400 billion (Goldman Sachs, *US Daily Financial Market Comment*, November 15, 2007), and Merrill Lynch puts them at around $500 billion (David A. Rosenberg, "A Daily Snapshot of Market Moving Developments," *Morning Market Memo*, New York, Merrill Lynch, December 19, 2007).

3. Rates on ARMs are subject to change when market interest rates change. (Rates are frequently tied to the rates banks charge each other for short-term loans.) Many subprime ARMs are hybrid products in which rates are fixed for the first two or three years and are reset annually thereafter.

Figure 2-1.

Mortgage Delinquencies

(Percentage of loans)

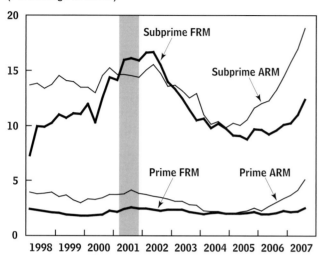

Sources: Congressional Budget Office; Mortgage Bankers Association.

Notes: Data are quarterly and are plotted through the third quarter of 2007.

ARM = adjustable-rate mortgage; FRM = fixed-rate mortgage.

subprime mortgages has grown rapidly in recent years: In 2005 and 2006, such loans made up about one-fifth of all originations of home mortgages (in dollar terms); they accounted for about 13 percent of all home mortgages at the end of that latter year.[4] Although the expansion of subprime mortgage lending allowed more people to buy homes, that outcome was achieved in large part by significantly lowering credit standards and offering terms on such lending that were more favorable than had been seen in the past. For example, lenders sometimes made loans to borrowers who would not be able to make their scheduled future payments after their very low introductory interest rates (known as "teaser rates") expired. The fall in housing prices that has occurred over the past year combined with a tightening of lending standards has greatly diminished borrowers' ability to sell their homes or refinance their mortgage loans, leaving many of them with repayment problems.

As a result, the number of delinquencies and foreclosures on subprime ARMs began to rise dramatically after 2005. By the third quarter of 2007, almost 19 percent of subprime ARMs were considered delinquent, up from a recent low of 10 percent in the second quarter of 2005 (see Figure 2-1). In addition, the share of subprime ARMs entering foreclosure more than tripled, rising from an average of 1.5 percent in 2004 and 2005 to 4.7 percent in the third quarter of 2007. Although the share of delinquent fixed-rate subprime loans has also grown, it is still smaller and has grown more slowly than the share of delinquent subprime ARMs.

The very high rates of delinquency on recent subprime mortgage loans surprised investors, and lenders have virtually stopped making new subprime loans. Trading of existing subprime mortgage-backed securities (MBSs) has diminished, and their prices have fallen sharply, to as low as 14 cents on the dollar for the riskiest of those securities, because of uncertainty about their value, particularly in view of investors' loss of confidence in the securities' credit ratings. The price declines were steepest for subprime MBSs that had been issued more recently, suggesting that lenders have significantly lowered their standards for making loans in the past few years.

Mortgage delinquencies and foreclosures could be a problem for the economy and the financial markets for several years. In the case of subprime ARMs, rates for some loans have already been reset, but those on an additional 1.7 million mortgages will be reset during 2008 and 2009.[5] Those changes, plus the ones occurring in later years (most before the end of 2010), could eventually add about $40 billion to borrowers' annual payments.[6] Although that increase is not large relative to households' total after-tax income ($10 trillion), many households will be hard-pressed to make the higher payments, and some will default on their mortgages and go into foreclosure. The risk of a sharp increase in foreclosures has led to various actions and proposals to help the market cope with the repayment problems among borrowers with subprime ARMs.[7]

---

4. For additional information on the problems in the market for subprime mortgages and their impact on financial markets, see the statement of Peter R. Orszag, Director, Congressional Budget Office, *The Current Economic Situation*, before the House Committee on the Budget, December 5, 2007.

5. Sheila C. Bair, "The Case for Loan Modification," *FDIC Quarterly*, vol. 1, no. 3 (2007), pp. 22–29.

6. See Christopher L. Cagan, *Mortgage Payment Reset: The Issue and the Impact* (Santa Ana, Calif.: First American CoreLogic, March 19, 2007).

7. See Congressional Budget Office, *Options for Responding to Short-Term Economic Weakness* (January 2008).

Spillovers Into Other Financial Markets

The problems of the subprime mortgage market have undermined the confidence of many investors and caused them to reduce their holdings of mortgage loans and of other asset-backed securities associated with particularly risky lending to businesses and consumers. That contagion effect has been intensified by the lack of transparency about which financial instruments and institutions face losses from defaults on subprime mortgages, forcing investors and financial institutions to reevaluate the risk of their investments in a wide range of financial assets. That reassessment has subsequently lessened investors' willingness to bear such risk and driven down the value of suspect assets, some of which were once thought to have little possibility of default.

Some of that reassessment can be seen as a correction to the underpricing of risk that had occurred in recent years and that contributed to the current turmoil in the financial markets. For example, because the revaluation of risk led to what the markets term a "flight to quality" (that is, a shift from riskier investments to such instruments as U.S. Treasury securities, which investors consider safe), interest rates on prime mortgage loans have actually declined in recent months. To date, the market for conforming mortgages (mortgages that are no greater than $417,000), which make up the bulk of all mortgage loans, has seen no significant adverse effects from the subprime mortgage troubles (see Box 2-1).[8] Some people fear, however, that the reassessment will go too far and jeopardize economic growth by indiscriminately reducing funding for profitable investments.

Jumbo Mortgages. In the mortgage markets, the spillover from subprime defaults has been most pronounced for jumbo mortgages—those in amounts greater than those for conforming loans. The availability of funds in the market for existing jumbo loans (a so-called secondary market that resells such loans in the form of securities) has sharply declined; consequently, rates on new jumbo loans in the (primary) market have risen. Borrowers now pay roughly one percentage point more for jumbo loans than for conforming loans (see Figure 2-2). Relatively few new jumbo loans are now securitized.[9]

Figure 2-2.

Corporate Bond Yields and Mortgage Rates

(Percent)

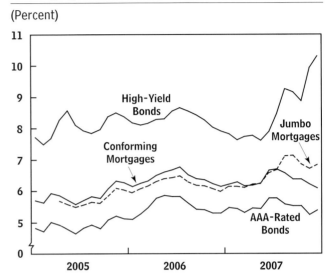

Sources: Congressional Budget Office; Federal Reserve Board; Bloomberg; *Wall Street Journal*.

Note: Data are monthly and are plotted through December 2007.

Corporate Bonds. Spillovers from the troubles in the mortgage markets have also raised the cost of borrowing for businesses that have low credit ratings. In the corporate sector, interest rates on high-yield or speculative-grade bonds—those whose risk of default is judged to be high—jumped last summer when the subprime market's problems emerged, and the rates remain elevated. By contrast, the average interest rate on investment-grade bonds (those with a low risk of default) was essentially the same last year as in 2006. Nevertheless, the difference between the interest rate on investment-grade bonds and that on 10-year Treasury notes, an indication of the riskiness of those bonds, has risen compared with what it was last year, suggesting that repricing of risk has occurred even in the market for the safest corporate debt.

Commercial Paper. The market for commercial paper, a kind of loan that plays a key role in providing short-term

---

8. Some other indicators, though, such as the October Senior Loan Officer Opinion Survey by the Federal Reserve, suggest that lending standards have been tightened for all mortgage borrowers.

9. Securitization is the process by which loans (student loans, mortgages, commercial loans, and automobile loans) and other receivables (credit card payments) are assembled into pools and then their cash flows sold as tradable asset-backed securities that are purchased by different classes of investors who accept different levels of risk.

Box 2-1.

Conforming Mortgages and the Role of Fannie Mae and Freddie Mac

The problems in the subprime mortgage market have not affected the availability of conforming mortgages—that is, mortgages that are eligible to be purchased on the secondary mortgage market by Fannie Mae and Freddie Mac. In fact, mortgage rates in the latter market have fallen because investors have bid up the price of the mortgage-backed securities (MBSs) offered by those two government-sponsored enterprises, or GSEs. GSEs are private financial institutions chartered by the federal government to promote the flow of credit for targeted uses—in this case, housing. To do that, they raise funds in the capital markets partly on the strength of an implied federal guarantee against the risk of default (which reduces their borrowing costs and enables them to hold less capital than other borrowers and yet still borrow large sums).

Although losses resulting from the subprime troubles have affected the potential of the GSEs to hold loans, they are unlikely to affect Fannie's and Freddie's ability to guarantee MBSs. The two GSEs' concentration in the prime mortgage market helps insulate them from losses, but as of fall 2007, they still held about $230 billion in subprime and Alt-A mortgages.[1] (In terms of their level of risk, Alt-A mortgages carry a higher rating than do subprime mortgages but a lower rating than prime mortgages.) Because of their subprime-related losses, the GSEs' capital cushion in the third quarter of 2007 had dropped to just about $3 billion—on top, that is, of the $73 billion in capital that current laws and regulations require to safeguard the $1.6 trillion in assets carried on their balance sheets and the $3.3 trillion in off-balance-sheet guarantees of MBSs for which they are responsible.[2]

That modest cushion of $3 billion left little capacity to absorb further losses.

Consequently, Fannie Mae and Freddie Mac have raised $13 billion in new capital and cut their dividends. However, even if they had chosen not to raise more capital, the GSEs could have continued to guarantee returns on MBSs as long as they reduced their portfolios of mortgages—because the capital they are required to maintain for the mortgages held on their balance sheets is about five times higher than the capital required for their guarantees. Because the implicit federal backing that the GSEs' guarantees carry is the source of the lower costs for borrowing that they obtain in the conforming mortgage market, any problems that the GSEs encounter will probably not affect that market but could affect their ability to buy more subprime and Alt-A mortgages.

Fannie Mae and Freddie Mac have announced risk-based increases in some of their fees, which will probably be passed on to most borrowers—in the form of higher origination costs—beginning in March 2008. For some borrowers who have low credit scores and small down payments, the additional amounts they will have to pay could be several thousand dollars. For other borrowers who appear more creditworthy and make bigger down payments, the amounts will be much smaller.

Pending legislation would raise the conforming loan limits to assist borrowers in regions of the country (such as the West Coast) where home prices are high. Other proposals would increase the assistance that the GSEs provide to the subprime market. However, unless those initiatives are accompanied by higher capital requirements and regulatory reform, the implicit risk for the GSEs' operations that is borne by taxpayers will increase.

---

1. Alt-A mortgage loans, which share many of the same problems as subprime mortgage loans, were often made on the basis of undocumented income. Recently, Alt-A mortgages have included low-down-payment loans, interest-only loans, and loans whose balances rise over time. Those loans are defaulting at sharply rising rates.

2. For more information, see Congressional Budget Office, *Measuring the Capital Position of Fannie Mae and Freddie Mac* (June 2006).

Box 2-2.

Structured Investment Vehicles

Structured investment vehicles (SIVs) are entities that issue short-term commercial paper as well as medium-term notes to finance the purchase of longer-maturity, higher-yielding assets. (Such assets include asset-backed securities, which are made up of bank loans, mortgage-backed securities, and debt obligations backed by credit card receivables, automobile and other loans, and, in some cases, subprime mortgages.) Estimates are that in the summer of 2007, SIVs represented about $400 billion. However, the recent difficulties that those entities have encountered as a result of the subprime-related turmoil in the financial markets have caused a steady decline in that amount, to less than $150 billion as of early December 2007.[1]

Because the maturities of their assets are longer than the maturities of their liabilities, SIVs periodically need to roll over, or "re-fund," their debt (that is, pay off their old debt with new debt). That re-funding requires that lenders be willing to take on the risks associated with a SIV's investment portfolio. However, when markets are disrupted and the value of such a portfolio becomes difficult to establish, re-funding also becomes difficult—or impossible. In that case, a SIV may have to sell its most marketable assets to pay off its commercial paper and debt—as many SIVs may have done in recent months.

SIVs are known as off-balance-sheet entities because they are legally separate from the banks (or other institutions) that have created them and typically are not carried on the banks' balance sheets. Although such banks may have backup agreements with the SIVs to extend credit if requested, they have no legal obligation to cover the SIVs' losses. They may choose to do so, though, to protect their reputations. As long as the SIV does not appear on the bank's balance sheet, it has little or no effect on the bank's capital requirements. Those requirements, promulgated by bank regulators, stipulate (as a ratio) the amount of equity that a bank must hold in relation to the amount of assets on its balance sheet and the riskiness of those assets.

SIVs are often required to start selling their assets if their losses exceed certain threshold percentages of their capital or if they violate provisions that specify the liquidity (broadly, the available funds) they must maintain. Those involuntary sales may then push down the prices of the SIVs' assets, which could cause losses in the value of similar types of assets held by other SIVs and force those SIVs into such involuntary sales as well. The losses could also trigger defaults on commercial paper already issued by the SIVs and further impede their ability to borrow money.

Recent actions by some large banks to resolve the troubles of their sponsored SIVs have included bringing the SIVs' assets—and losses—back onto the banks' balance sheets. Those actions reduce a bank's capital ratio and absorb some of the bank's lending capacity—because the assets become either a loan or an investment of the bank, potentially crowding out other loans or investments.

---

1. Those estimates were drawn from "Remarks by Treasury Secretary Henry M. Paulson Jr. on housing and capital markets before the New York Society of Securities Analysts" (January 7, 2008), available at www.treasury.gov/press/releases/hp757.htm.

---

credit to both financial and nonfinancial businesses, has been especially affected by losses in the subprime mortgage market. In particular, those losses have severely curtailed the asset-backed segment of the commercial paper market, which has provided financing for structured investment vehicles (SIVs) and other investment funds

(or conduits) sponsored by banks (see Box 2-2). The total amount of outstanding commercial paper has dropped sharply since the summer of 2007, which indicates that businesses' access to short-term credit has been constricted. That constriction is primarily due to the decline in the amount of asset-backed commercial paper;

Figure 2-3.

Outstanding Amounts of Commercial Paper, by Issuer

(Billions of dollars)

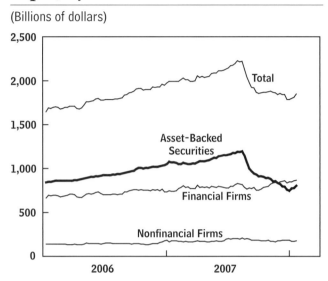

Sources: Congressional Budget Office; Federal Reserve Board.

Note: Data are weekly and are plotted through January 18, 2008.

other commercial paper markets have not been as significantly affected by the subprime losses (see Figure 2-3).

Bank Loans. Some banks have been hit hard by their exposure to subprime mortgage lending, both directly and indirectly through the activities of SIVs, raising concerns that banks might substantially restrict their lending. Banks are an important conduit for channeling credit to businesses and consumers, acting variously as originators of loans, securitizers, providers of backup credit lines to issuers of commercial paper, and investors in bonds. Although no one yet knows the share of subprime-related losses that banks will ultimately have to absorb, the losses announced to date have been significant. Those losses have reduced banks' capital and forced banks to tighten their credit terms on business and consumer loans. That tightening could curb the growth of the overall economy if many banks cannot easily raise additional capital to fund new lending.

Banks' capacity to lend to businesses and consumers might already be under stress. Commercial and industrial loans have increased sharply since the turmoil began last summer (see Figure 2-4). That increase probably in large part reflects lending that the banks are committed to make when backup credit lines are activated by failed asset-backed commercial paper programs. At the same

time, banks' investment in securities has increased, as they have brought some of the assets of their sponsored SIVs back onto their balance sheets, displacing other loans they might have made.

The severity of subprime-related losses and their effect on banks' lending capacity are open questions and likely to remain so throughout 2008, but expectations are that the banking system as a whole will not be imperiled. Thus far, some major financial institutions have been able to raise new capital; also, the tightening of credit standards to date has been less extreme than the tightening that occurred during the banking crisis of the early 1990s. Furthermore, because assets backed by subprime mortgages are widely held, other financial institutions besides banks—including hedge funds, pension funds, and other investment funds—as well as financial institutions in the rest of the world will also absorb some portion of the subprime-related losses.

Federal Reserve Actions and Interest Rates

Since its actions in August, when the turbulence in the financial markets began, the Federal Reserve has taken additional steps to increase the availability of credit and keep the economy growing. In August, it injected

Figure 2-4.

Banks' Commercial and Industrial Loans and Investment in Securities

(Billions of dollars)

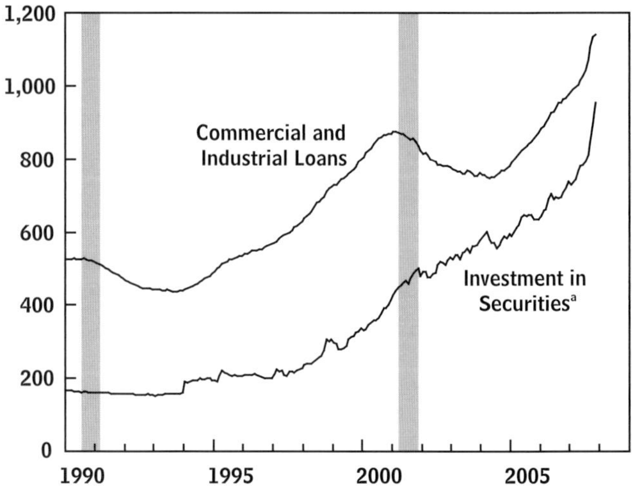

Sources: Congressional Budget Office; Federal Reserve Board.

Note: Data are monthly and are plotted through November 2007.

a. Other than U.S. government and government agency securities.

temporary reserves into the banking system—which moved the federal funds rate (the interest rate that financial institutions charge each other for overnight loans of their monetary reserves held at the central bank) below its target—and it lowered the discount rate (the interest rate that the Federal Reserve charges on a loan it makes to a bank). With conditions in financial markets still turbulent in the fall of 2007, the central bank cut its target rate, ending the year at 4.25 percent.

Late last year, the Federal Reserve took additional action to lessen the persistent stress on the money markets and announced a new policy instrument called the term auction facility, or TAF. In December, the TAF auctioned $40 billion in short-term financing to depository institutions that are eligible to borrow from the Federal Reserve's discount window; by the end of January, it will have auctioned another $60 billion (see Box 2-3).

Short-term credit markets have benefited significantly from the Federal Reserve's actions and its assurances of support for financial institutions. The international interbank market and the domestic commercial paper market—the short-term markets most affected by the subprime problems—have recovered from the summer's upsets (although in the case of asset-backed commercial paper, spreads, or differences, between borrowing rates and the federal funds rate are still larger than normal, and the number of transactions is smaller than usual.)

CBO expects that the Federal Reserve will further reduce the federal funds rate to prevent credit shortages in 2008 from retarding the growth of the economy and to counter the negative effects arising from a fragile housing market and high oil prices. In CBO's forecast, the target federal funds rate falls to 3.5 percent by the middle of 2008 and holds at that level for the rest of the year. As the economy recovers, the rate will gradually rise to 4.75 percent in early 2010, CBO anticipates.

CBO's assumptions about monetary policy and the economy underpin its forecast for interest rates on Treasury bills and notes. CBO estimates that the rate on 3 month Treasury bills will average 3.2 percent in 2008, reflecting the lower federal funds rate and the heightened demand for Treasury securities arising from the subprime-related troubles in the commercial paper market. CBO expects the rate to move higher, to 4.2 percent, in 2009 as the economy recovers and financial market problems ease. For many of the same reasons, CBO forecasts that the

rate on 10-year Treasury notes will climb from an average of 4.2 percent in 2008 to 4.9 percent in 2009. That estimate for the 10-year note incorporates the assumption that investors will remain confident that the Federal Reserve is committed to keeping inflation low.

How the U.S. Subprime-Related Turmoil Has Affected Other Countries

The troubles in the U.S. subprime mortgage market have directly affected financial institutions in other industrialized countries, particularly those that had invested heavily in U.S. securities backed by subprime mortgages or those that were relying on short-term interbank financing for longer-term loans. The international interbank market facilitates domestic and international transactions and provides payment and settlement services to businesses, consumers, and governments. A measure of perceptions of risk among banks in that market is the spread of the three-month dollar interbank rate—known as the dollar LIBOR rate—relative to the expected federal funds rate over that interval.[10] That LIBOR spread jumped during last summer's turmoil and again in November and early December. Spreads also increased between LIBOR rates for other major currencies and the expected policy rates of the corresponding central banks. A key factor in those hikes was concern about the adequacy of the capital held by banks that have had to absorb subprime-related losses—concern fueled by uncertainty about how much larger those losses might turn out to be.

The European Central Bank, the Bank of Canada, and the Bank of England have each injected substantial amounts of cash into their countries' financial markets to contain the credit crisis and bolster liquidity. Besides liquidity injections, the Bank of England cut its policy interest rate (similar to the federal funds rate) by 25 basis points on December 6 (a basis point is one-hundredth of a percentage point), acknowledging that the deterioration in financial conditions and the subsequent tightening of credit had increased the risk that economic growth might slow. (So far, other central banks have held off on previously planned hikes in interest rates.) As a result of those and other policy actions, the spread between the three-month dollar LIBOR rate and the expected federal funds rate (like the corresponding spreads in other currencies) has now narrowed but remains high relative to its normal level.

---

10. The dollar LIBOR (London Interbank Offered Rate) is the rate at which banks lend to each other for transactions in dollars.

Box 2-3.

The Federal Reserve's Term Auction Facility

On December 12, the Federal Reserve introduced a new policy tool, the term auction facility (TAF), to supply funds to financial institutions. The TAF was designed to address the wider-than-normal spread, or difference, that the subprime-related problems in the financial markets induced between the markets' expectations about the federal funds rate (the rate that financial institutions charge for overnight loans of their monetary reserves) and the dollar LIBOR, or London Interbank Offered Rate (which banks charge each other for short-term loans and which is widely used as a reference rate for financial instruments). Similar discrepancies occurred in LIBOR markets for other currencies.

The TAF has elements of two other mechanisms that have long been part of the Federal Reserve's monetary policymaking apparatus: open market operations and discount window lending. In its open market operations, which constitute the central bank's main tool for implementing monetary policy, the Federal Reserve buys and sells U.S. Treasury and federal agency securities through an auction involving representatives of member institutions (known as primary securities dealers). In that way, the Federal Reserve adjusts the supply of monetary reserves in the bank-

ing system in order to influence the federal funds rate. (The Federal Reserve's Open Market Committee establishes a target for that rate.)

In contrast, at the discount window, the Federal Reserve accepts requests for short-term loans by commercial banks and other depository institutions that have short-term liquidity needs or that face severe financial difficulties. For most banks, the discount rate is set as a spread (a certain number of basis points, or hundredths of a percentage point) above the target federal funds rate.[1] The rate that the Federal Reserve charges banks that are in good financial shape is lower than the rate it charges other banks. In times of financial market stress, however, banks have sometimes been reluctant to borrow through the discount window for fear of being stigmatized as weak and thus losing access to private sources of funds (such as other banks).

The TAF, which was designed to overcome that hesitation, is similar to open market operations in that funds are supplied through an auction. However, it differs in that under the TAF, the Federal Reserve

---

1. Small banks in agricultural or resort communities pay a rate that is an average of selected market rates.

As in the United States, housing prices in many other parts of the world have soared, but the financial disturbances here are unlikely to trigger a collapse in housing markets abroad. Most countries do not have subprime mortgage markets like those in the United States; also, they do not have an oversupply of housing, as this country does, because land is more limited and mortgage financing standards are more conservative. Nevertheless, shortages of credit in some countries may require action by those nations' central banks.

The Prospect of Slow Economic Growth in the Near Term

The pace of economic growth slowed in late 2007, and CBO anticipates additional slackening in 2008. Chief

causes of that slowdown are the problems in the housing and financial markets and high oil prices. If those factors continue to worsen, they could further weaken consumers' and businesses' confidence about the future, which might constrain economic activity even more than CBO now anticipates. Indeed, some indicators imply that the risk of a recession is high (see Box 2-4). However, the stronger growth of the nation's major trading partners combined with the dollar's decline will partially offset weak domestic demand and support growth by increasing U.S. exports.

Although the troubles in the oil, financial, and housing markets pose a serious risk to the nation's economic health, the economy may navigate those obstacles more successfully than CBO now expects. Despite some

Box 2-3.
Continued

announces the amount of funds that will be supplied and the auction determines the interest rate that will be paid by successful bidders, which in effect pushes that set amount of funds into the credit markets. (In contrast, in open market operations, the amount supplied and the interest rate that successful bidders pay are closely connected to the target for the federal funds rate.) Another difference between open market operations and the TAF is that the Federal Reserve will accept a broader range of securities in payment for TAF-supplied funds than it does for funds supplied through open market operations (for which only U.S. Treasury and government agency securities are accepted). Securities eligible under the TAF are the same as those eligible as collateral for the central bank's discount window lending. However, the open market-type auction of the TAF may eliminate the perceived stigma of using discount window borrowing in times of financial stress and make banks more willing to bid for funds to enhance their liquidity.

The interest rate on TAF-supplied funds in December was between the federal funds rate and the discount window lending rate, but the rate on the funds

auctioned on January 14 was below the federal funds target. The two TAF auctions, on December 17 and December 20, each added $20 billion in liquidity to the banking system at respective rates of 4.65 percent and 4.67 percent (compared with a federal funds target rate of 4.25 percent and a discount window rate of 4.75 percent). The auction on January 14 supplied $30 billion at a rate of 3.95 percent. Another auction on January 28 is scheduled to add another $30 billion.

In addition to the implementation of the TAF, the Federal Reserve set up reciprocal currency swap lines with the central banks of the European Community and Switzerland. The swaps, in which the Federal Reserve temporarily exchanges dollars for the respective central banks' currencies, have facilitated dollar-denominated borrowing by those banks' member institutions.

As a result of the TAF, the swap lines, and other actions, the spread of the dollar LIBOR over the expected federal funds rate has narrowed significantly.

adverse shocks, the economy has been naturally resilient during the past 25 years (although part of that resiliency can be attributed to well-functioning financial markets, and their ability to continue to function well is one of the risks of the current situation). Moreover, employers in the nonhousing portion of the business sector have not accumulated excess workers, capital, or inventories in recent years, implying that firms will not need to cut back as much as they would have in the past in response to ebbing demand. In addition, although globalization has increased the risk that the United States' economic troubles might spill over to other nations, it has also allowed the impact of the decline in U.S. consumer spending to be shared globally, reducing its adverse effects on U.S. producers and workers.

Continued Weakness in the Housing Sector
The housing sector will continue to be a drag on the growth of output in the first half of 2008, CBO forecasts, but it will probably have little direct effect on growth in the second half. The slowdown in residential investment has reduced the annual rate of growth of real GDP by about a percentage point in the past year and a half. However, as lower housing prices make home ownership more affordable and lower rates of construction help reduce the inventory of unsold homes, the numbers of housing "starts" (new housing units beginning construction) and of sales of new and existing homes will stop falling late in 2008 and then start growing in 2009.

Box 2-4.
Recession Signals

Two relatively reliable indicators of a recession, one based on the unemployment rate and the other on a relationship between long- and short-term interest rates, imply that a recession in 2008 is likely. The first such indicator is the change in the three-month moving average of the unemployment rate. Whenever the change in the average from the previous year has been 0.4 percentage points or more, the economy has been in a recession (see the figure to the right). For all recessions since 1975, the 0.4 percentage-point signal came within one to three months of the onset of the recession.

In the current business cycle, the 0.4 percentage-point threshold was reached when the Bureau of Labor Statistics released the December 2007 unemployment data on January 4. Yet the signal is partially undercut by the lack of support from some other labor-market data. For example, in past recessions, the number of layoffs usually increased around the time that the recession began. The most prominent measure of layoffs, the four-week moving average of initial claims for unemployment benefits, has begun to edge upward, but the increase to date is small and does not seem to indicate a recession. Moreover, surveys of employers thus far do not suggest that they plan large future reductions in hiring. Still, such labor-market indicators could deteriorate suddenly, once it became clear that demand was substantially weakening.[1]

Changes in the Unemployment Rate

(Percentage points)

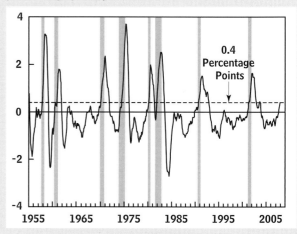

Sources: Congressional Budget Office; Department of Labor, Bureau of Labor Statistics.

Note: Changes are from the previous year in the three-month moving average of the civilian unemployment rate. Data are plotted through December 2007.

---

1. Some economists have argued that patterns of hiring and firing over the course of the business cycle have changed in recent years. See Robert Shimer, *Reassessing the Ins and Outs of Unemployment*, NBER Working Paper No. 13421 (Cambridge, Mass.: National Bureau of Economic Research, September 2007); and Robert Hall, "How Much Do We Understand About the Modern Recession?" (paper prepared for the Brookings Panel on Economic Activity, September 2007).

Housing Construction and Sales. During 2007, the numbers of housing starts and home sales continued to fall. The number of starts dropped by more than 38 percent for the year ending in December 2007, after sinking by 18 percent for the year ending in December 2006. Sales of new single-family homes for the year ending in November 2007 fell by 34 percent and are down by 53 percent from their peak in 2005. The ratio of unsold homes to monthly home sales has risen to the level observed in most recessions in the past: In November, it stood at 9.3 months, slightly higher than its level during

the recession of 1990 and 1991, for example. Sales of existing single-family homes have also continued to drop: They fell by 20 percent in the year ending in November 2007 and are down by about 30 percent from their peak in 2005.

CBO expects an upturn in the number of housing starts in 2009, in part because currently they are considerably below the underlying demand for new units (see Figure 2-5). Underlying demand—that is, the need for new housing units—is based on growth in the number of

Box 2-4.

Continued

Another relatively reliable signal of a recession is a negative yield spread, which occurs whenever a short-term interest rate (such as the rate for one-year Treasury bills) is above a long-term interest rate (such as the rate on 10-year Treasury notes). All but one occurrence of a negative yield spread since 1955 have foreshadowed an upcoming recession (see the figure to the right). From mid-2006 to mid-2007, the yield spread was continuously negative.

Again, though, that signal may be misleading this time, for two reasons. First, the yield-spread signal incorporates the assumption that high short-term rates and low long-term rates have the same impact on the probability of a downturn. If high short-term rates are more important, then the degree of monetary restraint normally implied by a negative yield spread may not be present this time.

Second, the long period of relatively mild inflation since 1985 may have caused investors to be more confident than in the past about the ability and commitment of the Federal Reserve to control inflation. If concerns about a possible sustained increase in inflation have ebbed over the years, the long-term interest rate would tend to be closer to the short-term rate even if no recession was in the offing—that is,

long-term rates would not have to reflect as large an "inflation risk premium" as they have in the past. Less volatility in economic activity can have a similar effect. Therefore, a slight inversion of the yield curve may be less of a recession signal now than in the past.

Yield Spread

(Percentage points)

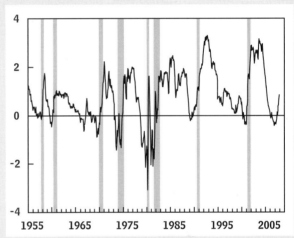

Sources: Congressional Budget Office; Federal Reserve Board.

Note: The spread is calculated as the difference between the rates on the 10-year Treasury note and the 1-year Treasury bill. Data are monthly and are plotted through December 2007.

households and estimates of the replacements required to cover the net removal of old units from the stock of usable housing. The number of starts is currently well below the estimate of underlying demand because of the unusually large excess inventory of vacant units. As those vacant units are sold, starts are expected to gradually return to the level of underlying demand.

Prices and Affordability. House prices have fallen sharply since their peak in the middle of 2006. A number of indexes are available to track prices; each is flawed, but together they give a sense of trends. One measure—the Standard & Poor's (S&P)/Case-Shiller national price index for single-family homes, originally developed by financial economists Karl Case and Robert Shiller—was

down by 5 percent in the third quarter of 2007 from its peak in the second quarter of 2006. (Those are the latest data available for that index.) In real terms, that amounts to an 8 percent drop over the period (see Figure 2-6). Rapid declines in home prices continued in the fourth quarter of 2007: By October, a narrower S&P/Case-Shiller index for just 20 cities (but available monthly) had fallen by 6.5 percent from its peak. Those trends are generally confirmed by a third price index, published by Radar Logic, Incorporated, a real estate and data analysis firm. (Another widely used index, the purchase-only index published by the Office of Federal Housing Enterprise Oversight, or OFHEO, did not begin to decline until the third quarter of 2007. The difference between

Figure 2-5.

Housing Starts and the Underlying Demand for New Housing

(Millions of units)

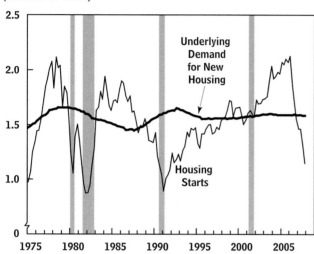

Sources: Congressional Budget Office; Department of Commerce, Bureau of the Census.

Notes: Housing starts include both single- and multifamily homes. The underlying demand for new housing is based on the growth in the number of households and the depreciation of the housing stock.

Data are quarterly and are plotted through the fourth quarter of 2007.

its movement and that of the other indexes may reflect the fact that the OFHEO index does not include homes with jumbo or subprime mortgages and thus excludes parts of the market that have seen the greatest difficulties in recent months.)[11]

The outlook for home prices is highly uncertain, but they are likely to continue to fall during 2008. Expectations of

---

11. Measures of home prices differ substantially in their coverage and how they handle changes in quality. The OFHEO index covers all areas of the country and has a relatively sophisticated adjustment for quality—a major issue in measuring home prices—but it is restricted to houses with conforming mortgages, thus missing the parts of the market that have been most affected by the recent turmoil. The S&P/Case-Shiller indexes use the same adjustment for quality and cover fewer markets and only single-family homes. However, they include all such homes in a covered area, whatever their type of mortgage. The Radar Logic composite index covers just 25 metropolitan housing markets and is not intended to represent the national market. It picks up all transactions, including condominiums, and is updated daily. Its only quality adjustment, however, is for the size of the residence.

such a decline are widespread. Futures markets, for example, anticipate large additional drops in house prices ranging from 5 percent to 10 percent for the coming year and 13 percent to 20 percent over the next three years. (Such expectations may not be a reliable guide, though, particularly for longer periods, because futures contracts of this kind do not trade frequently or in large numbers and therefore may not represent a broad consensus of investors.)

Private forecasters and investment firms also expect significant declines in nominal house prices. Macroeconomic Advisers, for its December 2007 forecast, assumed a 6.3 percent fall in prices between the middle of 2007 and the end of 2009. Goldman Sachs projects a total decline of 20 percent to 25 percent before an upturn occurs.

Such price declines will help make buying a home more affordable. According to the affordability index compiled by the National Association of Realtors, affordability

Figure 2-6.

Inflation-Adjusted Prices of Houses

(Index, 1990Q1 = 100)

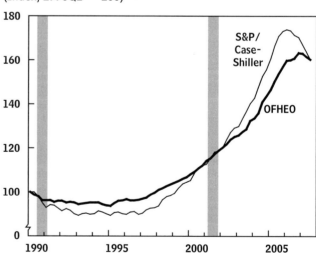

Sources: Congressional Budget Office; Office of Federal Housing Enterprise Oversight; Standard & Poor's; Fiserv; Macro-Markets, LLC; Department of Commerce, Bureau of Economic Analysis.

Notes: Both indexes have been adjusted for inflation by dividing them by the chained price index for personal consumption expenditures.

Data are quarterly and are plotted through the third quarter of 2007.

increased between 2006 and 2007 but remained considerably below its recent high in 2003.[12] The declines in house prices now occurring will contribute to greater affordability, and eventually the number of house sales is likely to increase as buyers start to expect that prices will no longer fall and that their housing investment will yield a positive return in the future.

A Slowdown in Consumer Spending

The growth of real consumer spending slowed last year, and CBO forecasts that its pace will decline further in 2008. The growth of real disposable personal income, a major determinant of consumer spending, is expected to slacken, given the less vigorous economic activity forecast for this year, and households' net wealth, another important determinant, is likely to decline in response to the continuing fall in house prices. Stricter lending standards and terms for borrowing may also slow the growth of consumer spending overall, and the high cost of energy—particularly gasoline—could further dampen spending for nonenergy goods and services.

The Effect of Declines in Housing Wealth. Housing wealth supported consumer spending through 2006, but falling home prices are likely to undercut spending over the next few years. Between 2003 and mid-2006, the rapid growth of housing prices increased homeowners' housing wealth, and many owners made use of that wealth by securing home-equity loans or taking cash out when refinancing their mortgages. The amount of housing equity withdrawn (net of mortgage fees, points, and taxes) totaled an estimated $663 billion in 2005 and $696 billion in 2006, down slightly from a peak of $739 billion in 2004. In 2007, lower prices for houses and stricter lending standards contributed to a slide in the amount of withdrawn equity—those withdrawals were about $550 billion (measured on an annual basis) in the first three quarters of the year. Probably only a small fraction of that amount was used for consumer spending; homeowners used the majority of it for such purposes as home improvements and debt repayment.

CBO expects that by the first quarter of 2009, house prices nationwide will have fallen by about 10 percent from their peak. The decline in housing wealth will lower the growth of real consumer spending in 2008 and 2009 by about 1 percentage point and half a percentage point, respectively.[13]

The Growth of Employment and Household Income. Employment growth declined throughout 2007, and CBO anticipates that its pace will slow further in the near future. Current data show that during 2007, the economy added 111,000 jobs per month—a rate substantially below the 189,000 jobs added monthly during 2006 and the 212,000 jobs per month that were added during 2005.[14] With the slowing of employment growth, the unemployment rate has crept up from an average of 4.5 percent during the first half of 2007 to an average of 4.8 percent during the fourth quarter (with a jump from 4.7 percent to 5.0 percent in December).

Thus far, much of the decline in the growth of employment has been attributed to housing-related industries, such as residential construction and mortgage lending. Since early 2006, employment in residential construction has fallen by about 300,000 jobs (8 percent); about half of that decline occurred during the second half of 2007. However, further large job losses in that sector are quite possible because residential investment has declined much more rapidly than employment over the past two years.[15]

CBO's forecast implies that the pace of job growth will fall further, to an average of about 55,000 jobs added per

---

12. The index measures the financial ability of households to purchase homes. An index of 100 implies that the median household income is just enough (with a 20 percent down payment) to qualify for a mortgage loan on a median-priced, existing single-family home. Higher values of the index imply greater affordability.

13. A significant amount of uncertainty exists about how much spending changes when wealth changes (known as the marginal propensity to consume out of wealth). See Congressional Budget Office, *Housing Wealth and Consumer Spending* (January 2007).

14. In February 2008, the Bureau of Labor Statistics (BLS) will revise the employment data for nonfarm business establishments for 2006 and 2007. BLS has indicated that it will revise the March 2007 employment level downward by 297,000 jobs, or 0.2 percent. That revision would reduce the average monthly growth in establishment employment in the 12 months through March 2007 by roughly 25,000 jobs. It is also likely that, after BLS incorporates information from its benchmark revisions, it will post additional downward revisions to employment growth for the period since March 2007.

15. Why a further drop in measured employment in residential construction has not already occurred remains something of a puzzle. One possible explanation is that some establishments classified by BLS as being involved in residential construction may have shifted many of their resources to unrelated activities.

Figure 2-7.

Consumer Expectations

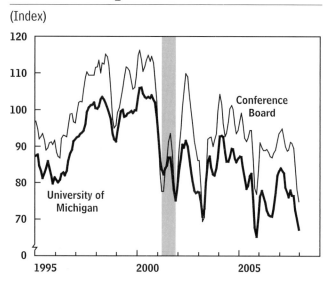

(Index)

Sources: Congressional Budget Office; Conference Board; University of Michigan.

Note: Data are monthly, smoothed using a three-month moving average, and plotted through December 2007.

month during the first half of 2008, and remain sluggish throughout the rest of the year. The unemployment rate, according to CBO's forecast, will rise to 5.3 percent by the end of 2008 and peak at 5.4 percent during 2009.

Despite the increase in unemployment, layoffs may not rise as much as they did in previous slowdowns. In the past few years, firms apparently did not hire excess workers. Much of the slowing in job growth appears to have taken place because of a drop in hiring rather than a rise in layoffs. Rates of both job creation and job destruction have been lower in the past several years than they were in the 1990s, suggesting that employers will need to shed fewer workers when demand weakens than they did during past episodes of ebbing economic activity. That factor, in turn, could prevent the economy's initial weakening from turning into a self-reinforcing downward spiral in the growth of spending, output, and employment.

CBO expects that the rate of growth of hourly wages will decline in the near term. Wages have grown rapidly over the past few years, helping to sustain a rise in consumer spending in the face of a reduction in housing wealth. But hourly wage growth has already started to inch downward, possibly reflecting the slowdown in job creation. For its forecast, CBO assumed that the slow

growth in hourly wages would continue throughout this year. Expectations are that the tepid rise in wages, when combined with a fall in the growth of the number of hours worked, will reduce the growth of household income and consumer spending in the near term.

The High Price of Energy. The price index for consumer spending on energy goods and services rose during 2007, and the increased prices that such a rise reflects are likely to curtail consumer spending on nonenergy goods and services. Consumers' expenditures for energy were about $50 billion higher in the second half of 2007 than in the second half of 2006. Although the increase in oil prices does not seem to have affected spending for goods and services thus far, the persistently high level of energy prices is expected to weaken consumer spending this year.

Consumer Expectations. Consumers' attitudes about their future economic circumstances have deteriorated in the past year. Two commonly used indexes of such attitudes are maintained by the University of Michigan and the Conference Board. Both show that consumer expectations are at their lowest point since the aftermath of the 2005 hurricanes, suggesting that consumer spending is likely to be weak in the near term (see Figure 2-7).

Slower Growth in Investment by Businesses. Stalling domestic demand and the tightening of credit conditions for businesses are likely to reduce the growth rates of firms' spending on investment this year. However, the growth of investment, in CBO's forecast, will improve in 2009, as consumer spending rebounds.

The patterns of growth of the two major categories of business fixed investment have diverged in recent years. The nonresidential-structure component provided solid support for the growth of GDP in 2006 and 2007, but spending for producers' durable equipment and software has been much less robust (see Figure 2-8). The differences in the growth of the two categories can be explained by their cyclical dynamics. In response to the faster growth of demand in 2003 and 2004, businesses boosted the rate of growth of the capital stock by increasing investment. But firms can shift their investment, particularly investment in structures, only slowly because of the time it takes to make such changes and the cost of those adjustments. Investment in equipment and software did not fully catch up to the higher level of demand until early 2006, and nonresidential construction is only now catching up. Just as the growth of investment in

Figure 2-8.

Real Business Fixed Investment

(Percentage change from previous year)

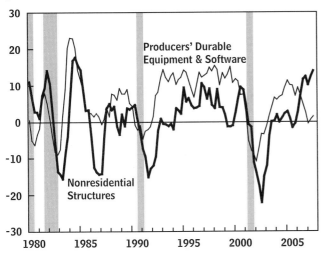

Sources: Congressional Budget Office; Department of Commerce, Bureau of Economic Analysis.

Note: Data are quarterly and are plotted through the third quarter of 2007.

equipment and software slowed in 2006 and 2007, the growth of nonresidential construction will slow in 2008, in CBO's estimation. Also, investment in producers' durable equipment and software will remain weak throughout 2008, CBO forecasts.

Part of that anticipated weakness stems from the increase, for some businesses, in the cost of financing their investment. As mentioned earlier, the risk premium paid by borrowers with a speculative-grade credit rating has risen sharply. Lending standards for business loans, including commercial real estate and commercial and industrial loans, have been tightened. In addition, although the growth of corporate profits, which provide internal funds and lessen the need for borrowing, has been remarkably strong for several years, it has recently slowed.

Nevertheless, the risk of a collapse in business fixed investment—such as those that occurred in the last two recessions—is small. The situation today is much more favorable than it was in the late 1990s, when after many years of rapid growth, investment was overdue for a downturn. This time, profits of many firms have grown briskly for many years, and many nonfinancial companies have large cash holdings that will partially insulate them from the credit crunch. Buyouts still occur frequently

(although those that use private equity occur less often). In addition, the level of the capital stock does not appear excessive in relation to the fundamentals of investment—demand, productivity, and employment—so the slowdown in the growth of demand that CBO anticipates is unlikely to be exacerbated by a major retrenchment in businesses' investment.

Strengthening of Net Exports

Although the growth of domestic demand will slow in 2008, the growth of domestic output and employment will be partially buoyed, CBO forecasts, by an increase in net exports. The decline in domestic demand growth will reduce U.S. consumers' spending on imports as well, and relatively strong economic expansion abroad will keep sales of U.S. products there rising. As a result, the trade deficit is forecast to decline (that is, net exports will become less negative), and the current-account deficit is also expected to shrink.[16] CBO forecasts that the rise in net exports will directly boost GDP growth this year by about three-quarters of a percentage point.

Stronger Growth Among the United States' Trading Partners. CBO expects that despite some slowing, economic growth abroad in the near term will remain more robust than growth in the United States. The outlook for the industrialized economies, in particular, is now subject to a higher degree of uncertainty as a result of the continuing vulnerability of global financial markets to the subprime-related troubles in the United States. Emerging economies, however, are expected to continue their strong economic expansions.

The turmoil in the financial markets will affect foreign economies less than it will affect the U.S. economy. With a few exceptions, foreign countries had not relied on the kinds of subprime financing methods that precipitated the market's turbulence in the United States. Some foreign banks and other financial institutions invested in, and suffered losses from, U.S. mortgage-backed securities. However, such losses affect a smaller proportion of those countries' financial institutions than they do in the United States, and thus far, other nations' central banks have avoided widespread financial difficulties by injecting, as noted earlier, a significant amount of liquidity into their financial markets.

16. The current account consists of net exports, net unilateral transfers, and net capital and labor income flows between the United States and the rest of the world.

Figure 2-9.

Nominal Trade-Weighted Value of the Dollar

(Index, January 1997 = 100)

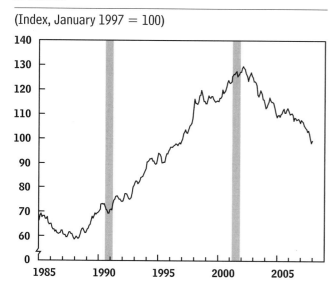

Sources: Congressional Budget Office; Federal Reserve Board.

Note: Data are monthly and are plotted through December 2007.

Similarly, the adverse effects of higher energy prices may be more muted abroad. The impact of increased oil prices overseas has been dampened by the rise in the value of foreign currencies relative to the dollar. European economies, moreover, export more goods and services to the oil-exporting countries than the United States does and thus are likely to benefit more from those countries' spending.

Some analysts fear that a downturn in domestic demand here will trigger much weaker growth abroad because the strength of some of those economies depends heavily on selling goods and services to the United States. It appears, however, that such nations have built up the growth of their own domestic demand over the past few years and have gradually lessened their dependence on exports to the United States. The persistence of rapid foreign growth last year in the face of a reduction in the growth of exports to the United States and a decline in the United States' real trade deficit indicate that growth abroad has, at least to some degree, been decoupled from the growth of U.S. domestic demand.

The growth of emerging economies, in particular, has been quite strong in recent years, and that momentum will help to soften the global effects of the slowdown in

the United States. Financial problems in this country have not caused a credit shortage in emerging economies' financial markets but instead have channeled capital to those countries (especially to Brazil and India).

The Recent Decline in the Exchange Value of the Dollar. The fall in the value of the dollar as measured against foreign currencies will also tend to reduce the trade deficit by encouraging exports and discouraging imports. The dollar has been on a downward trend since early 2002, but the pace of its decline against the currencies of major trading partners quickened last year (see Figure 2-9).

That acceleration of the past several months largely reflects the effects of the current turmoil in the financial markets:

■ The Federal Reserve lowered the relative rate of return on U.S. short-term securities by cutting interest rates more aggressively than other central banks did. The prospect of a further cut in the target federal funds rate may also have put downward pressure on the value of the dollar.

■ A loss of confidence in the U.S. financial markets, arising from the lack of transparency about the true scale of U.S. financial institutions' exposure to losses from the subprime-related troubles as well as the fear of a recession in the United States, has led to an increased flow of capital from this country and into other economies.

■ Because the recent instability in the dollar has undermined the dollar's status as the main reserve currency, central banks abroad are rebalancing their official portfolios of reserves in various currencies by reducing the amount that they hold in dollar-denominated assets.

For its forecast, CBO assumes that, once the financial disturbances have subsided, the exchange rate will return to a more gradually declining path that reflects the United States' economic relationships with the rest of the world.

Steady Growth Projected in Government Purchases
Total real purchases (consumption plus investment) by all levels of government grew by about 2 percent in 2007. CBO forecasts that in 2008, purchases will grow at about the same pace but that in 2009, the pace will decline slightly.

Figure 2-10.

Overall and Core PCE Price Indexes

(Percentage change from previous year)

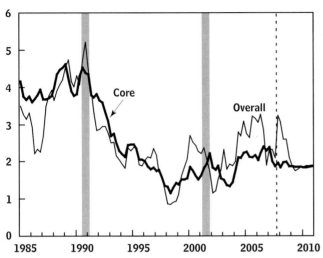

Sources: Congressional Budget Office; Department of Commerce,
          Bureau of Economic Analysis.

Notes: The overall PCE price index is the chained price index for
        personal consumption expenditures. The core index
        excludes prices for food and energy.

        Data are quarterly and are plotted through 2010.

The assumptions that CBO makes about the growth of federal spending imply real growth in federal purchases of about 3 percent in fiscal year 2008 and a slowing of that pace by half in fiscal year 2009.[17] Federal appropriations for 2008 so far include only $88 billion for military operations and other activities in Iraq and Afghanistan—more than $80 billion less than the amount policymakers provided last year for such purposes. However, some of last year's funds remain to be spent this year (and in future years), which will boost the growth of government purchases in 2008. (Similar effects hold for calendar years.) The slowing projected for fiscal year 2009 reflects the current-law assumptions that CBO uses in its budget and economic projections: CBO bases its projections only on the funds provided thus far for 2008 and therefore estimates that the growth of defense outlays in 2009 will be slower than it is in 2008. (The outlook for federal spending is discussed in detail in Chapter 3.) It is likely, however, that policymakers will provide additional funds for military operations in the months ahead, which would

increase the growth of defense spending (relative to the rate incorporated in CBO's baseline projections) both this fiscal year and next.[18]

CBO's forecast assumes that the growth of spending by state and local governments will slow. Purchases of goods and services by states and localities increased by more than 2 percent in calendar year 2007, the fourth year of steady growth, but spending is likely to be trimmed this year because of the weaker revenues associated with a slowdown in general economic activity. In addition, continued declines in property values will tend to lower receipts from property taxes and real estate transactions.

The Persistent Risk of Higher Inflation

Although CBO anticipates that inflation will be moderate, on average, in 2008 and 2009, increases in the prices of commodities (such as oil and grains) and the fall in the value of the dollar last year heighten the risk that inflation will rise. Core consumer price inflation, which excludes the volatile prices of food and energy, eased last year, and in CBO's forecast, it remains moderate, given that the feeble pace of economic growth anticipated in 2008 will reduce upward pressure on both wages and prices. In addition, high vacancy rates in the residential housing market imply that the growth of rents for housing, which account for a large portion of core inflation, will be slow in the near term. The outlook for overall inflation is more uncertain than that for core inflation because it takes account of the ups and downs of energy and food prices. However, CBO expects that consumer price inflation for both energy and food will ease by the end of 2008 and that inflation will be moderate in 2009 (see Figure 2-10).

Indicators of Moderate Inflation: Measures of Resource Constraints and Rents

Traditional measures of the inflationary pressures that stem from resource constraints indicate that core inflation will subside in 2008. The unemployment rate rose over the past year, and the growth of wages slowed. In addition, productivity growth in 2007 remained solid, and the combination of slower wage growth and a relatively sturdy rise in productivity implies that the growth of unit

---

17. Appendix D discusses the differences in the accounting treatment of federal spending in the federal budget and in the national income and product accounts.

18. According to CBO's estimate of the cyclically adjusted budget (the budget minus the effects of the business cycle), federal fiscal policy currently is essentially neutral—neither stimulative nor restrictive. For more discussion, see Congressional Budget Office, *The Cyclically Adjusted and Standardized Budget Measures* (forthcoming).

Figure 2-11.

Inflation-Adjusted Price of Crude Oil

(2007 dollars per barrel)

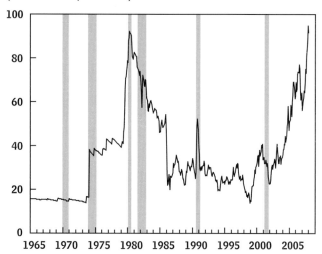

Sources: Congressional Budget Office; *Wall Street Journal;* Department of Commerce, Bureau of Economic Analysis.

Notes: The price is for West Texas intermediate crude oil. Before 1982, it refers to the posted price; for later years, the spot price. The price is adjusted for inflation by dividing it by the chained price index for personal consumption expenditures.

Data are monthly and are plotted through December 2007 (the December value for the price index is an estimate).

labor costs—the rise in hourly compensation in excess of labor productivity growth—was about 2 percent during 2007. In addition, capacity utilization in the manufacturing sector stayed below the level that suggests a high level of demand for goods that in turn can lead to inflationary pressures.

The outlook for rents reinforces the likelihood that inflation in the near term will be low. Rents, including the imputed rent for owner-occupied homes, are particularly important in considering inflation because they account for substantial portions of the most commonly used measures of underlying inflation in the prices of consumer goods: 38 percent of the core CPI-U and 14 percent of the core personal consumption expenditure (PCE) price index. Rent inflation slowed during 2007 as vacancy rates remained high for traditional rental units and for houses that are usually owner-occupied. Those rates are likely to remain elevated because of a general surplus of housing and the possibility that some people who cannot sell their houses will try to rent them. Also a possibility, though, is that increased demand for rental units as a result of the

rising number of foreclosures may partly offset that effect. Although the growth of rents is difficult to predict, CBO expects that high vacancy rates will constrain such growth throughout 2008 and 2009.

Risks of Higher Inflation: Commodity Prices and the Falling Dollar

The price of petroleum—specifically, the price of West Texas Intermediate crude oil—jumped late last year and in December averaged about $92 a barrel. In inflation-adjusted terms, the price surpassed its previous peak in 1980 (see Figure 2-11). Accounting for much of the recent surge in prices is burgeoning demand for crude oil from fast-growing developing countries in combination with the slow growth of supply. But geopolitical tensions and increases in demand as a result of speculative and precautionary purchases have also exerted upward pressure on prices. The rise in the price of crude oil has pushed the price of petroleum products—such as gasoline and heating oil—higher. For example, the national average price of a gallon of gasoline went from $2.31 in December 2006 to $3.02 in December 2007.

For its forecast, CBO has assumed that the price of petroleum will fall during 2008 to about $84 a barrel by year's end. That assumption was based on prices in the futures market at the time that the forecast was completed, in early December. If that drop does, indeed, occur, the prices paid by consumers for heating oil and gasoline will be lower at the end of the year than they are today (despite the seasonal hike in gasoline prices during the summer), which will dampen the overall growth of consumer prices. The volatility of those prices in recent years, however, suggests that changes in petroleum prices could affect the accuracy—in either direction—of CBO's forecast for inflation.

Inflation in food prices is expected to fall slightly from the 4½ percent to 5 percent rate of the past year to about 3 percent by the end of 2008. But inventories of grains were small at the end of 2007, and that increases the risk that poor harvests might cause food prices to rise more than CBO anticipates. A large number of prices for foodstuffs (such as corn, wheat, milk, and eggs) rose in 2007, and those increases boosted consumer food price inflation (see Figure 2-12). The prices of various grains are high in part because of continued concerns about small global stocks. In its forecast, CBO assumes that overall food commodity prices will stabilize or ease slightly during the

Figure 2-12.

Food Price Inflation and Foodstuffs Prices

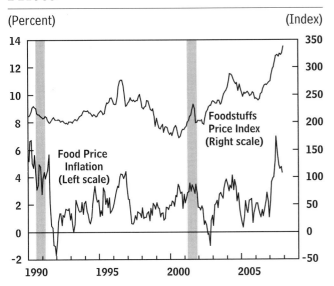

(Percent)   (Index)

Sources: Congressional Budget Office; Commodity Research
          Bureau; Department of Commerce, Bureau of Economic
          Analysis.

Notes: The food price inflation measure is the growth of the six-
        month moving average of the chained price index for per-
        sonal consumption expenditures on food. The foodstuffs
        index includes butter, cocoa beans, corn, hogs, lard, soybean
        oil, steers, sugar, and wheat.

        Data are monthly. For food price inflation, they are plotted
        through November 2007; for the foodstuffs price index, they
        are plotted through December of that year.

first half of this year, reducing upward pressure on consumer prices by the end of 2008.

The declining dollar will tend to increase core consumer price inflation, but CBO expects that its overall effect will be muted. Several recent studies indicate that the effect on inflation of changes in exchange rates has been smaller over the past several years than it was in the past. That shift arises mainly because foreign exporters have responded to the dollar's depreciation by reducing the prices of their goods and services (through increases in productivity or reductions in their profits).[19] Nevertheless, the losses that those exporters can absorb are limited. Given how much and how fast the value of the dollar has declined recently, some of the effects of the drop in the exchange rate may be passed through to consumer prices in the near term. However, in CBO's forecast, the upward

pressure on prices from the dollar's decline is offset by the moderating effects of slow economic growth.

The Outlook Through 2018

CBO's economic projections for the period beyond the next two years, to 2018, do not explicitly incorporate any ups and downs in the business cycle. Instead, they reflect the average effects of typical cycles, thereby including the likelihood that at least one recession will occur in any 10-year interval. The projections for that medium-term period extend historical trends in such underlying factors as the growth of the labor force, the growth of productivity, and the rate of national saving. CBO's projections for real GDP, inflation, real interest rates, and tax revenues are based on the projections of those underlying factors, including how current fiscal policy might affect the way those factors evolve.

CBO's projection of growth in real GDP averages 2.7 percent annually during the 2010–2018 period, a pace that exceeds the rate of growth of potential GDP during the same time. Weak growth in 2008 leaves real GDP below its potential level at the end of 2009, even though CBO expects that growth will pick up during that year. Thus, to bring actual and potential GDP back to their average historical relationship, CBO assumes that the rate of growth of the economy will be faster than its potential growth rate during the years after 2009.

CBO's current projections for inflation, unemployment, and interest rates after 2009 are similar to the ones that it published last August.[20] Inflation, as measured by the CPI-U, will average 2.2 percent during the 2010–2018 period, CBO projects, and growth in the PCE price index will average 1.9 percent. For most of the medium term, unemployment rates will average 4.8 percent, and interest rates on Treasury securities will average 4.6 percent for 3-month bills and 5.2 percent for 10-year notes.

19. See Mario Marazzi and others, *Exchange Rate Pass-Through to U.S. Import Prices: Some New Evidence*, International Finance Discussion Paper No. 833 (Washington, D.C.: Board of Governors of the Federal Reserve System, April 2005), available at www.federalreserve.gov/pubs/ifdp/2005/833/ifdp833.pdf. See also Mario Marazzi and Nathan Sheets, "Declining Exchange Rate Pass-Through to U.S. Import Prices: The Potential Role of Global Factors," *Journal of International Money and Finance*, vol. 26, no. 6 (October 2007), pp. 924–947.

20. See Congressional Budget Office, *The Budget and Economic Outlook: An Update* (August 2007).

Table 2-2.

Key Assumptions in CBO's Projection of Potential Output

(By calendar year, in percent)

	Average Annual Growth						Projected Average Annual Growth		
	1950–1973	1974–1981	1982–1990	1991–2001	2002–2007	Total, 1950–2007	2008–2013	2014–2018	Total, 2008–2018
	Overall Economy								
Potential Output	3.9	3.2	3.1	3.1	2.8	3.4	2.7	2.5	2.6
Potential Labor Force	1.6	2.5	1.6	1.2	1.1	1.6	0.8	0.5	0.7
Potential Labor Force Productivity[a]	2.3	0.7	1.5	1.9	1.6	1.8	1.8	2.0	1.9
	Nonfarm Business Sector								
Potential Output	4.0	3.6	3.3	3.5	3.0	3.6	3.0	2.9	2.9
Potential Hours Worked	1.4	2.3	1.7	1.1	1.1	1.5	0.8	0.5	0.7
Capital Input	3.8	4.2	4.1	4.6	2.5	3.9	3.5	3.5	3.5
Potential TFP	1.9	0.7	0.9	1.3	1.5	1.4	1.4	1.4	1.4
Potential TFP excluding adjustments	1.9	0.7	0.9	1.3	1.3	1.4	1.3	1.3	1.3
TFP adjustments	0	0	0	0.1	0.2	*	0.1	0.1	0.1
Price measurement[b]	0	0	0	0.1	0.1	*	0.1	0.1	0.1
Temporary adjustment[c]	0	0	0	*	*	*	0	0	0
Contributions to the Growth of Potential Output (Percentage points)									
Potential hours worked	0.9	1.6	1.2	0.8	0.7	1.0	0.5	0.4	0.5
Capital input	1.1	1.3	1.2	1.4	0.8	1.2	1.1	1.1	1.1
Potential TFP	1.9	0.7	0.9	1.3	1.5	1.4	1.4	1.4	1.4
Total Contributions	4.0	3.6	3.3	3.5	3.0	3.6	3.0	2.8	2.9
Potential Labor Productivity in the Nonfarm Business Sector[d]	2.6	1.3	1.5	2.4	1.9	2.1	2.2	2.3	2.3

Source: Congressional Budget Office.

Notes: TFP = total factor productivity; * = between zero and 0.05 percent.

a.   The ratio of potential output to the potential labor force.

b.   An adjustment for a conceptual change in the official measure of the gross domestic product chained price index.

c.   An adjustment for the unusually rapid growth of TFP between 2001 and 2003.

d.   The estimated trend in the ratio of output to hours worked in the nonfarm business sector.

Potential Output

In CBO's projection, potential output grows at an annual rate of 2.6 percent, on average, during the 2008–2018 period, or about eight-tenths of a percentage point slower than its long-run average pace of 3.4 percent (see Table 2-2). Growth will be slower than the historical average, in CBO's estimation, primarily because of the sharp slowdown expected in the rate of expansion of the potential labor force, as the large cohort of workers born

during the postwar baby boom (from 1946 to 1964) begins to reach the traditional age for retirement. In addition, the rate of capital accumulation, which averages 3.5 percent annually in CBO's 10-year projection, is slower than its average rate of growth since 1950. By contrast, productivity growth rises at a rate that is close to its long-run average. CBO's projection for the growth of potential GDP has been revised downward since CBO

Figure 2-13.

Total Factor Productivity

(Index, 1996 = 1.00)

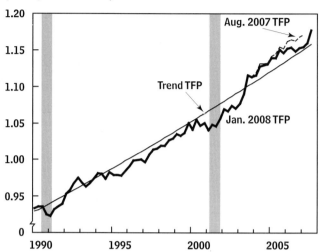

Source: Congressional Budget Office.

Note: Data are quarterly and are plotted through the first quarter of 2007 (for August 2007 TFP) and the third quarter of 2007 (for January 2008 TFP and trend TFP).

last updated its forecast, in August 2007, largely because revisions to the source data on which CBO bases its economic estimates have revealed a somewhat slower trend in potential total factor productivity, or TFP (average real output per unit of combined labor and capital services).

CBO now projects that the potential labor force—the labor force after an adjustment for movements in the business cycle—will grow at an average annual rate of 0.7 percent during the 2008–2018 period. That rate, which is almost identical to CBO's projection in August, is considerably lower than the 1.6 percent rate of growth experienced during the 1950–2007 period. Labor force growth is expected to slow because the rate of labor force participation is likely to decline during the next decade with the baby boomers' retirement; in addition, the rate of participation by women in the labor force is unlikely to increase during the next 10 years as it did in the past. (After a large surge during the 1960s, 1970s, and 1980s, women's participation leveled off during the 1990s and has remained flat since then.) In addition to the demographic effects, CBO's projection for growth of the labor force incorporates a slight slowing because of the increase in marginal personal tax rates scheduled under current law. (Rates increase over the medium term because of the growing reach of the alternative minimum tax, real

bracket creep—in which inflation pushes income into higher tax brackets—and the expiration of provisions originally enacted in the Economic Growth and Tax Relief Reconciliation Act of 2001.) CBO assumes that the increase in marginal tax rates will modestly lessen people's incentive to work.

The average rate of capital accumulation that CBO projects for the 2008–2018 period—3.5 percent—is almost identical to the rate it projected last August, but it is slower than the long-run average rate, largely because of the projected slowdown in labor force growth. One by-product of that slowdown is that firms will not need to increase the stock of capital at the same rate as in the past—because there will be relatively fewer workers to provide with structures, equipment, and software. Hence, firms can maintain the same growth in the amount of capital per worker but with less investment than in other periods.

CBO's projections show potential TFP growing by 1.4 percent, on average, during the 2008–2018 period. That rate, which is similar to both the historical average and the rate in last August's projection, results from largely offsetting changes caused by revisions to source data—specifically, the national income and product accounts (NIPAs)—and data that have become newly available.

In August, the Department of Commerce's Bureau of Economic Analysis (BEA), which maintains the NIPAs, released a set of revisions to the accounts that revealed that the growth of TFP since 2003 was significantly slower than previously thought. According to the data available last summer, before BEA's revision, TFP grew at an average annual rate of 1.5 percent between the third quarter of 2003 and the first quarter of 2007; according to the most recent, revised data, the growth rate was 1.1 percent (see Figure 2-13). By itself, that change would tend to lower CBO's projection of potential TFP. However, other data released since August indicate that total factor productivity grew strongly in the second and third quarters of 2007 (4.1 percent at an annual rate). The addition of the latter data improve the outlook for potential TFP and largely offset the effects of BEA's revisions to the NIPAs.

Inflation, Unemployment, and Interest Rates

CBO's projections for inflation have changed little since last August. Inflation, as measured by the CPI-U, will average 2.2 percent annually during the 2010–2018 period, CBO now estimates, and growth in the PCE and core PCE price indexes will average 1.9 percent per year. In general, CBO assumes that in the medium term, monetary policy will determine what happens to inflation, and that the Federal Reserve will seek to maintain core inflation in the PCE price index at just under 2 percent, on average. CBO projects that the rate of unemployment will average 4.8 percent during the 2010–2018 period.

CBO's medium-term projections for interest rates are also quite similar to those it published in August. CBO estimates those rates by adding its projection for inflation to its projection for real interest rates. The real rate on 3-month Treasury bills will average 2.5 percent during the latter years of the projection period, CBO forecasts, and the real rate on 10-year Treasury notes will average 3.0 percent. When combined with the projected rates of CPI-U inflation, those real rates imply nominal rates of 4.7 percent for 3-month Treasury bills and 5.2 percent for 10-year Treasury notes.

Projections of Income

CBO's projections of federal revenues are based on its projections of various categories of income as measured in the NIPAs. The outlook for revenues is most directly affected by projections of wages and salaries, corporate profits, proprietors' income, and interest and dividend income. However, CBO makes numerous adjustments to the NIPA categories to project the income reported on tax forms for calculating tax liability (see Chapter 4 for details of CBO's outlook for revenues).

Data Problems

Before-tax profits (which are also known as book profits) required an unusual adjustment for CBO's current forecast. Corporate tax returns are the primary source of data for the NIPAs' estimates of profits and book depreciation (the depreciation that the tax code allows businesses to deduct when they calculate their taxable profits), but at the time that BEA released its August revisions, the most recent complete data for those returns were for 2004. BEA, in developing its estimate of depreciation and book profits for 2005, relied on preliminary information from the Internal Revenue Service gathered from corporate tax returns for 2005 and on other data, such as the Bureau of the Census's surveys on corporate profits for years after that.

Since August, more-complete data for 2005 have become available. As a result, CBO's estimate of book depreciation for 2005 and subsequent years is higher than BEA's estimate, and CBO's estimate of book profits between 2005 and 2007 is lower. Because of that, CBO has used a different historical pattern for book profits in its projections of revenues than the pattern provided by the NIPAs. (See Chapter 4 for additional detail on the effects of profits on CBO's revenue outlook.) CBO includes only economic profits in its forecast tables this year because that measure is not affected by differences in assumptions about historical book depreciation and is a better measure of profits from current production.

Income Shares

CBO projects the income categories from the NIPAs as shares of output, or GDP. At the broadest level, GDP can be divided into a share for labor income and a share for domestic capital income.[21]

The labor share of GDP has averaged 62.3 percent since 1950. CBO's measure of labor income consists of the total compensation that employers pay their employees— that is, the sum of wages and salaries and supplemental benefits—and 65 percent of proprietors' income. Supplements include employers' payments for health and other insurance premiums, employers' contributions to pension funds, and the employer's share of payroll taxes (for Social Security and Medicare). Most stock options are included in the wage and salary component of labor income when they are exercised.[22] (Stock options were a factor in the rise in the GDP labor share in the late 1990s.)

Recent data from the NIPAs indicate that the labor income share of GDP over the four quarters ending in the third quarter of 2007 averaged about 61.9 percent, or about half a percentage point less than its long-term average. The relatively low unemployment rate nationwide during 2007 encouraged faster growth of compensation last year, but the slowdown in economic growth that CBO expects this year is likely to suppress the growth of wages. Therefore, CBO projects that labor income will

---

21. For more details on CBO's projection methods, see Congressional Budget Office, *How CBO Forecasts Income* (August 2006).

22. The most common stock options used in the United States, nonqualified stock options, are treated as part of labor compensation in the NIPAs.

Figure 2-14.

Total Labor Income and Wages and Salaries

(Percentage of gross domestic product)

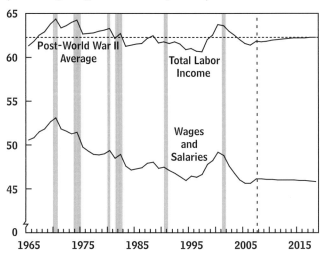

Sources: Congressional Budget Office; Department of Commerce, Bureau of Economic Analysis.

Note: Data are annual and are plotted through 2018.

grow only slightly faster this year than the slow growth it has forecast for nominal GDP. However, CBO assumes that the labor share of GDP will return to its long-run average during the 2008–2018 period (see Figure 2-14).

The GDP share of domestic capital income is essentially the opposite of the labor share, and so it falls slowly in CBO's forecast. Capital income consists of domestic corporate profits, depreciation charges, interest and transfer payments made by domestic businesses, rental income, and the remaining 35 percent of proprietors' income. Within the capital share, CBO's forecast anticipates a decline in domestic economic profits relative to GDP and an increase in domestic businesses' interest payments (see Figure 2-15). In the past, the growth of profits has weakened when the growth of GDP slowed, and CBO's forecast reflects that historical pattern. Profits have been high relative to GDP in recent years, in part because businesses' interest payments have been unusually low, reflecting both low corporate interest rates and the slower accumulation of debt in the corporate sector compared with past periods. In the latter years of the projection period (2010 to 2018), the shares of domestic profits and interest payments in CBO's projections are expected to move

to levels that are similar to their averages over the past 20 years.

Changes in the Outlook Since August 2007

Compared with its August projections, CBO's current forecast for 2008 and 2009 indicates much weaker growth, significantly higher inflation in 2008, lower interest rates, and a smaller GDP share for profits (see Table 2-3). Real growth in the middle of 2007 turned out to be faster than CBO had anticipated in its forecast last summer; also, during the second half of 2007, housing activity declined more than CBO had expected and energy prices rose by much more. In addition, the repercussions from the subprime shock to the financial markets now appear to be more severe than CBO had initially thought they would be. The weaker near-term outlook has also resulted in lower interest rates on Treasury securities in recent months (although interest rates on all low-rated private-sector securities are higher). Given the environment of very slow growth this year, CBO expects that interest rates on Treasury securities will remain lower in 2008 and 2009 than the rates it had forecast last August.

Figure 2-15.

Domestic Profits and Businesses' Interest Payments

(Percentage of gross domestic product)

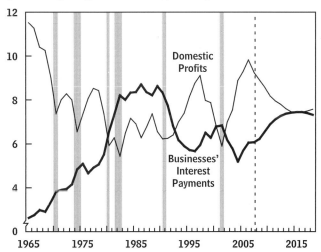

Sources: Congressional Budget Office; Department of Commerce, Bureau of Economic Analysis.

Note: Data are annual and are plotted through 2018.

Table 2-3.

CBO's Current and Previous Economic Projections for Calendar Years 2007 to 2017

	Estimated 2007	Forecast 2008	Forecast 2009	Projected Annual Average 2010 to 2013	Projected Annual Average 2014 to 2017
Nominal GDP (Billions of dollars)					
January 2008	13,828	14,330	14,997	18,243 [a]	21,654 [b]
August 2007	13,893	14,575	15,306	18,390 [a]	21,829 [b]
Nominal GDP (Percentage change)					
January 2008	4.8	3.6	4.7	5.0	4.4
August 2007	4.9	4.9	5.0	4.7	4.4
Real GDP (Percentage change)					
January 2008	2.2	1.7	2.8	3.1	2.5
August 2007	2.1	2.9	3.2	2.8	2.5
GDP Price Index (Percentage change)					
January 2008	2.5	1.9	1.8	1.9	1.9
August 2007	2.7	2.0	1.8	1.8	1.8
Consumer Price Index[c] (Percentage change)					
January 2008	2.8	2.9	2.3	2.2	2.2
August 2007	2.8	2.3	2.2	2.2	2.2
Unemployment Rate (Percent)					
January 2008	4.6	5.1	5.4	4.9	4.8
August 2007	4.5	4.7	4.8	4.8	4.8
Three-Month Treasury Bill Rate (Percent)					
January 2008	4.4	3.2	4.2	4.6	4.7
August 2007	4.8	4.8	4.8	4.7	4.7
Ten-Year Treasury Note Rate (Percent)					
January 2008	4.6	4.2	4.9	5.2	5.2
August 2007	4.9	5.2	5.2	5.2	5.2
Tax Bases (Billions of dollars)					
Economic profits					
January 2008	1,599	1,620	1,649	1,842 [a]	2,200 [b]
August 2007	1,702	1,751	1,788	2,004 [a]	2,330 [b]
Wages and salaries					
January 2008	6,368	6,615	6,913	8,401 [a]	9,936 [b]
August 2007	6,383	6,703	7,046	8,470 [a]	10,016 [b]
Tax Bases (Percentage of GDP)					
Economic profits					
January 2008	11.6	11.3	11.0	10.3	10.1
August 2007	12.3	12.0	11.7	11.2	10.7
Wages and salaries					
January 2008	46.0	46.2	46.1	46.1	46.0
August 2007	45.9	46.0	46.0	46.0	46.0
Memorandum:					
Real Potential GDP (Percentage change)					
January 2008	2.8	2.8	2.7	2.6	2.5
August 2007	2.8	2.8	2.8	2.7	2.5

Sources: Congressional Budget Office; Department of Commerce, Bureau of Economic Analysis; Department of Labor, Bureau of Labor Statistics; Federal Reserve Board.

Notes: GDP = gross domestic product; percentage changes are measured from one year to the next.

a.   Level in 2013.

b.   Level in 2017.

c.   The consumer price index for all urban consumers.

CPI-U inflation during the last few months of 2007 was much higher than CBO had anticipated because prices for motor fuel jumped unexpectedly. However, if price hikes for energy are excluded from that measure, inflation grew only slightly more during the last quarter of 2007 than CBO had previously estimated. The current forecast assumes that the large upticks in the prices of food and energy in 2007 were largely transitory; thus, CBO forecasts that growth in the CPI-U after 2008 will be essentially the same as the estimate of growth it published last August.

In the case of CBO's medium-term projections, the major changes relative to CBO's last outlook are the slight reduction in projected growth of real GDP and the lower profits share of GDP. Average inflation, the unemployment rate, and interest rates over the medium term are largely unchanged from CBO's August 2007 projections.

Changes in the economic outlook since last summer have reduced CBO's projections of revenues significantly, but they have also slightly curbed its projections of spending in the near term. The economic changes have worsened the overall budget outlook for 2008 by $17 billion, and the changes over the 10 years from 2008 to 2017 have increased the projection of the cumulative deficit for that period by $486 billion. The slower real growth of GDP and the lower profits share that CBO projects throughout the period account for the reduction in revenues. The drop in the projected rates on Treasury securities will reduce the government's net interest payments, CBO forecasts, particularly in 2008 and 2009. (The specific revisions to the budget outlook that can be attributed to changes in the economic forecast are described in more detail in Appendix A.)

How CBO's Forecast Compares With Others

CBO's forecast for real growth in 2008 is significantly more pessimistic than that of the Administration and somewhat more pessimistic than the current *Blue Chip* consensus forecast (see Table 2-4). (The *Blue Chip* consensus forecast is based on a survey of about 50 private-sector forecasters.) After 2008, the differences between the forecasts are not large for most categories of estimates, although CBO's shows markedly higher unemployment and short-term interest rates in 2009 compared with those of the *Blue Chip* consensus and the Administration.

The *Blue Chip* consensus forecast of January 10, 2008, projects a rate of growth for real output in 2008 that is about halfway between the forecasts of the Administration and CBO, but the publishers of the *Blue Chip* outlook note that their January survey was taken before the weak employment report of December 2007. Hence, they speculate, participants would probably have lowered their forecasts of economic growth for 2008 if they had been aware of those data.

CBO's lower forecast, relative to the *Blue Chip*'s, of real output growth in 2008 stems from a view of the growth of household real income and spending that is less robust than the one that the January *Blue Chip* outlook foresees. However, the two forecasts are nearly identical for CPI-U inflation in 2008 and 2009. Unemployment rates in the two outlooks are about the same for 2008, but that of the consensus shows no additional rise in 2009—whereas CBO's shows a significant further increase in that year. The consensus view of long-term Treasury rates differs only slightly from CBO's for both 2008 and 2009, but its outlook for the rates on 3-month Treasury bills follows a different path than CBO's: The *Blue Chip*'s average for interest rates on the 3-month Treasury bill is higher in 2008 by 0.2 percentage points and lower in 2009 by 0.3 percentage points than CBO's forecast for those rates.

Compared with the Administration, CBO expects slower real growth and a higher unemployment rate during 2008 as well as higher CPI-U inflation. CBO projects significantly lower interest rates on 3-month Treasury bills and 10-year Treasury notes during 2008 than does the Administration.

Because the Federal Reserve is now publishing its range of internal forecasts more frequently, CBO can compare the annual economic projections in its outlook with those of the central bank (see Table 2-5 on page 50). The Federal Reserve's Federal Open Market Committee compiles and releases its projections four times each year, but there is a delay between the time of the meeting and the actual report. Thus, the comparisons here (which consider CBO's forecast against the projections prepared for the committee's meeting last October) may differ substantially from those involving later projections by the FOMC. (The next time the projections will be released will be in February, after the committee's January meeting.)

Relative to the FOMC's October 2007 projections, CBO foresees real growth of GDP that is below the reported range of the Federal Reserve's estimates for 2008, whereas it forecasts real GDP growth for 2009 that is above the FOMC's range of estimates. In addition, CBO estimates that the unemployment rate will be above the range expected by the Federal Reserve for both 2008 and 2009.

CBO's inflation forecast for 2008 and 2009 is at the upper end of the central tendency for overall inflation reported by the Federal Reserve on the basis of the October FOMC meeting. Similarly, CBO's forecast for core inflation lies at the top end of the central tendency published by the central bank.

Table 2-4.

Comparison of Economic Forecasts by CBO, the Administration, and the *Blue Chip* Consensus for Calendar Years 2008 to 2013

	Estimated 2007	Forecast 2008	Forecast 2009	Projected Annual Average, 2010 to 2013
	Fourth Quarter to Fourth Quarter (Percentage Change)			
Nominal GDP				
CBO	4.7	3.7	5.1	5.0
Administration	5.1	4.8	5.1	4.9
Blue Chip consensus	5.2	4.2	5.1	n.a.
Real GDP				
CBO	2.5	1.5	3.3	3.0
Administration	2.7	2.7	3.0	2.9
Blue Chip consensus	2.6	2.0	2.9	n.a.
GDP Price Index				
CBO	2.2	2.1	1.8	1.9
Administration	2.3	2.0	2.0	2.0
Blue Chip consensus	2.6	2.1	2.1	n.a.
Consumer Price Index[a]				
CBO	3.8	2.5	2.2	2.2
Administration	3.9	2.1	2.2	2.3
Blue Chip consensus	3.9	2.4	2.3	n.a.
	Calendar Year Average (Percent)			
Unemployment Rate				
CBO	4.6	5.1	5.4	4.9
Administration	4.6	4.9	4.9	4.8
Blue Chip consensus	4.6	5.0	5.0	n.a.
Three-Month Treasury Bill Rate				
CBO	4.4	3.2	4.2	4.6
Administration	4.4	3.7	3.8	4.1
Blue Chip consensus	4.4	3.4	3.9	n.a.
Ten-Year Treasury Note Rate				
CBO	4.6	4.2	4.9	5.2
Administration	4.7	4.6	4.9	5.2
Blue Chip consensus	4.6	4.3	4.8	n.a.

Sources: Congressional Budget Office; Department of Commerce, Bureau of Economic Analysis; Department of Labor, Bureau of Labor Statistics; Federal Reserve Board; Aspen Publishers, Inc., *Blue Chip Economic Indicators* (January 10, 2008); Council of Economic Advisers, Department of the Treasury, and Office of Management and Budget, "Administration Economic Forecast" (joint press release, November 29, 2007).

Notes: The *Blue Chip* consensus is the average of about 50 forecasts by private-sector economists. The latest *Blue Chip* consensus does not extend past 2009.

GDP = gross domestic product; n.a. = not applicable.

a.   The consumer price index for all urban consumers.

Table 2-5.

Comparison of Economic Forecasts by the Federal Reserve and CBO for Calendar Years 2007, 2008, and 2009

	Federal Reserve[a]		CBO
	Range	Central Tendency	
Calendar Year 2007			
Percentage Change, Fourth Quarter to Fourth Quarter			
Real gross domestic product	2.2 to 2.7	2.4 to 2.5	2.5
PCE price index	2.7 to 3.2	2.9 to 3.0	3.2
Core PCE price index[b]	1.8 to 2.1	1.8 to 1.9	2.0
Average Level, Fourth Quarter (Percent)			
Civilian unemployment rate	4.7 to 4.8	4.7 to 4.8	4.7
Calendar Year 2008			
Percentage Change, Fourth Quarter to Fourth Quarter			
Real gross domestic product	1.6 to 2.6	1.8 to 2.5	1.5
PCE price index	1.7 to 2.3	1.8 to 2.1	2.1
Core PCE price index[b]	1.7 to 2.0	1.7 to 1.9	1.9
Average Level, Fourth Quarter (Percent)			
Civilian unemployment rate	4.6 to 5.0	4.8 to 4.9	5.3
Calendar Year 2009			
Percentage Change, Fourth Quarter to Fourth Quarter			
Real gross domestic product	2.0 to 2.8	2.3 to 2.7	3.3
PCE price index	1.5 to 2.2	1.7 to 2.0	1.9
Core PCE price index[b]	1.5 to 2.0	1.7 to 1.9	1.9
Average Level, Fourth Quarter (Percent)			
Civilian unemployment rate	4.6 to 5.0	4.8 to 4.9	5.3

Sources: Congressional Budget Office; Federal Reserve Board of Governors, "Minutes of the Federal Open Market Committee, October 30–31, 2007" (November 20, 2007), available at www.federalreserve.gov/monetarypolicy/files/fomcminutes20071031.pdf.

Note: PCE = personal consumption expenditure.

a. The range of estimates from the Federal Reserve reflects all views of the members of the Federal Open Market Committee. The central tendency reflects the most common views of the committee's members.

b. Excluding food and energy.

The Spending Outlook

Under an assumption that current laws and policies will remain in effect, the baseline projections prepared by the Congressional Budget Office for the next decade anticipate that, as it has for most of the past several years, mandatory spending will grow faster than the economy. In contrast, discretionary spending is projected to grow at the rate of inflation—and thus more slowly than the economy. Total outlays are projected to decline from 20.2 percent of gross domestic product in 2008 to 19.3 percent of GDP in 2018.

If current laws governing mandatory programs remain the same and if discretionary appropriations total $1,045 billion for fiscal year 2008—the amount provided thus far—outlays in 2008 will total $2.9 trillion, CBO estimates (see Table 3-1). Spending would grow by $143 billion—a 5.2 percent increase over 2007 (see Table 3-2). Excluding net interest, spending is estimated to rise by 5.9 percent in 2008. The increase for that category in 2007 was 2.7 percent, well below the average increase of 6.3 percent per year recorded between 1997 and 2006.

Additional funding is likely to be provided in 2008 for operations in Iraq and Afghanistan and for other activities associated with the war on terrorism, however, because the $88 billion in appropriations provided for such purposes so far is expected to cover costs for only part of the year. The Administration has requested an additional $105 billion for 2008 for operations in Iraq and Afghanistan and other activities related to the war on terrorism. That additional funding is not reflected in CBO's baseline projections and would boost discretionary outlays for defense in 2008 by about $30 billion, to around $600 billion. As a result, total outlays in 2008 would be 6 percent higher than in 2007. (The remainder of the additional 2008 funds would be spent in future years.) Also, legislation intended to bolster a weakening economy through fiscal stimulus could lift spending in other areas of the budget.

The increase in outlays for 2008 is fueled by increases in both mandatory and discretionary spending. Mandatory programs are projected to grow by 6.9 percent, faster than the average annual rate from 1997 to 2006. Discretionary outlays are projected to increase by 4.5 percent (even without additional funding for operations in Iraq and Afghanistan), 2 percentage points above last year's rate. However, funding for nondefense discretionary programs in 2007 was held well below the average increase over the previous 10 years because most agencies were covered by a continuing resolution that provided funding at or near the amounts provided for 2006. Lower payments for net interest, primarily because of lower interest rates, will partially offset other increases in outlays in 2008.

Under current law, overall federal spending is projected to grow slightly faster than the economy over the next two years: As a percentage of GDP, total outlays are projected to rise from 20.0 percent in 2007 to 20.2 percent this year and 20.4 percent in 2009 (nearly equal to the 20.6 percent average of the past 40 years). Those totals are likely to rise somewhat once additional funding to continue operations in Iraq and Afghanistan is enacted and if economic stimulus is provided.

For subsequent years, CBO estimates that total spending—under assumptions for the baseline—will grow slightly more slowly than the economy, and as a result, decline to 19.3 percent of GDP in 2018. In those projections, discretionary outlays, which grew by an average of 6.7 percent annually from 1997 to 2006, increase by 2.9 percent in 2009 and average just 2.2 percent annual growth from 2010 to 2018. (This chapter's section on discretionary spending describes the likely outcomes of other possible assumptions about growth in spending that is governed by the annual appropriation process.) In

Table 3-1.

CBO's Projections of Outlays Under Assumptions for the Baseline

	Actual 2007	2008	2009	2010	2011	2012	2013	2014	2015	2016	2017	2018	Total, 2009-2013	Total, 2009-2018
						In Billions of Dollars								
Mandatory Outlays														
Social Security	581	611	646	682	719	761	807	856	908	965	1,027	1,092	3,615	8,464
Medicare	436	454	485	512	561	565	629	671	719	803	841	879	2,752	6,666
Medicaid	191	208	225	243	261	282	304	328	353	381	412	445	1,314	3,232
Other spending	420	463	481	490	504	485	503	515	530	555	567	575	2,463	5,204
Offsetting receipts	-178	-186	-183	-190	-200	-209	-220	-231	-241	-254	-268	-285	-1,001	-2,281
Subtotal	1,450	1,550	1,654	1,737	1,846	1,884	2,022	2,138	2,270	2,451	2,578	2,706	9,142	21,285
Discretionary Outlays														
Defense	549	572	590	603	620	626	645	660	677	698	710	723	3,084	6,552
Nondefense	493	517	531	542	550	560	571	583	596	610	624	637	2,754	5,804
Subtotal	1,042	1,089	1,121	1,145	1,170	1,186	1,216	1,243	1,272	1,307	1,335	1,360	5,838	12,356
Net Interest	238	234	241	266	283	286	285	285	282	278	271	259	1,360	2,735
Total	**2,731**	**2,873**	**3,015**	**3,148**	**3,299**	**3,355**	**3,524**	**3,666**	**3,824**	**4,037**	**4,183**	**4,325**	**16,341**	**36,376**
On-budget	2,277	2,404	2,519	2,628	2,757	2,788	2,926	3,037	3,160	3,334	3,439	3,536	13,618	30,124
Off-budget	454	469	496	520	541	568	597	629	664	702	744	789	2,723	6,251
						As a Percentage of GDP								
Mandatory Outlays														
Social Security	4.3	4.3	4.4	4.4	4.4	4.4	4.5	4.5	4.6	4.7	4.8	4.9	4.4	4.6
Medicare	3.2	3.2	3.3	3.3	3.4	3.3	3.5	3.6	3.7	3.9	3.9	3.9	3.3	3.6
Medicaid	1.4	1.5	1.5	1.6	1.6	1.6	1.7	1.7	1.8	1.9	1.9	2.0	1.6	1.7
Other spending	3.1	3.3	3.2	3.1	3.1	2.8	2.8	2.7	2.7	2.7	2.6	2.6	3.0	2.8
Offsetting receipts	-1.3	-1.3	-1.2	-1.2	-1.2	-1.2	-1.2	-1.2	-1.2	-1.2	-1.3	-1.3	-1.2	-1.2
Subtotal	10.6	10.9	11.2	11.1	11.2	10.9	11.2	11.3	11.5	11.9	12.0	12.1	11.1	11.5
Discretionary Outlays														
Defense	4.0	4.0	4.0	3.9	3.8	3.6	3.6	3.5	3.4	3.4	3.3	3.2	3.8	3.5
Nondefense	3.6	3.6	3.6	3.5	3.3	3.2	3.2	3.1	3.0	3.0	2.9	2.8	3.4	3.1
Subtotal	7.6	7.7	7.6	7.3	7.1	6.9	6.7	6.6	6.5	6.4	6.2	6.1	7.1	6.7
Net Interest	1.7	1.6	1.6	1.7	1.7	1.7	1.6	1.5	1.4	1.4	1.3	1.2	1.7	1.5
Total	**20.0**	**20.2**	**20.4**	**20.2**	**20.1**	**19.4**	**19.5**	**19.4**	**19.4**	**19.7**	**19.5**	**19.3**	**19.9**	**19.7**
On-budget	16.7	16.9	17.0	16.8	16.8	16.2	16.2	16.1	16.1	16.2	16.1	15.8	16.6	16.3
Off-budget	3.3	3.3	3.3	3.3	3.3	3.3	3.3	3.3	3.4	3.4	3.5	3.5	3.3	3.4
Memorandum:														
Gross Domestic Product (Billions of dollars)	13,670	14,201	14,812	15,600	16,445	17,256	18,043	18,856	19,685	20,540	21,426	22,355	82,156	185,018

Source: Congressional Budget Office.

Table 3-2.

Average Annual Rates of Growth in Outlays Since 1997 and Under CBO's Baseline

(Percent)

	Actual 1997 to 2006	Actual 2007	Estimated 2008	Projected[a] 2009	Projected[a] 2010 to 2018
Mandatory Outlays	6.0	2.7	6.9	6.7	5.6
Social Security	4.6	6.9	5.1	5.6	6.0
Medicare	6.9	16.7	4.0	6.9	6.8
Medicaid	7.0	5.5	8.9	8.3	7.9
Other[b]	7.2	-22.8	14.5	7.4	-0.3
Discretionary Outlays	6.7	2.6	4.5	2.9	2.2
Defense	6.9	5.5	4.3	3.1	2.3
Nondefense	6.4	-0.5	4.8	2.6	2.0
Net Interest	-0.6	5.0	-1.6	3.1	0.8
Total Outlays	5.5	2.9	5.2	4.9	4.1
Total Outlays Excluding Net Interest	6.3	2.7	5.9	5.1	4.3
Memorandum:					
Consumer Price Index	2.6	2.3	3.2	2.3	2.2
Nominal Gross Domestic Product	5.4	4.6	3.9	4.3	4.7
Discretionary Budget Authority	7.2	6.4	-2.1	3.0	2.3
Defense	7.7	11.8	-5.8	2.4	2.4
Nondefense	6.6	-0.4	2.9	3.8	2.3

Source: Congressional Budget Office.

Note: The growth rates include the effects of shifts in the timing of some payments.

a.   When constructing its baseline, CBO uses the employment cost index for wages and salaries to inflate discretionary spending related to federal personnel and the gross domestic product price index to adjust other discretionary spending.

b.   Includes offsetting receipts.

contrast, over the same period, mandatory spending is projected to grow at more than double that rate— 5.6 percent per year—slightly below the average annual rate recorded over the past decade. (See Box 3-1 for descriptions of the various types of federal spending.)

The differences in the projected growth of mandatory and discretionary spending stem largely from long-standing procedures for preparing baseline projections. CBO continues to follow now-expired provisions of the Balanced Budget and Emergency Deficit Control Act of 1985 that have governed its baseline procedures for more than 20 years. Therefore, CBO projects spending for mandatory programs under the assumption that they will continue to operate as currently specified in law and according to its estimates of various parameters that

govern payments for those programs—including caseloads and benefit costs. For discretionary programs, the Deficit Control Act specified that estimates for the future should assume that current appropriations grow with inflation, which produces a significantly slower rate of growth than has actually occurred in most recent years; discretionary outlays have grown by less than the rate of inflation in just 1 of the past 10 years and in only 14 of the past 40 years.

The share of federal spending categorized as discretionary declined from almost 14 percent of GDP in 1968 to about 6 percent in 1999. Discretionary outlays began to rise in 2001, and they totaled 7.6 percent of GDP in 2007 (see Figure 3-1). Because discretionary funding in the baseline projections is increased only in line with

Box 3-1.
Categories of Federal Spending

On the basis of its treatment in the budget process, federal spending can be divided into three broad categories:

Mandatory spending consists primarily of benefit programs, such as Social Security, Medicare, and Medicaid. The Congress generally determines spending for those programs by setting rules for eligibility, benefit formulas, and other parameters rather than by appropriating specific amounts each year. In making baseline projections, the Congressional Budget Office (CBO) assumes that existing laws and policies for those programs will remain unchanged and that most expiring programs will be extended. Mandatory spending also includes offsetting receipts—fees and other charges that are recorded as negative budget authority and outlays. Offsetting receipts differ from revenues in that revenues are collected in the exercise of the government's sovereign powers (for example, in the form of income taxes) whereas offsetting receipts generally are collected from other government accounts or from members of the public for business-like transactions (for example, as premiums for Medicare or as rental payments and royalties for oil or gas drilling on public lands).

Discretionary spending is controlled by annual appropriation acts; policymakers decide each year how much money to provide for given activities. Appropriations fund all manner of government activities, such as those for defense, law enforcement, and transportation. They also fund the national park system, disaster relief, and foreign aid. Some fees and other charges that are triggered by appropriation action are classified as offsetting collections, which are credited against discretionary spending.

CBO's baseline depicts the path of discretionary spending as directed by the provisions of the Balanced Budget and Emergency Deficit Control Act of 1985. The act stated that current spending should be

assumed to grow with inflation in the future.[1] Although those provisions (contained in section 257 of the act) expired at the end of September 2006, CBO continues to follow their requirements in preparing its baseline for discretionary spending. Appropriations to date have provided a total of $1,045 billion in budget authority for fiscal year 2008: $586 billion for defense and $458 billion for nondefense activities.

In addition to spending from those appropriations, the baseline includes discretionary spending for highway infrastructure, highway and motor carrier safety, public transit, and airport infrastructure programs that receive mandatory budget authority from authorizing legislation. Each year, however, the annual appropriation acts control spending for those programs by limiting how much of the budget authority the Department of Transportation can obligate. For that reason, such obligation limitations are treated as a measure of discretionary resources, and the resulting outlays are considered discretionary spending. Transportation obligation limitations for 2008 total $54 billion.

Net interest includes interest paid on Treasury securities and other interest the government pays (for example, on late refunds issued by the Internal Revenue Service) minus interest that the government collects from various sources (such as from commercial banks that maintain Treasury tax and loan accounts). Net interest is determined by the size and composition of the government's debt, annual budget deficits or surpluses, and market interest rates.

---

1. The inflation rates used in CBO's baseline, as specified by the Deficit Control Act, are the employment cost index for wages and salaries (applied to expenditures related to federal personnel) and the gross domestic product price index (for other expenditures).

Figure 3-1.

Major Components of Spending, 1968 to 2018

(Percentage of gross domestic product)

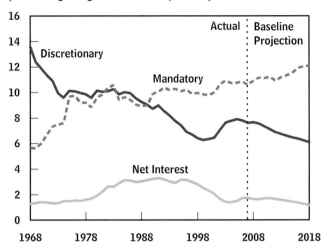

Sources: Congressional Budget Office; Office of Management and
          Budget.

inflation and not overall economic growth, the baseline projection for that category of spending falls to 6.1 percent of GDP by 2018. CBO estimates, however, that mandatory spending—which has more than doubled over the past 40 years as a percentage of GDP—will continue to increase over the next decade (led by growth in Medicare, Medicaid, and Social Security), climbing from its current share of 10.9 percent of GDP to 12.1 percent in 2018. The largest drivers of such growth are the rapid increase in the cost of health care and, to a lesser degree, the rising numbers of the nation's elderly population.

In 1991, net interest as a percentage of GDP reached a 40-year peak (3.3 percent). It declined each year from 1996 through 2004, bottoming out at 1.4 percent in 2004 (because of lower interest rates and either declining deficits or budget surpluses in most of those years). Since 2005, however, interest payments have increased slightly, measuring 1.7 percent of GDP in 2007. Under assumptions for the baseline, net interest will change little as a percentage of GDP through 2013 and then fall as projected surpluses emerge.

Mandatory Spending

Mandatory—or direct—spending makes up more than half of the federal budget. This category includes

payments to people and entities such as businesses, non-profit institutions, and state and local governments. In general, those payments are governed by statutory criteria and they are not normally constrained by the annual appropriation process. Offsetting receipts (certain types of payments that federal agencies receive from the public and other government agencies) are classified as offsets to mandatory spending. In 2007, mandatory outlays were $1.5 trillion, a figure that CBO projects will rise steadily to reach $2.7 trillion by 2018 (see Table 3-3).

From 1997 to 2006, mandatory spending increased at an average annual rate of 6.0 percent. Increases in spending for health care programs, for the refundable portion of the earned income tax credit and the child tax credit, and for farm programs all contributed to the high rate of growth over the period. Also, 2006 witnessed particularly large increases in spending for flood insurance resulting from Hurricane Katrina and for the subsidy costs of student loans. In addition, several other federal agencies revised previous estimates of subsidy costs for loans and loan guarantees issued in the past, which also boosted 2006 outlays significantly.[1] Spending in all three areas returned to more typical levels in 2007.

As a result of those unusually high payments in 2006 and their return to more normal levels in 2007, mandatory spending in 2007 grew by only 2.7 percent. It is projected to return to a higher growth rate in 2008 and 2009, increasing by 6.9 percent and 6.7 percent, respectively. Over the following nine years, mandatory outlays are expected to climb at a faster rate than the economy—by 5.6 percent per year, on average—thereby increasing as a share of GDP from 10.6 percent in 2007 to 12.1 percent by 2018. Over that same period, Medicare and Medicaid outlays together are projected to increase from 4.6 percent of GDP to 5.9 percent; Social Security spending is expected to rise from 4.3 percent in 2007 to 4.9 percent of GDP by 2018. Outlays for other mandatory programs (under an assumption that the law does not change) are projected to decline as a percentage of GDP from 3.1 percent in 2007 to 2.6 percent in 2018.

Mandatory spending is dominated by income-support payments and health care programs for the elderly, persons with disabilities, and the poor. The three largest

---

1. Such "credit reestimates" occur each year, but those in 2006
    were particularly large, exceeding the 2007 reestimates by about
    $16 billion.

Table 3-3.

CBO's Baseline Projections of Mandatory Outlays

(Billions of dollars)

	Actual 2007	2008	2009	2010	2011	2012	2013	2014	2015	2016	2017	2018	Total, 2009-2013	Total, 2009-2018
Social Security	581	611	646	682	719	761	807	856	908	965	1,027	1,092	3,615	8,464
Medicare[a]	436	454	485	512	561	565	629	671	719	803	841	879	2,752	6,666
Medicaid	191	208	225	243	261	282	304	328	353	381	412	445	1,314	3,232
Income Security														
Supplemental Security Income	36	41	43	45	51	44	50	52	53	60	57	53	234	509
Earned income and child tax credits	54	56	56	57	58	40	41	41	41	41	41	41	252	458
Unemployment compensation	33	39	46	43	40	43	45	48	50	52	54	56	217	476
Food Stamps	35	38	41	42	42	43	44	44	45	46	48	49	212	445
Family support[b]	24	24	24	24	24	24	24	25	25	25	25	25	121	246
Child nutrition	14	15	16	16	17	18	18	19	20	21	22	23	85	190
Foster care	7	7	7	7	7	8	8	8	9	9	9	9	37	81
Subtotal	202	221	233	235	240	220	230	237	243	254	256	257	1,159	2,406
Other Retirement and Disability														
Federal civilian[c]	72	75	78	82	85	89	92	96	100	104	107	111	426	945
Military	44	46	49	50	51	53	54	55	56	58	59	61	257	546
Veteran[d]	36	40	41	42	47	42	46	47	49	54	52	49	218	470
Other	8	9	8	9	9	10	10	10	11	11	11	11	46	99
Subtotal	159	169	177	183	192	193	202	209	216	226	229	233	947	2,060

Continued

programs, Medicare, Medicaid, and Social Security, were responsible for nearly 75 percent of direct spending in 2007—$1.2 trillion (excluding income from offsetting receipts). Other income-security programs (such as the refundable portions of the EITC and the child tax credit, food assistance, Supplemental Security Income [SSI], and unemployment compensation) made up about 12 percent of direct spending ($202 billion); other retirement and disability programs (including federal civilian and military retirement and veterans' compensation programs) made up almost 10 percent ($159 billion). All other mandatory programs (such as agriculture subsidies, health care benefits for retirees of the uniformed services, and student loans) made up less than 4 percent of mandatory spending, with outlays of $59 billion in 2007.

Medicare and Medicaid

Taken together, gross federal outlays for the two major health programs, Medicare and Medicaid, totaled $627 billion in 2007, or 23 percent of all federal outlays.

Spending for those two health programs is projected to grow briskly over the next decade—at an average rate of 7 percent and 8 percent per year, respectively.

Medicare. The larger of the two major health care programs, Medicare provides subsidized medical insurance for the elderly and some people with disabilities. Medicare has three programs: Part A (Hospital Insurance), Part B (Supplementary Medical Insurance), and Part D (the subsidy for outpatient prescription drugs).[2] People generally become eligible for Medicare at age 65 or two years after they become eligible for Social Security Disability Insurance benefits. In 2007, Medicare had about 44 million beneficiaries; it is expected to enroll 58 million by 2018.

2. Medicare Part C specifies the rules under which private health care plans can assume responsibility for and be paid for providing the benefits covered under Parts A, B, and D.

Table 3-3.

Continued

- -
(Billions of dollars)

	Actual 2007	2008	2009	2010	2011	2012	2013	2014	2015	2016	2017	2018	Total, 2009- 2013	Total, 2009- 2018
Other Programs														
Commodity Credit Corporation Fund	8	7	7	7	7	7	7	8	8	8	8	8	37	77
TRICARE For Life	8	8	8	8	9	9	10	11	12	13	13	15	45	108
Student loans	7	3	2	4	5	5	3	3	3	2	2	2	20	32
Universal Service Fund	7	8	8	8	8	9	9	9	9	9	9	9	42	87
State Children's Health Insurance Program	6	7	6	6	5	5	5	5	5	5	5	5	28	53
Social services	5	5	5	5	5	5	5	5	5	5	6	6	26	53
Other	18	34	35	33	31	31	31	29	30	32	38	40	161	329
Subtotal	59	73	71	72	72	72	71	69	72	74	81	85	357	739
Offsetting Receipts														
Medicare[e]	-66	-69	-74	-79	-84	-90	-96	-103	-110	-119	-129	-139	-423	-1,024
Employers' share of employees' retirement	-48	-51	-55	-57	-59	-62	-64	-67	-70	-73	-82	-86	-297	-674
Other	-64	-65	-54	-54	-56	-57	-60	-62	-61	-62	-57	-60	-282	-583
Subtotal	-178	-186	-183	-190	-200	-209	-220	-231	-241	-254	-268	-285	-1,001	-2,281
Total Mandatory Outlays	**1,450**	**1,550**	**1,654**	**1,737**	**1,846**	**1,884**	**2,022**	**2,138**	**2,270**	**2,451**	**2,578**	**2,706**	**9,142**	**21,285**
Memorandum:														
Mandatory Outlays Excluding Offsetting Receipts	1,628	1,736	1,836	1,927	2,046	2,092	2,243	2,369	2,511	2,705	2,846	2,991	10,143	23,566
Medicare Outlays Net of Offsetting Receipts	370	385	411	433	477	475	533	569	609	684	712	740	2,329	5,642

Source: Congressional Budget Office.

Note: Spending for the benefit programs shown above generally excludes administrative costs, which are discretionary.

a. Excludes offsetting receipts.

b. Includes Temporary Assistance for Needy Families and various programs that involve payments to states for child support enforcement and family support.

c. Includes Civil Service, Foreign Service, Coast Guard, and other small retirement programs and annuitants' health benefits.

d. Includes veterans' compensation, pensions, and life insurance programs.

e. Includes Medicare premiums and amounts paid by states from savings on Medicaid prescription drug costs.

Medicare spending will increase by about 4 percent in 2008, CBO estimates, a slower pace than in recent years. The slowdown has four main causes: First, spending under Part D will have been in place for nearly two years and will no longer be experiencing the rapid growth associated with the program's introduction. Second, shifts in the timing of certain payments to providers at the beginning of 2007 boosted Medicare outlays in that year and thereby will reduce growth in 2008.[3] Third, payments to

prescription drug plans have been adjusted to reconcile estimated and actual costs for 2006. The initial payments to those plans were based on projected expenses. Actual prescription drug costs in 2006 were lower than projected, resulting in a reduction (of about $4 billion) in the net amounts paid to plans so far this year.

---

3. Excluding those shifts, Medicare outlays in 2008 would increase by 5.2 percent, CBO estimates.

Box 3-2.

Medicare's Prescription Drug Benefit

In January 2006, Medicare began to subsidize prescription drug coverage under its new Part D program. Coverage comes from private prescription drug plans available to all enrollees in a geographic area, from managed care plans that participate in the Medicare Advantage program, and from employer- or union-sponsored plans. Part D enrollment is voluntary, and participants pay premiums to cover a portion of the program's cost. Part D also provides additional federal subsidies to cover the cost of drugs for some low-income Medicare beneficiaries.

During 2007, almost 30 million people—about 73 percent of all Medicare beneficiaries—were enrolled in the drug benefit, and Part D spent a total of $49 billion on prescription drug coverage. Those costs were partly offset by $2 billion in premiums withheld from some enrollees' Social Security benefits (most

enrollees pay their premiums directly to the plans), and by $7 billion in "clawback" payments from states, leaving a net cost of $41 billion (see the table to the right). The state payments are intended to reflect the savings accruing to states from Medicare's coverage of drug costs previously paid by Medicaid; they are based on historical Medicaid spending on prescription drugs for people who are eligible for both programs.

The Congressional Budget Office (CBO) estimates that payments under Part D for prescription drugs will total $45 billion in 2008 and that they will reach $136 billion by 2018. The 2008 costs will be lower than those in 2007; the Centers for Medicare and Medicaid Services will collect more than $4 billion from drug plans because of lower-than-anticipated spending in 2006.

Finally, Medicare's payment rates for physicians are set to be reduced by about 10 percent in July 2008, and the baseline projections assume those reductions take effect. (Such a reduction was previously scheduled for January 2008 but was delayed by six months in recently enacted legislation.)

Under current law, additional cuts in the rates paid to physicians will follow for several years (as explained later in this chapter). Nevertheless, CBO anticipates that growth in Medicare outlays will average 6.8 percent annually, from 2009 to 2018, and it estimates that Medicare outlays as a share of GDP will rise from 3.2 percent this year to 3.9 percent in 2018. Over that period federal spending per beneficiary for Parts A and B will grow in nominal terms by more than 40 percent, from about $9,300 in 2008 to $13,200 in 2018. Gross Medicare outlays will total $879 billion in 2018, CBO projects. That amount does not include the effects of premiums and some payments from states, which are discussed in the section on offsetting receipts. Those receipts will total an estimated $139 billion by 2018.

About 73 percent of Medicare beneficiaries had Part D coverage for prescription drugs for 2007; CBO projects that share will grow to about 78 percent of Medicare beneficiaries over the next few years. (Box 3-2 discusses CBO's estimates of spending for Part D.)

In 2007, the Medicare trustees issued a "Medicare funding warning" after projecting, for the second consecutive year, that payments from the general fund will account for more than 45 percent of total Medicare outlays within seven years. In accordance with the Medicare Modernization Act (Public Law 108-173), such a determination requires the President to submit to the Congress a proposal to reduce the payments from the general fund below the 45 percent threshold. The proposal would require Congressional action to become law.

Medicaid. Medicaid is a joint federal and state program that funds medical care for many of the nation's poor, elderly, and people with disabilities. The federal government shares costs with states for approved services, but the proportion varies from state to state, averaging 57 percent nationwide. Federal outlays for Medicaid totaled $191 billion in 2007—about 12 percent of direct

Box 3-2.

Continued

CBO's Projections of Spending for Medicare Part D
(Billions of dollars)

	2007	2008	2009	2010	2011	2012	2013	2014	2015	2016	2017	2018	Total, 2009-2013	Total, 2009-2018
Gross Medicare Part D Outlays	49	45	57	62	74	70	85	95	106	129	134	136	348	948
Offsetting Receipts														
Premiums	-2	-2	-2	-3	-3	-4	-4	-4	-5	-6	-6	-7	-15	-44
Payments from States	-7	-7	-8	-9	-10	-10	-11	-12	-13	-15	-16	-18	-48	-122
Subtotal	-8	-9	-10	-11	-13	-14	-15	-17	-18	-20	-23	-25	-63	-166
Total	**41**	**36**	**46**	**51**	**62**	**56**	**69**	**78**	**88**	**109**	**112**	**112**	**284**	**782**
Memorandum:														
Net Part D Outlays Adjusted for the Timing of Certain Payments	41	36	46	51	56	62	69	78	88	98	110	124	284	782

Source: Congressional Budget Office.

CBO also estimates that the federal government will collect $9 billion in offsetting receipts in 2008 from premiums and clawback payments. That amount will rise to $25 billion in 2018. Overall, by CBO's estimates, net spending for Part D will increase from $36 billion in 2008 to $112 billion in 2018. (Spending appears relatively flat over the last three years of the projection period because the number of monthly payments in those years will drop from 13 in 2016 to 12 in 2017 and 11 in 2018 because of shifts in the timing of payments to drug plans.)

The current estimate for Part D spending is lower than CBO's August 2007 estimate because bids that drug plans submitted to provide drug coverage in calendar year 2008 are lower than expected—on average, only about 2 percent higher than the 2007 bids. As a result, CBO reduced its projection of the per capita costs of providing drug coverage.

spending that year. Like Medicare, Medicaid has a history of rapid cost growth, with annual increases averaging 7.0 percent from 1997 to 2006, even though spending declined slightly in 2006. Medicaid outlays increased by 5.5 percent in 2007.

CBO estimates that Medicaid outlays will increase by 8.9 percent and 8.3 percent, respectively, over 2008 and 2009 and will average 7.9 percent annual growth over the remainder of the projection period. Medicaid had about 60 million enrollees in 2007; the program is expected to enroll 72 million by 2018. That increasing caseload and the states' response to providers' demands for rate increases are the primary drivers of the growth. (Because the federal government shares costs with the states, state spending for Medicaid will rise at similar rates.) CBO projects that federal spending for Medicaid as a share of GDP will rise from 1.5 percent in 2008 to 2.0 percent in 2018, reaching $445 billion in that year.

Social Security

Social Security, which pays cash benefits to the elderly, to people with disabilities, and to their dependents, is the largest federal spending program. Social Security encompasses two programs: Old-Age and Survivors Insurance (OASI) and Disability Insurance (DI). In 2007, Social Security outlays came to $581 billion, more than 20 percent of all federal spending and more than 35 percent of mandatory spending (excluding offsetting receipts). Spending for Social Security, currently about 4.3 percent of GDP, will increase steadily over the next decade (and beyond) as the nation's elderly population increases. CBO expects that, between 2009 and 2018, the pool of recipients will grow by an average of 2.5 percent per year and that outlays will rise by an average of about 6 percent annually. By 2018, CBO estimates, Social Security will claim 4.9 percent of GDP.

Old-Age and Survivors Insurance. OASI, the larger of the two components, pays benefits to workers who reach a specific age (they become eligible for reduced benefits at age 62). It also makes payments to eligible spouses and children and to some survivors (primarily elderly widows and young children) of deceased workers. OASI benefits totaled $483 billion in 2007, a figure that will climb increasingly rapidly, reaching an estimated $918 billion by 2018. The growth in outlays for OASI is projected to average 6.1 percent a year between 2009 and 2018.

About one-third of the growth in OASI is attributable to a rising caseload. About 40.9 million people received OASI payments in December 2007, and CBO estimates that some 54.2 million people will do so in 2018, an increase of nearly 33 percent. The oldest members of the baby-boom generation (those born in 1946) will qualify for initial OASI benefits in 2008, when they reach age 62. (Typically, 40 percent to 50 percent of retired workers claim their benefits at the age of 62.) The rate of growth in the population of OASI recipients is projected to jump from about 1.5 percent in 2008 to 2.1 percent in 2009 and to accelerate each year thereafter, rising to 3.0 percent by 2018.

The rest of the growth in spending for OASI stems from benefit increases, which are projected to average 3.4 percent per year over the coming decade. Initial benefits are based on a retiree's lifetime wages, adjusted for overall wage growth in the economy. After a person becomes eligible, benefits also rise each year according to a cost-of-living adjustment (COLA). The January 2008 COLA is 2.3 percent, down from 3.3 percent in 2007. CBO projects that the COLA for Social Security programs will be 2.8 percent in January 2009, 2.3 percent in 2010, and 2.2 percent each year from 2011 through 2018.

Disability Insurance. Social Security's disability benefits go to workers who suffer debilitating health conditions before they are old enough for OASI enrollment.

(Payments also are made to the eligible spouses and children of those recipients.) In 2007, the government paid out nearly $97 billion in disability benefits. That figure will increase to $104 billion in 2008, CBO projects, and rise to $174 billion by 2018, an annual rate of increase of 5.3 percent.

As with OASI, burgeoning caseloads and rising average benefits (as a result of wage growth and COLAs) contribute to the increase in DI spending. Another factor is the continuing rise in Social Security's "normal retirement age"—from 65 to 66 and eventually to 67. Because the age increase delays the reclassification of disabled workers as retired workers, older people with disabilities will receive DI benefits for a longer period before making the transition to OASI. That increase also lengthens the period during which workers can apply for DI benefits.

Other Income-Security Programs

The federal government also provides payments to people and to other government entities through programs that assist various populations—people with disabilities, the poor, the unemployed, needy families with children, and children who have been abused and neglected. Federal spending for SSI, unemployment compensation, the EITC and the child tax credit, Food Stamps, family support, and foster care, among other services, totaled $202 billion in 2007, about 1.5 percent of GDP.

Under the assumptions for CBO's baseline, spending for other income-security programs—in contrast to the rapid growth in spending for Medicare, Medicaid, and Social Security—will increase by just 1.5 percent per year, on average, and will constitute 1.2 percent of GDP by 2018. Outlays for some programs (SSI, unemployment compensation, Food Stamps, child nutrition, and foster care) will grow more quickly than the average for the category, but spending for family support will barely increase. EITC and child tax credit outlays are projected to decline over the next 10 years with the scheduled expiration of statutory provisions that affect those credits.

Supplemental Security Income. SSI provides cash benefits to low-income people who are elderly or have disabilities. SSI outlays totaled $36 billion in 2007, a year in which 11 (rather than 12) monthly payments were made because October 1, 2006, was a Sunday. Under the assumptions that govern the baseline, spending on SSI is projected to reach $41 billion in 2008 and to increase at an annual rate of 2.6 percent over the next decade. The program's growth is driven mainly by COLAs and by a rise in the number of people with disabilities.

Earned Income and Child Tax Credits. The EITC and the child tax credit are partially refundable tax credits available to people who earn wages below an established maximum and to qualifying families with dependent children. Either credit can reduce a filer's overall tax liability; if the credit exceeds the liability, the excess may be refunded to the taxpayer, depending on the filer's earnings. The refundable portions (which are categorized as outlays) totaled $54 billion in 2007 and are projected to rise to $56 billion in 2008 and to $57 billion by 2010. In 2012—the first full fiscal year in which tax receipts will reflect the expiration of provisions initially enacted in the Economic Growth and Tax Relief Reconciliation Act of 2001—the refundability of the child tax credit will be virtually eliminated under current law. In addition, scheduled higher tax rates will reduce the EITC's refundable portion because more of the credit will offset tax liability and be reflected as a reduction in revenues. As a result, CBO estimates, outlays for those credits will decline—under current law—to $41 billion in 2018.

Unemployment Compensation. Outlays for unemployment compensation rose slightly last year, to nearly $33 billion, from $31 billion in 2006. CBO estimates that the unemployment rate will continue to rise throughout 2008, reaching 5.2 percent by the end of the fiscal year (up from an average of 4.5 percent last year). Consequently, spending for unemployment compensation will increase to nearly $39 billion in 2008. The unemployment rate is projected to rise again in 2009, to 5.3 percent, and then to fall over the next three years to 4.8 percent, where it is assumed to remain through 2018. As the unemployment rate rises, the proportion of people who are eligible for and collect unemployment benefits also rises. In addition, as the labor force increases, more people become eligible for unemployment compensation. And, although individual states are responsible for setting benefit amounts, benefit growth tends to reflect the growth in wages. CBO estimates that outlays for unemployment compensation will grow by more than 20 percent in 2008 and by over 15 percent in 2009 (reaching $46 billion). Such payments are projected to fall in 2010 and 2011 as a result of lower projected unemployment; between 2012 and 2018, they rise by an average annual rate of nearly 5 percent.

Food Stamps. CBO anticipates that outlays for the Food Stamp program will rise by more than 10 percent in 2008 (to $38 billion) and by nearly 7 percent the next year (reaching $41 billion). Much of that growth is the result of significant near-term increases that are anticipated in the cost of food at home. In 2006 and 2007, the average monthly benefit rose by 1.6 percent per year.[4] The benefit is projected to rise by 6.2 percent in 2008 and by an additional 5.8 percent in 2009. Over the remaining nine years of its baseline period, CBO projects growth to slow to 2.2 percent annually. CBO expects participation to increase in 2008 and 2009—reflecting recent trends— and to average 27.3 million between 2008 and 2018. Overall, spending for the program will grow by 2.5 percent per year, reaching nearly $49 billion by 2018, CBO projects.

Family Support. Spending for family support programs— grants to states to help fund welfare programs, child support enforcement, and child care entitlements—is projected to remain fairly flat, rising from $24 billion in 2008 to $25 billion by 2018. The largest program in this category, Temporary Assistance for Needy Families (TANF), is capped by law at roughly $17 billion per year. TANF is authorized through 2010, but in keeping with rules governing the treatment of programs set to expire, CBO's baseline assumes that TANF funding will continue at its most recently authorized level.

Child Nutrition and Foster Care. Spending for child nutrition, which provides cash and commodity assistance for meals and snacks through a variety of programs in schools, day care settings, and summer programs, is projected to rise by more than 4 percent annually through 2018. Outlays for child nutrition totaled $14 billion in 2007 and are projected to rise to $23 billion by 2018. Per-meal reimbursements for the school lunch program are projected to rise by 2.5 percent annually through 2018.

CBO estimates that spending for foster care and adoption assistance, almost $7 billion in 2007, will increase by 3.3 percent annually, reaching about $9 billion by 2018. Income eligibility standards for federal foster care and adoption assistance are becoming more difficult to meet because they are not indexed for inflation; as a result, CBO anticipates that the foster care caseload will

---

4. The maximum benefit is tied to the June-over-June change in the cost of the Department of Agriculture's Thrifty Food Plan.

continue to decline but that the decline will be more than offset by increases in spending for average benefits, administration, and adoption assistance.

Other Federal Retirement and Disability Programs

Benefits for federal civilian and military retirees and for veterans' pension and disability totaled $159 billion in 2007—about 10 percent of gross mandatory spending and 1.2 percent of GDP. CBO projects those outlays will grow at a rate of 3.2 percent annually over the next 10 years, reaching $233 billion (but falling to 1.0 percent of GDP) by 2018.

Retirement and survivor benefits paid through the federal civilian retirement program (along with several smaller retirement programs for employees of various government agencies and for retired railroad workers) amounted to $72 billion in 2007. CBO projects such outlays will grow at an annual average rate of 4.0 percent over the projection period and total $111 billion by 2018. Growth in federal retirement benefits is attributable primarily to COLAs and to rising federal salaries, which boost future benefits.

One factor that restrains growth in retirement programs is the gradual replacement of the Civil Service Retirement System (CSRS) with the Federal Employees' Retirement System (FERS). FERS covers employees hired after 1983 and provides a smaller defined benefit than that provided by CSRS. FERS recipients, however, are eligible to receive Social Security benefits through their federal employment (CSRS employees are not), and their contributions to the federal Thrift Savings Plan are matched in part by their employing agencies.

The federal government also provides retirement and disability benefits to retired military personnel and to veterans.[5] Military annuities totaled $44 billion in 2007, and they are projected to rise to $46 billion this year and to grow by an average of 2.8 percent each year thereafter. Most of the growth in military retirement programs results from COLAs and other benefit increases. Mandatory spending for veterans' benefits—disability compensation, pensions, life insurance, and dependency and indemnity compensation to surviving spouses and children—totaled $36 billion in 2007. Those payments are

projected to grow by an average of 2.2 percent annually, again because of COLAs and other benefit increases. The veterans' disability compensation caseload is projected to grow by about 1 percent annually.

Other Mandatory Spending

Other mandatory spending programs include farm price and income support programs administered by the Commodity Credit Corporation (CCC), TRICARE For Life,[6] student loans, the Universal Service Fund,[7] and the State Children's Health Insurance Program (SCHIP). Spending for this category was about $59 billion in 2007 and is projected to increase by almost 25 percent this year, to $73 billion. Revisions to previous estimates of subsidy costs for loans and loan guarantees (or "credit reestimates") account for almost $6 billion of that increase, and higher spending for disaster assistance (mostly for crops and livestock) accounts for another $3 billion. Outlays for the category will grow at a much slower average annual rate of 1.5 percent a year for the remainder of the projection period, CBO estimates.

CCC payments to agricultural producers totaled $8 billion in 2007, after varying between $9 billion and $30 billion in the preceding seven years. CBO estimates those outlays will range between $7 billion and $8 billion per year through 2018. The relatively low level of spending primarily reflects lower income-support payments to farmers because of historically high crop prices that are attributable in part to the strong market demand for ethanol (which is made from corn). Following directions established by the Deficit Control Act, CBO's baseline assumes most major farm programs, which are set to expire on March 15, 2008, will continue in their current form throughout the 2008–2018 period. (For a more detailed discussion of agriculture programs, see Box 3-3.)

In 2007, federal student loan subsidies and administrative costs for the program totaled almost $7 billion. With interest rates that are more favorable to the government and with the implementation of major program reforms, CBO estimates that student loan costs will decline in 2008; outlays for student loans are estimated to fall to

---

5. Veterans also receive education and housing benefits, which are included in other mandatory spending. Veterans' health care is a discretionary program.

6. TRICARE For Life provides health care benefits to retirees of the uniformed services (and to their dependents and surviving spouses) who are eligible for Medicare.

7. Spending for universal telecommunications service is roughly matched by revenues deposited into this fund, resulting in little net budgetary impact.

$3 billion in 2008 and to fluctuate within a range of $2 billion to $5 billion per year for the next decade as some program reforms are phased in and others are phased out.[8]

SCHIP is a federal and state program that provides health coverage to low-income children who are uninsured but are not poor enough to qualify for Medicaid. On average, the federal government pays about 69 percent of the program's costs. SCHIP is authorized through March 2009 and total funding for the basic program is capped by law at $5 billion annually, with each state's share determined by a formula. Consistent with the Deficit Control Act, CBO's baseline assumes that SCHIP funding will continue at that level in later years. Since 2006, SCHIP also has provided extra funding to states that have exhausted their available funds, but those additional amounts are structured by law to be temporary and are not continued in CBO's baseline.[9] Federal SCHIP outlays totaled $6 billion in 2007 and are projected to rise to more than $7 billion in 2008 before gradually declining to $5 billion annually in later years.

What Causes Growth in Mandatory Spending?
Excluding offsetting receipts, CBO projects that mandatory spending will total $1.7 trillion in 2008 and that it will grow faster than the economy over the coming decade. By 2018, $1.3 trillion will be added to annual mandatory spending. Several factors account for that growth, mainly COLAs, other benefit increases, and rising caseloads (see Table 3-4 on page 66).

COLAs and Other Automatic Adjustments. Annual changes in benefits that are pegged to inflation and other automatic adjustments account for more than one-

quarter of the projected growth in mandatory spending. All major retirement programs grant automatic COLAs (the 2008 adjustment is 2.3 percent). CBO estimates that the consumer price index (the economic indicator of inflation to which COLAs are tied) will increase by 2.8 percent in 2009, by 2.3 percent in 2010, and by 2.2 percent annually from 2011 through 2018. The Food Stamp program and the EITC are indexed to other measures of inflation. In total, automatic adjustments for inflation in programs other than Medicare are projected to raise mandatory outlays by $22 billion in 2009 and by $238 billion by 2018, accounting for 19 percent of the growth in mandatory spending estimated for the period.

Payment rates for many Medicare services also are adjusted annually to reflect changes in the costs of goods and services used by providers and changes in economic factors such as GDP and productivity. The effect of those automatic increases on Medicare spending is dampened by the sustainable growth rate (SGR) formula, which is used to establish a fee schedule for physicians' services. The SGR formula sets a cumulative spending target for payments to physicians and for services related to medical visits (such as laboratory tests and drugs administered by physicians).

Left unaltered, the SGR formula ultimately recoups spending that exceeds the cumulative target by reducing payment rates for physicians' services or by holding increases below inflation (as measured by the Medicare economic index).[10] Under an assumption that current law remains in effect, CBO anticipates that the SGR formula will reduce payment rates for physicians' services by about 10 percent beginning in July 2008 and by approximately 5 percent annually for much of the rest of the 2009–2018 period. At the end of that time, cumulative Medicare spending measured under the SGR will be nearly back in line with the formula's cumulative targets,

---

8. The College Cost Reduction and Access Act (Public Law 110-84), which was enacted in September 2007, made significant changes to the federal financial assistance programs for postsecondary education. It reduced the government's payments to lenders in the Federal Family Education Loan Program and to guaranty agencies, it modified fees for lenders, it reduced the cost of federal loans for some borrowers, and it increased funding for the Pell Grant program. The budgetary effects of those changes largely offset one another.

9. The Congress appropriated additional funds of up to $1.6 billion for 2008 and $275 million for 2009.

---

10. The Medicare economic index tracks the costs of physicians' time and operating expenses. Most of the components of the index come from the Bureau of Labor Statistics. Changes in the costs of physicians' time are measured through changes in nonfarm labor costs. Changes in productivity also are factored directly into the index.

Box 3-3.

CBO's Baseline Projections of Spending to Support Agriculture

The latest baseline projections of the Congressional Budget Office (CBO) anticipate significantly higher prices for most crops in 2008 and over the next decade than estimated in CBO's August 2007 update of *The Budget and Economic Outlook*. Nevertheless, the current baseline contains projections of federal outlays for agriculture that are only 1 percent lower than those estimated in August (see the table to the right).[1]

In general, federal farm and income support programs guarantee the producers of a range of commodities a certain minimum price for their crops. When the prices in the marketplace top those amounts, federal spending falls for farm and income support programs. The higher prices for certain commodities assumed in the January baseline are the result of current and projected market conditions and a provision of the Energy Independence and Security Act of 2007 (Public Law 110-40) that requires increased use of alternative fuels for motor vehicles. That requirement will boost demand for corn and

soybeans, which are the primary feedstocks used to produce biomass-based fuel. CBO therefore projects reduced spending on farm and income support programs over the next decade—about 9 percent less than it anticipated in August.

At the same time, however, higher commodity prices are leading to greater spending for the federal crop insurance program because of the increased value of insured crops. Under the terms of that program, the federal government pays administrative expenses and about 60 percent of the indemnity costs for producers who purchase coverage. The higher the value of those crops, the higher those costs. As a result, CBO's forecast for lower-cost farm price and income support programs is mostly offset by higher government costs for crop insurance.

Many of the farm programs authorized in the Farm Security and Rural Investment Act of 2002 were set to expire at the end of 2007 but were extended through March 15, 2008. The House and Senate have passed different versions of legislation to amend and reauthorize farm income support, land conservation, trade, crop insurance, rural development, and nutrition programs.

---

1. CBO's August 2007 projection of agriculture outlays from 2008 through 2017 were, in total, about 3 percent above its previous estimates, issued in March 2007. In 2007, federal outlays for agriculture totaled nearly $18 billion.

---

but payment rates for physicians in 2018 will be less than three-quarters of what they will be in 2008.[11]

When combined, the indexing and the SGR adjustments to Medicare payment rates result in increases of $6 billion in 2009 and $120 billion in 2018, relative to spending in 2008, and make up about 10 percent of projected growth in mandatory spending.[12]

Other Changes in Benefits. Other factors that contribute to rising benefits account for more than 40 percent of the increase of $538 billion in mandatory spending over the projection period. About two-thirds of that figure (and 29 percent of all increases in mandatory spending) is attributable to growth in spending for Medicare and Medicaid that cannot be tied to statutory adjustments in payments or to the rising caseload. Increased use of services—more frequent visits to doctors, for example—

---

11. For more detail on the SGR, see Congressional Budget Office, *The Sustainable Growth Rate Formula for Setting Medicare's Physician Payment Rates* (September 7, 2006) and the statement by Peter R. Orszag, Director, Congressional Budget Office, *Medicare's Payments to Physicians: Options for Changing the Sustainable Growth Rate*, before the Senate Committee on Finance (March 1, 2007).

---

12. Amounts discussed for Medicare are gross spending and do not include the offsetting effects of premium payments. Those payments are set to cover about one-quarter of the costs for Part B, the Supplementary Medical Insurance program. Premiums also are paid under Part D.

Box 3-3.

Continued

Changes in CBO's Baseline Projections of Agriculture Outlays
(Billions of dollars)

	2008	2009	2010	2011	2012	2013	2014	2015	2016	2017	Total, 2008- 2012	Total, 2008- 2017
Commodity Credit Corporation and Other												
January 2008	17	14	14	14	15	15	15	15	15	15	75	150
August 2007	18	16	16	16	16	16	17	16	17	18	81	165
Difference	-1	-1	-1	-1	-1	-1	-1	-2	-2	-2	-6	-14
Crop Insurance												
January 2008	4	7	7	7	7	7	7	7	7	7	31	65
August 2007	5	5	5	5	5	5	5	5	5	5	26	53
Difference	*	2	1	1	1	1	1	1	1	1	5	12
Total Agriculture												
January 2008	21	21	21	21	22	22	22	22	22	22	106	215
August 2007	22	21	21	21	21	22	22	22	22	23	106	218
Difference	-1	*	*	*	*	*	*	*	-1	-1	-1	-2

Source: Congressional Budget Office.

contributes to growth, as does increased use of costly medical technology. Federal Medicaid costs also rise as states expand coverage of services—for example, by raising limits on the number of home health visits the program will cover.

Benefits for other programs also experience growth beyond the automatic adjustments. Growth in wages, for example, affects Social Security benefits, federal retirement benefits, and unemployment compensation.

Wage growth also affects refundable tax credits. Outlays for the EITC and the child tax credit will shrink relative to payments made in 2008, CBO projects, because rising wages will reduce eligibility and increase the proportion of credits that will offset taxes rather than be refunded. Beginning in 2012, expiring provisions first enacted in EGTRRA also will affect the EITC and the child tax credit by reducing the refundable portion of those credits.

If current tax law remains unchanged, outlays for those tax credits in each year from 2012 to 2018 will be well below outlays in 2008.

Increases in Caseloads. A rise in the number of people who will be eligible for and claim benefits will add $387 billion to mandatory spending by 2018, CBO estimates. The three largest mandatory programs (Medicare, Medicaid, and Social Security) will be responsible for $372 billion—more than 95 percent of that total. In 2008, CBO estimates, 50 million people will collect Social Security benefits. By 2018, that number will be 64 million. Projected increases in Medicare caseloads are similar, rising from about 44 million in 2008 to 56 million in 2018 (see Figure 3-2 on page 68). Changes in caseloads for all major benefit programs will contribute about 30 percent to the growth in mandatory spending from 2008 to 2018.

Table 3-4.

Sources of Growth in Mandatory Outlays

(Billions of dollars)

	2009	2010	2011	2012	2013	2014	2015	2016	2017	2018
Estimated Spending in 2008	1,736	1,736	1,736	1,736	1,736	1,736	1,736	1,736	1,736	1,736
Sources of Growth										
Cost-of-living and other automatic adjustments										
Medicare	6	12	21	31	41	53	67	81	98	120
Social Security	13	29	43	59	75	91	107	123	139	156
Other programs[a]	9	18	26	33	41	49	57	67	75	82
Subtotal	28	59	91	123	157	193	230	271	312	358
Other changes in benefits										
Medicare and Medicaid	27	53	81	113	151	183	220	267	315	368
Social Security	10	18	26	37	50	66	84	106	131	159
Other programs[a]	5	6	7	-7	-5	-2	1	4	7	11
Subtotal	42	76	114	143	196	247	305	376	454	538
Increases in caseloads										
Medicare and Medicaid	16	28	41	59	79	101	124	149	176	205
Social Security	11	25	38	54	70	88	107	126	146	166
Other programs[a]	7	5	3	6	7	9	10	10	12	15
Subtotal	34	58	82	118	156	198	240	285	334	387
Shifts in payment dates[b]	0	0	25	-25	0	0	0	36	3	-38
Other	-3	-2	-2	-2	-3	-4	-1	1	8	11
Total	**100**	**191**	**310**	**356**	**507**	**634**	**775**	**969**	**1,110**	**1,255**
Projected Spending	1,836	1,927	2,046	2,092	2,243	2,369	2,511	2,705	2,846	2,991

Source: Congressional Budget Office.

Note: Amounts do not include the effects of offsetting receipts.

a.   This category includes unemployment compensation, earned income and child tax credits, military and civilian retirement, veterans' benefits, child nutrition, Food Stamps, and foster care.

b.   Represents differences attributable to assumptions about the number of benefit checks that will be issued in a fiscal year. Benefit payments normally are made once a month, but in 2011 and 2016 there will be 13 monthly payments for Medicare, Supplemental Security Income, and veterans' compensation; in 2012 and 2018 those programs will issue 11 monthly payments.

Shifts in Payment Dates. The timing of outlays for some mandatory programs depends on whether October 1, the first day of the fiscal year, falls on a weekday or on a weekend. If it falls on a Saturday or a Sunday, some benefits are paid at the end of September, increasing spending for the preceding year but decreasing outlays for the forthcoming year. SSI, veterans' compensation and pension programs, and Medicare payments to managed care plans and Part D plans are affected by such calendar shifts. Those programs can make 11, 12, or 13 monthly payments in a fiscal year. Irregular numbers of benefit payments will affect mandatory spending in 2011, 2012, 2016, 2017, and 2018.

Offsetting Receipts

Offsetting receipts—which are recorded as negative spending—are certain payments made to the federal government by citizens, businesses, or other federal agencies. They include beneficiaries' premiums for Medicare, federal agencies' retirement contributions, and payments for harvesting timber or extracting minerals from federal lands. In 2007, offsetting receipts totaled $178 billion—

Table 3-5.

CBO's Baseline Projections of Offsetting Receipts

(Billions of dollars)

	Actual 2007	2008	2009	2010	2011	2012	2013	2014	2015	2016	2017	2018	Total, 2009-2013	Total, 2009-2018
Medicare[a]	-66	-69	-74	-79	-84	-90	-96	-103	-110	-119	-129	-139	-423	-1,024
Employers' Share of Employees' Retirement														
Social Security	-12	-13	-14	-15	-16	-17	-17	-18	-19	-20	-21	-22	-78	-180
Military retirement	-14	-16	-18	-18	-19	-19	-20	-20	-21	-22	-22	-23	-93	-201
Civil service retirement and other	-21	-22	-23	-24	-25	-26	-27	-28	-30	-31	-39	-41	-125	-293
Subtotal	-48	-51	-55	-57	-59	-62	-64	-67	-70	-73	-82	-86	-297	-674
TRICARE For Life	-12	-11	-11	-12	-12	-13	-14	-15	-16	-17	-18	-19	-62	-145
Natural Resources-Related Receipts[b]	-13	-18	-17	-18	-19	-19	-21	-21	-21	-22	-21	-23	-93	-201
Electromagnetic Spectrum Auctions	-14	-11	-2	*	*	*	0	0	0	0	0	0	-3	-3
Other	-26	-25	-24	-25	-25	-25	-25	-26	-24	-23	-18	-19	-124	-234
Total	**-178**	**-186**	**-183**	**-190**	**-200**	**-209**	**-220**	**-231**	**-241**	**-254**	**-268**	**-285**	**-1,001**	**-2,281**

Source: Congressional Budget Office.

Note: * = between -$500 million and zero.

a.   Includes Medicare premiums and amounts paid by states from savings on Medicaid prescription drug costs.

b.   Includes timber, mineral, and Outer Continental Shelf receipts and proceeds from sales of public land.

about 11 percent of gross mandatory spending and 1.3 percent of GDP (see Table 3-5). Offsetting receipts are expected to climb by nearly 4.4 percent on average over the next 10 years, primarily because of Medicare Part B premiums. By 2018, offsetting receipts will equal 1.3 percent of GDP, CBO estimates, about the same as in 2008.

Medicare Premiums and Payments From States. Offsetting receipts for Medicare totaled $66 billion in 2007—about 35 percent of all offsetting receipts. Over the coming years, those receipts will grow substantially, to about $140 billion in 2018. The bulk is from premiums paid by beneficiaries, but the amount also includes payments made by states and recoveries of overpayments made to providers.

Prior to 2007, nearly all Medicare premiums were paid by people enrolled in Part B, the Supplementary Medical Insurance program, which covers physicians' and outpatient hospital services. Starting in 2007, premiums for

prescription drug benefits under Part D of Medicare began to account for a significant share of Medicare's premium receipts. (Although collection of Part D premiums began in 2006, 2007 was the first full year of operation of Part D.) Part B premiums for some higher-income enrollees also were raised above the standard premium. CBO estimates that premium payments for Medicare will rise from $53 billion in 2008 to $106 billion in 2018.

The annual premium amount for Medicare's Part B is announced in the fall of each year. Because those annual premiums are supposed to offset about 25 percent of projected spending for Medicare Part B, legislation to increase spending in Part B that is enacted after the premium is announced (for example, by increasing fees paid to physicians) tends to result in premium revenue that is a lower percentage of Part B spending than that assumed by the program's trustees when the premium was calculated initially. That will occur in 2008. In subsequent years, however, premiums will be increased so that—over

Figure 3-2.

Caseload Growth in Social Security and Medicare, 1995 to 2018

(Millions of people)

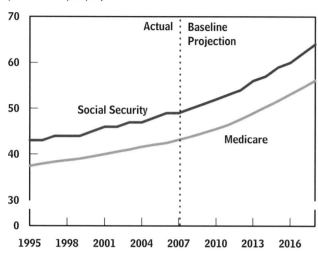

Sources: Congressional Budget Office; Office of Management and Budget.

a period of several years—standard premiums will, in fact, offset about 25 percent of Part B spending.

Medicare now pays some of the cost of providing prescription drug coverage for low-income enrollees. Previously, Medicaid covered that cost, which was split between beneficiaries' states and the federal government. A portion of the savings accruing to the states from that cost shifting is returned to the federal government and credited to the Part D program, and those payments from states are reflected in the budget as offsetting receipts. CBO expects that those payments will grow—primarily because of increases in the cost of prescription drugs—from $7 billion in 2008 to $18 billion in 2018.[13]

Other Offsetting Receipts. Other offsets to mandatory spending involve payments made by federal agencies to employees' retirement plans, proprietary receipts from royalties and other charges for oil and natural gas production on federal lands, sales arising from harvested timber

---

13. In 2006, states were required to pay back 90 percent of their estimated savings from shifting drug costs to the federal government; that portion will be reduced through 2015, when states will be required to pay back 75 percent of their estimated savings. It is scheduled to remain at that level thereafter.

and minerals extracted from federal land, and various fees paid by users of public property and services.

In 2007, $48 billion in offsetting receipts came in the form of intragovernmental transfers from federal agencies to employees' retirement plans (mostly trust funds for Social Security and for military and civil service retirement). CBO estimates that such payments will grow by about 5.3 percent annually, reaching $86 billion by 2018. Intragovernmental transfers also are made to the Uniformed Services Medicare-Eligible Retiree Health Care Fund under the TRICARE For Life program; those payments totaled $12 billion in 2007. CBO projects that rising health care costs will cause TRICARE For Life payments to rise by more than 5 percent each year, to $19 billion by 2018.

Receipts from programs to develop federally owned natural resources, particularly oil, natural gas, and minerals, totaled $13 billion in 2007. By 2018, CBO estimates, those receipts will total $23 billion.

CBO projects that the Federal Communications Commission's auctions of licenses to use the electromagnetic spectrum will boost offsetting receipts by $11 billion in 2008 and by another $2.9 billion over the 2009–2012 period. That total includes proceeds from the 2008 auction of licenses to use some of the frequencies currently used for television broadcasts as well as other auctions expected to occur before the agency's auction authority expires at the end of 2011.

Legislation Assumed in the Baseline
In keeping with precedents established by the Deficit Control Act, CBO's baseline projections assume that some mandatory programs will be extended when their authorization expires, although the assumptions apply differently to programs created before and after the Balanced Budget Act of 1997. All direct spending programs that predate mid-1997 and that have current-year outlays above $50 million are assumed to continue. For those established after 1997, continuation is assessed program by program, in consultation with the House and Senate Budget Committees. Smaller programs—those with current annual outlays below $50 million—are assumed to expire as authorization lapses. CBO's baseline projections therefore assume continuance of the Food Stamp program, TANF, SCHIP, rehabilitation services, child care entitlement grants to states, federal unemployment benefits and allowances (also known as trade adjustment

assistance for workers), child nutrition, and family preservation and support programs. Most CCC farm subsidies are assumed to continue.[14] In addition, the Deficit Control Act directed CBO to assume that a cost-of-living adjustment for veterans' compensation is granted each year. The assumption that expiring programs will continue accounts for outlays of nearly $4 billion in 2008 and $870 billion between 2009 and 2018 (see Table 3-6).

Discretionary Spending

Nearly 40 percent of federal spending is categorized as discretionary because it stems from spending authority provided in annual appropriation acts. That funding translates into outlays once the money is actually spent. Although some funds (for example, those designated for employees' salaries) are spent quickly, others (such as those intended for major construction projects) are disbursed over several years. In any given year, discretionary outlays include spending from new budget authority and from previous appropriations.

Recent Trends in Discretionary Funding and Outlays

In the mid-1980s, discretionary outlays were about 10 percent of GDP; by 1999 they had fallen to 6.3 percent (see Table 3-7 on page 72). In 2001, spending for discretionary programs began to move upward again as a share of the economy. The events of September 11, 2001, and military operations in Iraq and Afghanistan accelerated that trend. Discretionary outlays rose to 7.1 percent of GDP in 2002 and reached 7.9 percent in 2005. Such outlays have dipped slightly in the past two years and measured 7.6 percent of GDP in 2007. CBO projects that total discretionary outlays as a share of GDP will increase to 7.7 percent of GDP in 2008 in the absence of any additional appropriations for operations in Iraq and Afghanistan or other purposes.

Trends in overall discretionary spending have been heavily influenced by changes in spending on defense. During the late 1980s and the 1990s, defense outlays declined sharply as a share of the economy, sliding from 6.2 percent in 1986 to a low of 3.0 percent between 1999 and 2001. In 2002, defense outlays rose by 14 percent, to 3.4 percent of GDP, because of operations in Afghanistan, other activities related to the war on terrorism, and

defense initiatives that were planned or funded before September 11, 2001. Defense outlays continued to climb as military operations began in Iraq. After annual increases of 16 percent in 2003 and 12 percent in 2004, growth in defense outlays slowed to 9 percent in 2005 and to around 5 percent in both 2006 and 2007. CBO projects that, under current law, outlays will rise from $549 billion in 2007 to $572 billion in 2008. Actual defense outlays in 2008 are expected to be higher than $572 billion, however. Once additional appropriations are enacted to finance operations in Iraq and Afghanistan, defense outlays are likely to total about $600 billion—or 4.2 percent of GDP (compared with 4.0 percent of GDP in 2007). [15]

Nondefense discretionary programs encompass such activities as transportation, education grants, housing assistance, health-related research, most homeland security activities, foreign aid, and maintenance of national parks. Spending for such programs has ranged between 3.2 percent and 3.9 percent of GDP since the mid-1980s, although strong growth for most of this decade has pushed such outlays from the lower to the higher end of that range.

The recent growth in nondefense discretionary outlays came to a halt in 2007. Increases earlier in the decade were fueled initially by reconstruction costs in Iraq and, more recently, by costs related to hurricane damage from 2005. Funding for hurricane relief and recovery remained available in 2007, but outlays from such funding were significantly lower than in 2006.

In addition, with the exception of appropriations under the jurisdiction of the defense and homeland security subcommittees, appropriations funding the rest of the government's operations in 2007 were controlled by a continuing resolution that held appropriations at or near the amounts appropriated in 2006. Outlays for nondefense discretionary programs in 2007 thus dropped to $493 billion (0.5 percent lower than in 2006). With full-year appropriations enacted for all agencies in 2008, nondefense discretionary outlays will increase by 4.8 percent in 2008, CBO estimates.

---

14. Rehabilitation services and most CCC subsidies are due to expire under current law in 2008.

15. Although most spending for defense programs is classified as discretionary, about $4 billion a year in defense spending is mandatory.

Table 3-6.

Costs for Mandatory Programs That CBO's Baseline Assumes Will Continue Beyond Their Current Expiration Dates

(Billions of dollars)

	2008	2009	2010	2011	2012	2013	2014	2015	2016	2017	2018	Total, 2009-2013	Total, 2009-2018
Food Stamps													
Budget authority	n.a.	41.1	41.8	42.4	43.2	43.8	44.4	45.2	46.5	47.8	49.2	212.3	445.4
Outlays	n.a.	41.0	41.7	42.4	43.2	43.8	44.3	45.2	46.4	47.8	49.2	212.1	444.9
Temporary Assistance for Needy Families													
Budget authority	n.a.	n.a.	n.a.	16.8	16.8	16.8	16.8	16.8	16.8	16.8	16.8	50.3	134.2
Outlays	n.a.	n.a.	n.a.	11.6	16.8	16.8	16.8	16.8	16.8	16.8	16.8	45.2	129.1
Commodity Credit Corporation[a]													
Budget authority	0.4	8.2	8.3	9.8	10.5	11.1	11.8	12.0	13.8	15.7	17.6	47.9	118.8
Outlays	0.1	8.2	8.3	8.8	9.7	10.5	11.4	11.7	13.7	15.7	17.6	45.5	115.5
State Children's Health Insurance Program													
Budget authority	n.a.	0	5.0	5.0	5.0	5.0	5.0	5.0	5.0	5.0	5.0	20.2	45.4
Outlays	n.a.	1.7	5.3	5.4	5.2	5.2	5.2	5.3	5.1	5.1	5.1	22.7	48.5
Veterans' Compensation COLAs													
Budget authority	0.6	1.6	2.4	3.3	4.0	4.8	5.7	6.6	8.0	9.1	9.7	16.0	55.1
Outlays	0.6	1.5	2.3	3.3	3.9	4.7	5.6	6.4	8.0	9.0	9.6	15.6	54.2
Rehabilitation Services and Disability Research													
Budget authority	2.9	3.0	3.1	3.1	3.2	3.3	3.3	3.4	3.5	3.6	3.6	15.6	33.1
Outlays	2.8	2.9	3.0	3.1	3.2	3.2	3.3	3.4	3.4	3.5	3.6	15.4	32.6
Child Care Entitlements to States													
Budget authority	n.a.	n.a.	n.a.	2.9	2.9	2.9	2.9	2.9	2.9	2.9	2.9	8.8	23.3
Outlays	n.a.	n.a.	n.a.	2.1	2.8	2.9	2.9	2.9	2.9	2.9	2.9	7.8	22.4
Federal Unemployment Benefits and Allowances													
Budget authority	n.a.	0.9	1.0	1.0	1.0	1.1	1.1	1.1	1.1	1.2	1.2	5.0	10.7
Outlays	n.a.	0.7	0.9	1.0	1.0	1.0	1.1	1.1	1.1	1.2	1.2	4.7	10.3
Child Nutrition[b]													
Budget authority	n.a.	n.a.	0.5	0.5	0.5	0.6	0.6	0.6	0.6	0.6	0.6	2.1	5.1
Outlays	n.a.	n.a.	0.4	0.5	0.5	0.5	0.6	0.6	0.6	0.6	0.6	2.0	5.0

Continued

Table 3-6.

Continued

- -

(Billions of dollars)

	2008	2009	2010	2011	2012	2013	2014	2015	2016	2017	2018	Total, 2009-2013	Total, 2009-2018
Ground Transportation Programs Not Subject to Annual Obligation Limitations													
Budget authority	n.a.	n.a.	0.6	0.6	0.6	0.6	0.6	0.6	0.6	0.6	0.6	2.6	5.8
Outlays	n.a.	n.a.	0.2	0.4	0.6	0.6	0.6	0.6	0.6	0.6	0.6	1.8	4.9
Family Preservation and Support													
Budget authority	n.a.	n.a.	n.a.	n.a.	0.3	0.3	0.3	0.3	0.3	0.3	0.3	0.7	2.4
Outlays	n.a.	n.a.	n.a.	n.a.	0.1	0.3	0.3	0.3	0.3	0.3	0.3	0.4	2.1
Ground Transportation Programs Controlled by Obligation Limitations[c]													
Budget authority	n.a.	n.a.	42.8	42.8	42.8	42.8	42.8	42.8	42.8	42.8	33.9	171.1	376.1
Outlays	n.a.	n.a.	0	0	0	0	0	0	0	0	0	0	0
Air Transportation Programs Controlled by Obligation Limitations[c]													
Budget authority	2.8	3.4	3.4	3.4	3.4	3.4	3.4	3.4	3.4	3.4	3.4	17.0	34.1
Outlays	0	0	0	0	0	0	0	0	0	0	0	0	0
Other Natural Resources													
Budget authority	*	*	*	0.1	0.1	0.1	0.1	0.1	0.1	0.1	0.1	0.3	0.6
Outlays	*	*	0.1	0.1	0.1	0.1	0.1	-0.1	*	*	0.1	0.3	0.3
Total													
Budget authority	6.7	58.3	108.9	131.8	134.4	136.4	138.8	140.8	145.6	149.9	145.0	569.8	1,289.9
Outlays	3.6	56.0	62.2	78.7	86.9	89.5	92.1	94.2	99.1	103.6	107.6	373.4	869.9

Source: Congressional Budget Office.

Note: n.a. = not applicable; COLAs = cost-of-living adjustments; * = between -$50 million and $50 million.

a. Agricultural commodity price and income supports under the Farm Security and Rural Investment Act of 2002 (FSRIA) generally expire after 2007. Although permanent price support authority under the Agricultural Adjustment Act of 1939 and the Agricultural Act of 1949 would then become effective, CBO continues to adhere to the rule in section 257(b)(2)(iii) of the Deficit Control Act (now expired) which indicates that the baseline should assume that FSRIA's provisions remain in effect.

b. Includes the Summer Food Service program and states' administrative expenses.

c. Authorizing legislation provides contract authority, which is counted as mandatory budget authority. However, because spending is subject to obligation limitations specified in annual appropriation acts, outlays are considered discretionary.

Table 3-7.

Defense and Nondefense Discretionary Outlays, 1985 to 2008

	Defense Outlays			Nondefense Outlays			Total Discretionary Outlays		
	In Billions of Dollars	As a Percentage of GDP	Percentage Change From Previous Year	In Billions of Dollars	As a Percentage of GDP	Percentage Change From Previous Year	In Billions of Dollars	As a Percentage of GDP	Percentage Change From Previous Year
1985	253	6.1	11.0	163	3.9	7.4	416	10.0	9.6
1986	274	6.2	8.2	165	3.7	1.2	439	10.0	5.5
1987	283	6.1	3.2	162	3.5	-1.8	444	9.5	1.3
1988	291	5.8	3.0	174	3.5	7.3	464	9.3	4.6
1989	304	5.6	4.5	185	3.4	6.5	489	9.0	5.3
1990	300	5.2	-1.3	200	3.5	8.5	501	8.7	2.4
1991	320	5.4	6.5	214	3.6	6.6	533	9.0	6.5
1992	303	4.8	-5.3	231	3.7	8.2	534	8.6	0.1
1993	292	4.4	-3.4	247	3.8	6.8	539	8.2	1.0
1994	282	4.1	-3.5	259	3.7	4.9	541	7.8	0.4
1995	274	3.7	-3.1	271	3.7	4.7	545	7.4	0.6
1996	266	3.5	-2.8	267	3.5	-1.7	533	6.9	-2.2
1997	272	3.3	2.1	276	3.4	3.3	547	6.7	2.7
1998	270	3.1	-0.6	282	3.3	2.3	552	6.4	0.9
1999	276	3.0	2.0	296	3.2	5.2	572	6.3	3.6
2000	295	3.0	7.1	320	3.3	7.9	615	6.3	7.5
2001	306	3.0	3.8	343	3.4	7.3	649	6.5	5.6
2002	349	3.4	14.0	385	3.7	12.3	734	7.1	13.1
2003	405	3.7	16.0	420	3.9	9.1	825	7.6	12.4
2004	454	3.9	12.1	441	3.8	5.0	895	7.8	8.5
2005	494	4.0	8.7	475	3.9	7.6	968	7.9	8.2
2006	520	4.0	5.3	496	3.8	4.5	1016	7.8	4.9
2007	549	4.0	5.5	493	3.6	-0.5	1042	7.6	2.6
2008[a]	572	4.0	4.3	517	3.6	4.8	1089	7.7	4.5

Source: Congressional Budget Office.

Notes: GDP = gross domestic product.

The growth rates include the effects of shifts in the timing of some defense payments.

a. Estimated. If additional funding for operations in Iraq and Afghanistan is provided, defense outlays for 2008 could total about $600 billion.

Comparison of 2007 and 2008 Budget Authority. Total discretionary budget authority for 2007 was $1,068 billion; $23 billion above appropriations provided so far in 2008 (see Table 3-8). However, that comparison is distorted because only partial funding has been provided in 2008 for operations in Iraq and Afghanistan. With funding for those operations excluded, discretionary defense appropriations are $42 billion, or 9.2 percent, higher in 2008 than in 2007. Nondefense discretionary funding for 2008 is $17 billion (3.9 percent) more than the amount provided in 2007.

Composition of Nondefense Discretionary Funding. Four categories account for more than half of the $512 billion in funding provided thus far for nondefense discretionary activities in 2008 (see Table 3-9). Education, training, employment, and social services together will receive 16 percent of nondefense discretionary funding ($81 billion). Student loans and several other programs in that

Table 3-8.

Growth in Discretionary Budget Authority, 2007 to 2008

(Billions of dollars)

	Actual 2007	Estimated 2008	Percentage Change
Budget Authority			
Defense	622	586	-5.8
Nondefense	445	458	2.9
Total	**1,068**	**1,045** [a]	**-2.1**
Memorandum:			
Excluding Funding for Iraq and Afghanistan and Other			
Activites Related to the War on Terrorism			
Defense	458	500	9.2
Nondefense	440	457	3.9
Total	**898**	**957**	**6.6**

Source: Congressional Budget Office.

Note: Does not include obligation limitations for certain transportation programs.

a.   Includes $87 billion in defense funding and $1 billion in nondefense funding provided so far for military operations and other activities in Iraq and Afghanistan. However, the President has requested an additional $105 billion for 2008 for such purposes.

category are not included in that total because they are considered mandatory.

Funding for transportation programs adds another $81 billion (16 percent) to the total. That sum includes $54 billion in obligation limitations for several surface and air transportation programs. Although those programs receive mandatory budget authority through authorizing legislation, the annual appropriation acts limit how much of that authority the Department of Transportation can obligate and thereby govern annual spending. Those limitations are treated as a measure of discretionary budgetary resources, and the resulting outlays are classified as discretionary.

Appropriations for health research and public health total $54 billion and make up 11 percent of nondefense discretionary funding in 2008. Finally, at $53 billion, income-security programs (mostly for housing and nutrition assistance) claim 10 percent of nondefense discretionary funding. Other income-security programs, such as unemployment compensation and TANF, are not included in the total because they are included in mandatory spending.

Discretionary Spending from 2009 Through 2018

Under assumptions for the baseline, CBO projects that discretionary outlays will increase to $1.1 trillion in 2008

and continue rising each year as they reflect steadily increasing budget authority. Following the specifications in the Deficit Control Act, CBO assumes that discretionary resources (including funding for operations in Iraq and Afghanistan and obligation limitations for some transportation programs) will keep pace with inflation after 2008. Although provisions of that act expired at the end of September 2006, CBO continues to observe its requirements in preparing baseline projections of discretionary spending. As a result, such funding is projected to grow at a rate of 2.9 percent in 2009 and 2.2 percent annually through 2018. At that rate, CBO projects, discretionary outlays would reach $1.4 trillion by 2018. Discretionary outlays would decline as a percentage of GDP, however, falling from about 7.7 percent in 2008 to 6.1 percent in 2018.[16]

Alternative Paths for Discretionary Spending. CBO estimates that total discretionary budget authority in 2008 is about $1,045 billion and that transportation-related obligation limitations total $54 billion. In the projections of baseline spending, both are assumed to grow thereafter with inflation. To illustrate how future funding might differ from those assumptions, CBO presents alternative

---

16. If additional funding for operations in Iraq and Afghanistan adds about $30 billion to spending in fiscal year 2008, discretionary outlays this year will come to 7.9 percent of GDP.

Table 3-9.

Nondefense Discretionary Funding for 2008

	Amount of Funding (Billions of dollars)	Percentage of Total
Education, Training, Employment, and Social Services	81	16
Transportation	81	16
Health	54	11
Income Security	53	10
Administration of Justice	47	9
Veterans' Benefits and Services	43	8
International Affairs	37	7
Natural Resources and Environment	32	6
General Science, Space, and Technology	26	5
Community and Regional Development	20	4
General Government	17	3
Agriculture	6	1
Medicare	5	1
Social Security	5	1
Energy	5	1
Commerce and Housing Credit	3	1
Multiple Functions[a]	-3	-1
Total	**512**	**100**

Source: Congressional Budget Office.

Notes: Includes budgetary resources provided by obligation limitations for certain surface and air transportation programs.

a. The omnibus appropriations act included across-the-board cuts in several areas. Those cuts have not yet been assigned to specific programs.

paths for discretionary spending and shows their budgetary consequences (see Table 3-10).

The first alternative path assumes that most funding will grow at the average annual rate of nominal GDP after 2008 (an average of 4.6 percent a year, about twice as fast as the rate of growth assumed in the baseline). Funds provided for operations in Iraq and Afghanistan and other appropriations labeled as an emergency are assumed to grow more slowly—at the rate of inflation—as in baseline

projections. Under this scenario, total discretionary outlays would exceed the baseline figures by $1.4 trillion over the projection period. Added debt-service costs would bring the cumulative increase in outlays to $1.6 trillion.

The next two alternatives address possible funding for military operations in Iraq and Afghanistan and other activities related to the war on terrorism. CBO has constructed two possible paths of spending for such activities. Under both scenarios, the number of active-duty, Reserve, and National Guard personnel would average 205,000 in fiscal year 2008. The first alternative assumes that force levels will decline rapidly throughout 2009— falling to approximately 30,000 by the beginning of 2010 and remaining at that level thereafter. (Those service members might be involved in operations in Iraq, Afghanistan, or elsewhere in the world.) As described more fully in Chapter 1, that scenario would add about $30 billion to baseline outlays for 2008, but annual outlays would decline relative to the current baseline beginning in 2011. Projected 10-year outlays for that alternative path would be $426 billion lower than the amount in the baseline, including debt-service savings.

In the second scenario that describes operations in Iraq, Afghanistan, and the war on terrorism, funding would still decrease over the coming 10 years, but it would be higher than in the previous scenario because troops would return to the United States more slowly, and more troops (about 75,000) would remain deployed over the long term. Like the first alternative, that scenario would add about $30 billion to baseline outlays for 2008. Annual outlays, however, would decline relative to the current baseline beginning in 2014. Projected 10-year outlays, including debt-service costs, would be $226 billion higher than the amount in the baseline.

The final alternative shows lower spending relative to the baseline—it assumes that most discretionary budget authority and obligation limitations are frozen at the 2008 amount for the entire projection period.[17] Total discretionary outlays for the 10-year period would be $1.3 trillion lower than those in the baseline. Debt-service adjustments would reduce spending by another

---

17. In this scenario, budget authority for some items (such as offsetting collections and payments made by the Treasury on behalf of the Department of Defense for TRICARE For Life) is not held constant at the 2008 amount.

$235 billion, for a total of $1.6 trillion. Under that scenario, total discretionary spending would fall below 5 percent of GDP by 2018.

Net Interest

The federal government's interest payments depend primarily on market interest rates and on the amount of outstanding debt held by the public. The Congress and the President can influence the latter through legislation that governs spending and taxes and, thus, the extent of government borrowing. Interest rates are determined largely by market forces and by Federal Reserve Board policies.

For the third consecutive year, net interest grew much faster than the rest of the budget in 2007. Since 2004, interest outlays have risen by 14 percent, on average, which has been nearly triple the rate for all other outlays. The increase in interest costs in recent years is attributable mostly to higher short-term rates, although to a lesser extent additional debt held by the public was responsible as well. In 2007, net interest costs totaled $238 billion, 5 percent above the 2006 total, $227 billion (see Table 3-11 on page 78). Net interest stands at 1.7 percent of GDP, roughly the same as in 2006.

Despite higher debt, CBO projects that interest spending in 2008 will decline by 2 percent to $234 billion (or 1.6 percent of GDP). The decrease stems primarily from declining interest rates, which have fallen because of the recent turmoil in financial markets (see Chapter 2). The rates for both the 91-day Treasury bill and the 10-year Treasury note averaged 4.7 percent in 2007; they have since fallen and are projected to remain around 3 percent and 4 percent, respectively, for the rest of 2008.

Under the assumptions that govern its baseline, CBO projects that net interest costs will grow by an average of 5 percent per year from 2009 to 2012, which is 1 percentage point faster than spending in the rest of the budget, because of growth in federal debt and a projected rise in interest rates. CBO projects that, by 2010, the rate for the 91-day Treasury bill will increase gradually to 4.7 percent and the rate for the 10-year Treasury note will rise to 5.2 percent. As a percentage of GDP, net interest in CBO's baseline is projected to average 1.7 percent through 2012; thereafter, interest costs decline as projected deficits turn to surpluses—with net interest outlays falling to 1.2 percent of GDP in 2018.

Interest on Debt Held by the Public

Interest outlays also are affected by the composition of debt held by the public. For example, the Treasury adjusts the mix of marketable securities (bills with maturities of less than 6 months; notes with maturities of 2, 5, and 10 years; 30-year bonds; and 5-, 10- and 20-year inflation-protected securities) in response to market forces. As that mix changes, so does the average maturity of new issues, which has fluctuated significantly.[18] For instance, average maturity was nearly 90 months in the late 1990s, but it decreased to less than 30 months in 2003. In 2006, the Treasury began reissuing 30-year bonds, a practice it had suspended in 2001. As a result, the average maturity of new issues increased from nearly three years at the end of 2005 to about five years at the end of 2007.

In 2007, the Treasury stopped issuing three-year notes. Those quarterly sales, which ranged between $14 billion and $24 billion (exclusive of sales to the Federal Reserve) were small relative to the size of the public debt ($5 trillion at the end of 2007), and their elimination will not significantly affect the average maturity of the overall stock. For the next few years, that stock is projected to remain relatively stable, with Treasury notes accounting for more than half of it, Treasury bills accounting for around a quarter, and bonds and inflation-protected securities constituting the rest.

Interest on Intragovernmental Holdings

The federal government has issued about $3.9 trillion in securities to federal trust funds and other government accounts. Similar in composition to debt held by the public, those securities consist of bills, notes, bonds, inflation-protected securities, and zero-coupon bonds. However, the interest paid on those securities has no net budgetary impact because it is credited to accounts elsewhere in the budget. In 2008, trust funds will be credited with $195 billion of such intragovernmental interest, CBO estimates, mostly for the Social Security and Civil Service Retirement and Disability Insurance trust funds. Over the 10-year baseline period, CBO projects, trust fund interest receipts will total more than $2.6 trillion. (For a more detailed discussion of trust funds and other measures of debt, see Appendix B.)

---

18. The average maturity of new issues is a one-year rolling average of the maturities of all the marketable securities the Treasury has issued to the public. See www.treas.gov/offices/domestic-finance/debt-management/qrc/2007/2007-q4-chart-data.pdf.

Table 3-10.

CBO's Projections of Discretionary Spending Under Selected Policy Alternatives

(Billions of dollars)

	Actual 2007	2008	2009	2010	2011	2012	2013	2014	2015	2016	2017	2018	Total, 2009-2013	Total, 2009-2018
Baseline (Discretionary resources grow with inflation after 2008)[a]														
Budget Authority														
Defense	622	586	600	613	627	642	657	673	689	706	723	741	3,140	6,673
Nondefense	445	458	476	484	495	507	519	532	545	558	572	585	2,480	5,271
Total	**1,068**	**1,045**	**1,076**	**1,097**	**1,122**	**1,149**	**1,176**	**1,205**	**1,234**	**1,264**	**1,295**	**1,326**	**5,620**	**11,944**
Outlays														
Defense	549	572	590	603	620	626	645	660	677	698	710	723	3,084	6,552
Nondefense	493	517	531	542	550	560	571	583	596	610	624	637	2,754	5,804
Total	**1,042**	**1,089**	**1,121**	**1,145**	**1,170**	**1,186**	**1,216**	**1,243**	**1,272**	**1,307**	**1,335**	**1,360**	**5,838**	**12,356**
Most Discretionary Resources Grow at the Rate of Nominal Gross Domestic Product After 2008[b]														
Budget Authority														
Defense	622	586	609	638	669	700	729	760	791	823	857	892	3,345	7,467
Nondefense	445	458	482	509	537	565	592	620	648	677	708	739	2,686	6,077
Total	**1,068**	**1,045**	**1,091**	**1,147**	**1,207**	**1,265**	**1,321**	**1,379**	**1,439**	**1,500**	**1,564**	**1,630**	**6,031**	**13,544**
Outlays														
Defense	549	572	595	621	652	674	708	738	768	805	833	863	3,250	7,256
Nondefense	493	517	534	557	581	607	633	660	688	717	748	777	2,913	6,502
Total	**1,042**	**1,089**	**1,129**	**1,178**	**1,233**	**1,281**	**1,341**	**1,397**	**1,456**	**1,522**	**1,581**	**1,640**	**6,162**	**13,759**
Troops Deployed for Military Operations in Iraq and Afghanistan and for the War on Terrorism Decrease to 30,000 by 2010														
Budget Authority														
Defense	622	688	626	569	566	579	593	608	623	638	654	670	2,933	6,127
Nondefense	445	462	478	486	496	508	519	532	545	557	571	584	2,488	5,278
Total	**1,068**	**1,150**	**1,104**	**1,056**	**1,062**	**1,088**	**1,112**	**1,140**	**1,168**	**1,196**	**1,225**	**1,255**	**5,421**	**11,405**
Outlays														
Defense	549	602	631	616	596	580	588	600	613	632	643	654	3,011	6,152
Nondefense	493	518	532	544	552	561	573	584	597	610	624	636	2,762	5,813
Total	**1,042**	**1,119**	**1,163**	**1,159**	**1,148**	**1,141**	**1,161**	**1,183**	**1,210**	**1,242**	**1,267**	**1,290**	**5,773**	**11,966**

Continued

Table 3-10.

Continued

- -
(Billions of dollars)

	Actual 2007	2008	2009	2010	2011	2012	2013	2014	2015	2016	2017	2018	Total, 2009- 2013	Total, 2009- 2018
	Troops Deployed for Military Operations in Iraq and Afghanistan and for the War on Terrorism Decrease to 75,000 by 2013													
Budget Authority														
Defense	622	688	669	666	661	646	639	648	664	681	699	715	3,281	6,689
Nondefense	445	462	478	486	496	508	519	532	545	557	571	584	2,488	5,278
Total	1,068	1,150	1,147	1,153	1,157	1,155	1,158	1,180	1,209	1,239	1,270	1,300	5,769	11,967
Outlays														
Defense	549	602	646	661	669	654	656	656	659	676	687	699	3,286	6,662
Nondefense	493	518	532	544	552	561	573	584	597	610	624	636	2,762	5,813
Total	1,042	1,119	1,178	1,204	1,221	1,215	1,229	1,239	1,256	1,286	1,311	1,335	6,048	12,476
	Discretionary Resources Are Frozen at the 2008 Level													
Budget Authority														
Defense	622	586	586	586	587	588	589	590	591	591	592	594	2,936	5,894
Nondefense	445	458	465	462	462	462	462	462	462	461	461	460	2,313	4,619
Total	1,068	1,045	1,051	1,049	1,049	1,050	1,051	1,052	1,052	1,053	1,054	1,054	5,250	10,513
Outlays														
Defense	549	572	580	583	586	580	585	586	587	591	589	587	2,914	5,853
Nondefense	493	517	524	525	522	519	518	516	515	514	514	511	2,608	5,177
Total	1,042	1,089	1,104	1,108	1,108	1,099	1,102	1,101	1,102	1,105	1,103	1,097	5,522	11,030

Source: Congressional Budget Office.

Note: Nondefense discretionary outlays are usually higher than budget authority because of spending from the Highway Trust Fund and the Airport and Airway Trust Fund that is subject to obligation limitations set in appropriation acts. The budget authority for such programs is provided in authorizing legislation and is not considered discretionary.

a.   Inflation in CBO's baseline is projected using the inflators specified in the Balanced Budget and Emergency Deficit Control Act of 1985: the gross domestic product price index and the employment cost index for wages and salaries.

b.   This alternative assumes that appropriations declared as emergencies (including those for operations in Iraq and Afghanistan) enacted during 2008 are projected at baseline levels (that is, increased at the rate of inflation).

Table 3-11.

CBO's Baseline Projections of Federal Interest Outlays

(Billions of dollars)

	Actual 2007	2008	2009	2010	2011	2012	2013	2014	2015	2016	2017	2018	Total, 2009-2013	Total, 2009-2018
Interest on Treasury Debt Securities (Gross interest)[a]	430	447	453	493	526	547	564	582	598	613	624	634	2,581	5,632
Interest Received by Trust Funds														
Social Security	-106	-116	-121	-130	-140	-152	-164	-178	-192	-206	-221	-236	-707	-1,739
Other trust funds[b]	-72	-79	-77	-79	-83	-87	-89	-92	-95	-95	-96	-98	-415	-891
Subtotal	-178	-195	-198	-209	-223	-238	-254	-270	-286	-301	-317	-333	-1,122	-2,630
Other Interest[c]	-10	-15	-12	-17	-18	-21	-23	-26	-29	-32	-35	-40	-92	-253
Other Investment Income[d]	-4	-3	-1	-1	-1	-1	-1	-1	-1	-1	-1	-1	-7	-14
Total (Net interest)	**238**	**234**	**241**	**266**	**283**	**286**	**285**	**285**	**282**	**278**	**271**	**259**	**1,360**	**2,735**

Source: Congressional Budget Office.

a.   Excludes interest costs of debt issued by agencies other than the Treasury (primarily the Tennessee Valley Authority).

b.   Mainly the Civil Service Retirement, Military Retirement, Medicare, and Unemployment Insurance Trust Funds.

c.   Primarily interest on loans to the public.

d.   Earnings on private investments by the National Railroad Retirement Investment Trust.

Other Interest and Investment Income

The $15 billion in other interest CBO anticipates the government will receive in 2008 represents the net of many interest payments and interest collections. On balance, the government earns more of that interest than it pays out. Among the interest outflows are payments for interest on tax refunds that are issued more than 45 days after the date on which they were filed. On the collections side, one of the largest inflows is interest received from the financing accounts of credit programs, such as the direct student loan program. Although other interest is projected to increase rapidly through the projection period, almost all of that growth will come from interest on the accrued balances credited to the TRICARE For Life program. (Because those are intragovernmental payments between the Treasury and the Department of Defense, they have no net effect on the budget.) Such receipts are projected to grow from $6 billion in 2008 to $20 billion in 2018.

CBO also estimates that earnings from the Railroad Retirement Investment Trust will total $3 billion in 2008 and $14 billion between 2009 and 2018.

CHAPTER 4

The Revenue Outlook

The Congressional Budget Office expects a slow-down in the growth of revenues in 2008, largely because overall economic growth will slow markedly. If current laws and policies remained unchanged, federal revenues would reach about $2.7 trillion in 2008, which is about 3.4 percent higher than in 2007. As a share of gross domestic product, revenues would decline slightly, from 18.8 percent last year to 18.7 percent in 2008 (see Figure 4-1). That decline in revenues as a percentage of GDP would follow three consecutive years of increases.

In CBO's baseline projections, revenues rise to 19.0 percent of GDP in 2009 and then decline to 18.6 percent in 2010. The increase in 2009 stems largely from higher individual income tax receipts as the higher exemption amounts under the alternative minimum tax expire. The decline in 2010 occurs mainly because of falling corporate income tax receipts. After several years of very robust growth, taxable corporate profits declined in dollar terms in 2007, and CBO anticipates further declines from 2008 through 2010.

In the projections, revenues jump sharply in 2011 and 2012 upon the expiration of various tax provisions originally enacted in the Economic Growth and Tax Relief Reconciliation Act of 2001 and the Jobs and Growth Tax Relief Reconciliation Act of 2003. In addition, revenues continue growing faster than GDP through 2018, except in 2013, when legislated shifts in corporate payments between fiscal years decrease the growth of corporate receipts (see Figure 4-2). Because of the structure of the individual income tax system, revenues claim a higher fraction of income each year as real (inflation-adjusted) income grows. Those increases more than offset the projection of continued declines in corporate receipts as a share of GDP (itself driven by a projected decline in taxable corporate profits relative to GDP) and the downward effect on capital gains tax receipts from lower realizations relative to GDP.

Under the assumption that current laws and policies will remain the same, total revenues reach 20.3 percent of GDP in 2018, a level not reached since 2000, and prior to that, not since World War II. If the law was changed so that the expiring provisions of EGTRRA, JGTRRA, and other tax legislation were extended and the AMT was indexed for inflation, revenues would be lower—roughly 17.5 percent of GDP in 2018.

CBO has lowered its projections of revenues from those published in August 2007—by $116 billion in 2008 and between $35 billion and $44 billion each year thereafter through 2017. The largest change to the estimate for 2008 occurred because of legislation enacted in December 2007 that extended relief from the AMT for one year, leading CBO to reduce estimated revenues for 2008 by about $70 billion (and to increase its estimate for 2009 by about $19 billion). Most of the other changes to the revenue projections of five months ago reflect changes to the economic outlook. Because CBO lowered its forecast of economic growth over the 2008–2009 period, it lowered its projections of taxable incomes. In addition, a projected increase in business interest payments and a corresponding decrease in corporate profits reduced projected revenues over the 2008–2017 period because the marginal tax rates generally applied to the latter are higher than those applied to the former. (For more discussion of the changes to CBO's revenue baseline, see Appendix A.)

Sources of Revenues

Federal revenues derive from various sources: individual income taxes, social insurance (payroll) taxes, corporate income taxes, excise taxes, estate and gift taxes, customs duties, and miscellaneous receipts. Receipts from individual income taxes, which are the largest component of federal receipts, have historically accounted for much of the

Figure 4-1.

Total Revenues as a Share of Gross Domestic Product, 1968 to 2018

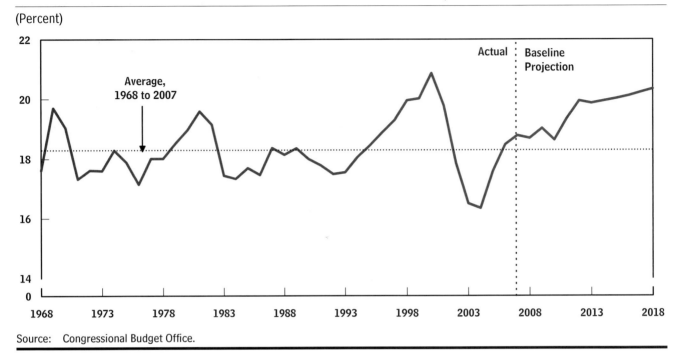

(Percent)

Source: Congressional Budget Office.

variation in receipts and account for most of the pro-jected movements in receipts over the 2008–2018 period.

Historical Perspective

Between 1968 and the late 1990s, individual income taxes produced nearly half of all federal revenues and typically claimed between 7.5 percent and 9.5 percent of GDP (see Figure 4-3). They have experienced dra-matic swings recently: They reached a historical high of 10.3 percent of GDP in 2000, fell to a more-than-50-year low of 7.0 percent in 2004, and then rebounded in the past three years to reach 8.5 percent of GDP.

Social insurance taxes (collected mainly for Social Secu-rity and Medicare) represent the second-largest source of revenues, accounting for about one-third of revenues. They grew as a share of GDP from 1968 to the late 1980s as a result of increases in tax rates and the tax base and since then have been relatively stable at between 6.4 per-cent and 6.9 percent of GDP. Corporate income taxes, the third-largest source, have averaged about 12 percent of federal revenues since 1968 and about 2.2 percent of GDP. They have fluctuated significantly over the period, however, including falling to a 20-year low in 2003, at

about 1.2 percent of GDP. Strong growth since then boosted those receipts to 2.7 percent of GDP in both 2006 and 2007, the highest level since the late 1970s. Growth in those receipts over the past four years accounted for about two-thirds of the increase in total revenues as a share of GDP—from 16.5 percent in 2003 to 18.8 percent in 2007. Revenues from other taxes, duties, and miscellaneous receipts (including those from the Federal Reserve System) make up the remainder of federal revenues and recently have amounted to a little less than 1.5 percent of GDP.

In sum, over the past 40 years, social insurance taxes have grown as a share of federal revenues, while the shares for corporate income taxes and excise taxes have declined. In the late 1960s, social insurance taxes and corporate income taxes contributed similar amounts of receipts: each roughly 20 percent of total receipts, or about 4 per-cent of GDP. In recent years, by contrast, social insurance tax receipts have accounted for more than 30 percent of total receipts, producing at least twice as much as corpo-rate income taxes. The contribution of excise taxes has declined from about 9 percent of revenues in 1968 to less than 3 percent today.

Figure 4-2.

Annual Growth of Federal Revenues and Gross Domestic Product, 1968 to 2018

(Percentage change from previous year)

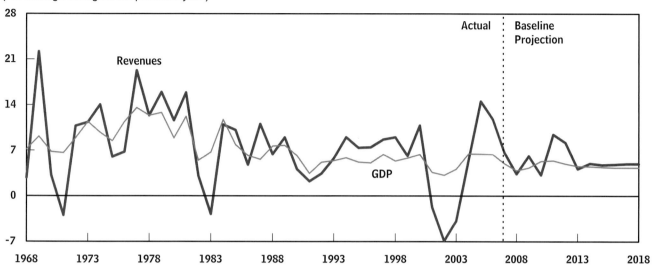

Source: Congressional Budget Office.

Projections in Brief

CBO projects that, under current law, receipts from individual income taxes will remain at 8.5 percent of GDP in 2008 and then climb to 10.9 percent in 2018, a gain of 2.4 percentage points. That increase more than accounts for the projected rise in total revenues, which are expected to climb by a smaller amount, 1.7 percentage points—from 18.7 percent of GDP in 2008 to 20.3 percent in 2018.

Of the projected increase in individual receipts relative to GDP, a little over half, or about 1.5 percentage points, results from scheduled changes in tax laws. The changes include a reduced exemption amount for the AMT beginning in 2008, followed by the expiration after 2010 of provisions originally enacted in EGTRRA and JGTRRA.

The remainder of the projected increase in individual receipts relative to GDP is largely attributable to the structure of the tax code—wherein effective tax rates rise as personal income rises—and to other factors, such as growth faster than that of GDP in distributions from tax-deferred 401(k) plans and individual retirement accounts as members of the baby-boom generation reach retirement age.[1] The projected rise in effective tax rates occurs in part because of the phenomenon known as "real bracket creep," in which the growth of real income causes

a greater proportion of a taxpayer's income to be taxed in higher brackets. Over the period from 2008 to 2018, that factor causes revenues as a share of GDP to rise by about 0.6 percentage points. Another factor causing increases is that, under current law, the AMT is not indexed for inflation, so an increasing number of taxpayers will have to pay it. The lack of indexation in the AMT boosts receipts from the individual income tax relative to GDP by about 0.4 percentage points over the upcoming decade. (In addition, the AMT's exemption levels have been temporarily increased; their scheduled decline beginning in 2008 boosts receipts further.) Projected growth in retirement incomes also leads to an increase in revenues relative to GDP of about 0.4 percentage points. Those increases in individual income tax receipts relative to GDP are partially offset by projected decreases in receipts from realizations of capital gains relative to GDP, which reduce projected revenues by 0.4 percentage points of GDP.

Consistent with an anticipated decline in corporate profits as a share of the economy, receipts from corporate income taxes are projected to fall steadily as a percentage of GDP over the next decade, reaching 1.7 percent in 2017 and 2018. In the past several years, profits have

---

1.   Effective tax rates are the ratio of tax liability to income.

Figure 4-3.

Revenues, by Source, as a Share of Gross Domestic Product, 1968 to 2018

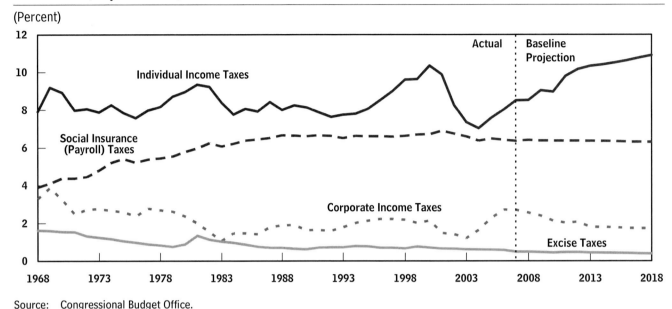

(Percent)

Source: Congressional Budget Office.

risen to levels relative to GDP not seen since the mid-1960s. Profit growth slowed markedly in 2007, and CBO expects profits to decline relative to GDP in the near term as a result of the expected economic slowdown, which normally affects profits more than other incomes. Over the longer term, profits are projected to decline relative to GDP because labor compensation is expected to climb as a share of GDP to a more historical level (lowering the capital income share of GDP), and business interest payments (which reduce profits) are expected to climb from their recent historically low levels relative to GDP.

CBO expects that the revenues arising from other tax sources combined will remain relatively stable as a share of GDP. In the agency's projections, social insurance receipts decline just slightly, from 6.4 percent of GDP in 2007 to 6.3 percent from 2015 to 2018. Those receipts follow the projection for wages and salaries, which also decline just slightly, from 46.0 percent of GDP in 2007 to 45.8 percent in 2018.[2] Other receipts fluctuate between 1.1 percent and 1.4 percent of GDP between 2008 and 2018. Receipts from excise taxes drop by about 0.1 percent of GDP over the next 10 years. In the

projections, receipts from estate and gift taxes are relatively stable as a share of GDP until 2012, when they jump as scheduled changes in law return the estate and gift tax to the form that existed before the enactment of EGTRRA in 2001. Miscellaneous receipts and customs duties also remain relatively stable.

CBO's Current Revenue Projections in Detail

According to CBO's baseline projections, under current law most of the movement in total receipts relative to GDP from 2008 to 2018 will result from changes in individual and corporate income tax receipts (see Table 4-1). In general, other sources of revenue will be much more stable relative to the size of the economy—although scheduled changes in tax law, the general design of the taxes, movements in the tax bases that are independent of GDP, and other factors do cause some sources of revenue to grow slightly differently than GDP.

Individual Income Taxes

Individual income tax receipts account for almost all of the projected increase in total revenues relative to GDP over the next 10 years. Historically, individual income tax receipts have been a key determinant of movements in total receipts. Between 1992 and 2000, they grew at an average annual rate of nearly 10 percent, reaching a

---

2. Relative to GDP, wages and salaries decline slightly and overall labor compensation increases because, according to CBO's projections, nontaxable fringe benefits, such as employer-paid health insurance, will rise over time relative to GDP.

Table 4-1.

CBO's Projections of Revenues

	Actual 2007	2008	2009	2010	2011	2012	2013	2014	2015	2016	2017	2018	Total, 2009-2013	Total, 2009-2018
	In Billions of Dollars													
Individual Income Taxes	1,163	1,211	1,340	1,399	1,611	1,753	1,863	1,962	2,070	2,184	2,307	2,438	7,966	18,928
Corporate Income Taxes	370	364	356	334	333	357	327	342	350	361	374	388	1,707	3,522
Social Insurance Taxes	870	910	947	997	1,049	1,101	1,149	1,199	1,249	1,301	1,355	1,411	5,244	11,758
Excise Taxes	65	68	68	69	75	79	80	82	83	85	86	87	372	794
Estate and Gift Taxes	26	27	27	22	21	55	63	70	76	83	90	97	188	604
Customs Duties	26	27	29	32	34	37	39	42	45	48	51	54	171	410
Miscellaneous	47	47	50	54	58	61	63	66	68	70	72	73	285	633
Total	**2,568**	**2,654**	**2,817**	**2,907**	**3,182**	**3,442**	**3,585**	**3,763**	**3,941**	**4,131**	**4,334**	**4,548**	**15,933**	**36,649**
On-budget	1,933	1,990	2,123	2,177	2,414	2,636	2,743	2,883	3,024	3,175	3,337	3,509	12,093	28,020
Off-budget[a]	635	665	694	730	768	806	842	880	918	957	997	1,039	3,839	8,629
Memorandum:														
Gross Domestic Product	13,670	14,201	14,812	15,600	16,445	17,256	18,043	18,856	19,685	20,540	21,426	22,355	82,156	185,018
	As a Percentage of Gross Domestic Product													
Individual Income Taxes	8.5	8.5	9.0	9.0	9.8	10.2	10.3	10.4	10.5	10.6	10.8	10.9	9.7	10.2
Corporate Income Taxes	2.7	2.6	2.4	2.1	2.0	2.1	1.8	1.8	1.8	1.8	1.7	1.7	2.1	1.9
Social Insurance Taxes	6.4	6.4	6.4	6.4	6.4	6.4	6.4	6.4	6.3	6.3	6.3	6.3	6.4	6.4
Excise Taxes	0.5	0.5	0.5	0.4	0.5	0.5	0.4	0.4	0.4	0.4	0.4	0.4	0.5	0.4
Estate and Gift Taxes	0.2	0.2	0.2	0.1	0.1	0.3	0.3	0.4	0.4	0.4	0.4	0.4	0.2	0.3
Customs Duties	0.2	0.2	0.2	0.2	0.2	0.2	0.2	0.2	0.2	0.2	0.2	0.2	0.2	0.2
Miscellaneous Receipts	0.3	0.3	0.3	0.3	0.4	0.4	0.3	0.3	0.3	0.3	0.3	0.3	0.3	0.3
Total	**18.8**	**18.7**	**19.0**	**18.6**	**19.3**	**19.9**	**19.9**	**20.0**	**20.0**	**20.1**	**20.2**	**20.3**	**19.4**	**19.8**
On-budget	14.1	14.0	14.3	14.0	14.7	15.3	15.2	15.3	15.4	15.5	15.6	15.7	14.7	15.1
Off-budget[a]	4.6	4.7	4.7	4.7	4.7	4.7	4.7	4.7	4.7	4.7	4.7	4.6	4.7	4.7

Source: Congressional Budget Office.

a.   The revenues of the two Social Security trust funds (the Old-Age and Survivors Insurance Trust Fund and the Disability Insurance Trust Fund) are off-budget.

historical peak of 10.3 percent of GDP (see Figure 4-3). After 2000, individual receipts fell as a share of GDP for four consecutive years. The downturn began as a result of the stock market decline and the 2001 recession and was reinforced by the tax legislation enacted in several stages between 2001 and 2004. Income growth picked up substantially in 2004, and tax receipts grew by an average of nearly 13 percent annually from 2005 to 2007. In that year, receipts as a share of GDP reached 8.5 percent.

CBO expects that individual income tax receipts in 2008 will grow at about the same rate as GDP (under an assumption that current laws and policies remain unchanged), keeping revenues at 8.5 percent of GDP. Then, CBO projects, revenues will climb relative to GDP in 2009 (in large part because of the expiration of temporary AMT provisions), stabilize again in 2010, and climb relative to GDP thereafter through 2018. The projected increase results from the structure of the income tax system and scheduled changes in tax law, including the expiration of most provisions of EGTRRA and JGTRRA in 2010. In CBO's projections, individual income tax receipts reach a new peak of 10.4 percent of GDP by 2014 and 10.9 percent by 2018.

Table 4-2.

CBO's Projections of Individual Income Tax Receipts and the NIPA Tax Base

	Actual 2007	2008	2009	2010	2011	2012	2013	2014	2015	2016	2017	2018	Total, 2009-2013[a]	Total, 2009-2018[a]
Individual Income Tax Receipts														
In billions of dollars	1,163	1,211	1,340	1,399	1,611	1,753	1,863	1,962	2,070	2,184	2,307	2,438	7,966	18,928
As a percentage of GDP	8.5	8.5	9.0	9.0	9.8	10.2	10.3	10.4	10.5	10.6	10.8	10.9	9.7	10.2
Annual growth rate	11.5	4.1	10.6	4.4	15.1	8.8	6.3	5.3	5.5	5.5	5.6	5.7	9.0	7.2
Taxable Personal Income														
In billions of dollars	9,285	9,695	10,125	10,692	11,247	11,793	12,333	12,887	13,446	14,019	14,615	15,236	56,191	126,393
As a percentage of GDP	67.9	68.3	68.4	68.5	68.4	68.3	68.4	68.3	68.3	68.3	68.2	68.2	68.4	68.3
Annual growth rate	6.1	4.4	4.4	5.6	5.2	4.9	4.6	4.5	4.3	4.3	4.3	4.2	4.9	4.6
Individual Receipts as a Percentage of Taxable Personal Income	12.5	12.5	13.2	13.1	14.3	14.9	15.1	15.2	15.4	15.6	15.8	16.0	14.2	15.0

Source: Congressional Budget Office.

Notes: GDP = gross domestic product.

The tax base in this table (taxable personal income) reflects income as measured by the national income and product accounts rather than as reported on tax returns. An important difference, therefore, is that it excludes capital gains realizations.

a.   Measures expressed in billions of dollars are the cumulative amounts over the period. Measures expressed as a percentage of GDP or taxable personal income are averages over the period. Measures expressed as annual growth rates are the average rates compounded annually over the period, including growth in 2009.

Projected Receipts in 2008 and 2009. The growth of individual income tax receipts, CBO projects, will slow substantially, to just over 4 percent in 2008 (see Table 4-2). In the projections, overall economic growth slows in 2008; the growth in taxable personal incomes does the same correspondingly. (Taxable personal income includes wages and salaries, dividends, interest, rental income, and proprietors' income. For a description of taxable personal income and other components of the tax base, see Box 4-1.) CBO expects taxable personal income—as measured in the national income and product accounts—to grow by 4.4 percent in 2008, just slightly more than the expected growth of GDP, at 3.9 percent. Wages and salaries, the largest source of personal income, will grow by 4.2 percent in 2008, CBO projects, which is less than the 6.0 percent averaged over the past two years. As a result, withholding from paychecks (including both income and payroll tax withholding), which grew at an average annual rate of 6.9 percent over the past two years, is projected to grow by about 5.0 percent in 2008.

In CBO's baseline projections, the expiration of the higher exemptions that mitigated the effects of the AMT on taxpayers boosts receipts sharply in 2009, and revenues grow by over 10 percent in that year as a result. The exemption amounts for the AMT were increased for 2007 in legislation enacted in December 2007 (the Tax Increase Prevention Act of 2007, P.L. 110-166). Because of that legislation, the share of taxpayers with AMT liability remained at about 3 percent in 2007 (the same share as in 2006), but the tax relief expired at the end of December 2007. Although relief from the AMT has been enacted for each of the past several years, CBO does not assume such future changes in law in its baseline. As a result, CBO projects that tax liabilities from the AMT will rise sharply in tax year 2008, by about $64 billion, and that tax receipts will rise sharply in fiscal year 2009, when almost all of those liabilities will be paid to the Internal Revenue Service.

Several factors lead CBO to assume in its projections that almost all of that additional AMT liability from 2008 will be paid in fiscal year 2009 rather than through additional payments in 2008. First, with the reduced exemption,

Figure 4-4.

Effects of the Individual Alternative Minimum Tax in CBO's Baseline

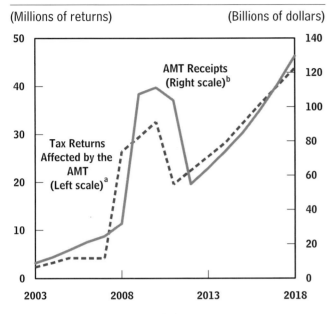

(Millions of returns)   (Billions of dollars)

Source: Congressional Budget Office.

Notes: The alternative minimum tax (AMT) requires some taxpayers to calculate their taxes using a more limited set of exemptions, deductions, and credits than is applicable under the regular individual income tax.

Some taxpayers are affected by the AMT not because it imposes a liability but because it limits their credits taken under the regular tax.

a.   Based on calendar year.

b.   Based on fiscal year.

many taxpayers may be surprised when they file their 2008 tax returns in the spring of 2009 and find that they have incurred substantial liability attributable to the AMT. Second, even if taxpayers know that they will face such liability, they may not have to increase their estimated payments or direct their employers to withhold more taxes from their paychecks in order to avoid penalties when filing their tax returns.[3] Finally, because legislative action to avoid substantial increases in AMT liability has occurred on a temporary basis several times now, taxpayers aware of their higher AMT liability may anticipate

---

3.   For example, taxpayers with income below $150,000 can avoid penalties by making estimated payments and withholding amounts equal to their prior year's tax liability. Taxpayers with income in excess of $150,000 must pay 110 percent of their prior year's liability to avoid penalties automatically.

---

such action again. As a result, they may not increase their estimated payments or tax withholding in 2008. Consequently, in CBO's projections, many taxpayers with substantial AMT liability in 2008 are assumed to pay insufficient estimated payments and tax withholding in that year and face substantial final payments when they file tax returns in 2009.

In CBO's baseline, receipts from the AMT jump from $32 billion in 2008 to $107 billion in 2009. Without that substantial increase, individual income tax receipts would be projected to grow at only 4.5 percent in 2009, about 6 percentage points more slowly than with the additional receipts from the AMT (see Figure 4-4). Under the baseline, not only will taxpayers make the much larger AMT payments required for tax year 2008 when they file their tax returns in 2009, but taxpayers will also respond in that year by raising their estimated payments to cover their AMT liability for 2009. A portion of the payments in 2009, therefore, represents a one-time shift of amounts that stem from tax liability for the previous year.

Projected Receipts Beyond 2009. For 2009 and beyond, projected revenues reflect steady growth in personal income, adjusted by scheduled changes in tax law in specific years. Receipts are expected to hold roughly steady as a share of GDP and of taxable personal income in 2010. They then rise sharply in 2011 with the expiration of tax provisions enacted in EGTRRA and JGTRRA and rise in each succeeding year of the projection period. They reach 10.9 percent of GDP by 2018, 2.4 percentage points higher than the level expected in 2008 and 1.9 percentage points higher than the level expected in 2009.

The projected increases in receipts as a share of GDP result primarily from two factors: scheduled changes in tax legislation and several characteristics inherent in the tax system. The projection for capital gains realizations works in the opposite direction to restrain the growth of revenues.

Tax Law Changes. Scheduled changes in tax law—principally the expiration of provisions originally enacted in 2001 (in EGTRRA) and 2003 (in JGTRRA)—will cause receipts to increase, especially in 2011 and 2012. As a result of such changes in 2011, the tax rates applied to capital gains and dividends will increase, statutory tax

Box 4-1.

Tax Bases and Tax Liability

Tax receipts vary with economic activity, but they do not move perfectly with gross domestic product (GDP). Although the bases for individual and corporate income taxes and for social insurance taxes are related to GDP, they sometimes grow faster or more slowly than the overall economy. As a result, the ratio of receipts to GDP may change even if tax laws remain the same.

The Individual Income Tax Base

A rough measure of the individual income tax base includes estimates of wages and salaries, dividends, interest, rental income, and proprietors' income from the national income and product accounts (NIPAs), which are maintained by the Department of Commerce's Bureau of Economic Analysis. That measure, referred to here as **taxable personal income,** excludes retained corporate profits and fringe benefits that workers do not receive in taxable form.

That income measure must be narrowed further to obtain the actual tax base of the income tax. Some of that income is earned in a form that is tax-exempt, such as income from state and local bonds; and some is tax-deferred, such as income earned in retirement accounts, on which taxes are paid not when the income is accrued but when the individual retires and begins to draw down the account. Also, NIPA estimates of personal interest and rental income contain large components of imputed income (income that is not earned in a cash transaction, including personal earnings within pension funds and life insurance policies and income from owner-occupied housing) that are not taxable. Consequently, a substantial amount of interest, dividend, and rental income is excluded from the taxable base of the income tax.

Further adjustments, both additions and subtractions, must be made to determine taxpayers' **adjusted gross income,** or AGI. **Capital gains realizations—** the increase in the value of assets between the time they are purchased and sold—are added because NIPA estimates of taxable personal income exclude them as unrelated to current production. Contributions from income made to tax-deductible individual retirement accounts and 401(k) plans are subtracted, but distributions to retirees from those plans are added.

A variety of other, smaller adjustments must be made to reflect the various adjustments that taxpayers make. **Exemptions** and **deductions** are subtracted from AGI to yield **taxable income,** to which progressive tax rates—rates that rise as income rises—are applied. (Those rates are known as statutory marginal tax rates; the range of taxable income over which a statutory marginal rate applies is known as an income tax bracket, of which there are now six.)

The tax that results from applying statutory rates to taxable income may then be subject to further adjustments in the form of **credits,** such as the child tax credit for taxpayers with children under age 17, which reduce taxpayers' **tax liability** (the amount of taxes they owe). An important factor in calculating individual tax liability is the **alternative minimum tax** (AMT), which requires some taxpayers to calculate their taxes under a more limited set of exemptions, deductions, and credits. Taxpayers then pay whichever is higher, the AMT or the regular tax. The ratio of tax liability to AGI is the **effective tax rate on AGI.**

Box 4-1.

Continued

The Social Insurance Tax Base

Social insurance taxes, the second-largest source of receipts, use payrolls as their base. Those taxes largely fund Social Security and the Hospital Insurance program, or HI (Part A of Medicare). Social Security taxes are imposed as a fixed percentage of pay up to an annual **taxable maximum** (currently $102,000) that is indexed for the growth of wages in the economy. HI taxes are not subject to a taxable maximum.

The Corporate Income Tax Base

Corporate profits form the tax base of the corporate income tax. Profits are measured in a variety of ways in the NIPAs. Several adjustments are made to those measures to better approximate what is taxed by the corporate income tax.

First, different measures of depreciation cause important differences in the measurement of corporate profits. **Economic profits** are measured to include the profit-reducing effects of **economic depreciation**—the dollar value of productive capital assets that is estimated to have been used up in the production process. (In the NIPAs, economic profits are referred to as profits before tax with inventory valuation and capital consumption adjustments.) For tax purposes, however, corporations calculate **book profits,** which include reductions for **book,** or **tax, depreciation.** (In the NIPAs, book profits are referred to as profits before tax.) Book depreciation is typically more front-loaded than economic depreciation; that is, the capital is assumed to decline in value at a faster rate than the best estimates of how fast its economic value actually falls, allowing firms to generally report taxable profits that are smaller than economic profits.

Second, the profits of the Federal Reserve System are included in economic and book profits, but they are not taxed under the corporate income tax. (Instead, they are generally remitted to the Treasury as miscellaneous receipts.)

Third, economic and book profits both include certain foreign-source income of U.S. multinational corporations. Such income is taxed at very low effective rates, in part because it is generally taxable only when it is "repatriated," or returned, to the U.S. parent company. In addition, it generates little revenue because corporations can offset their domestic tax by the amount of foreign taxes paid on that income, within limits.

Several other differences exist between book profits and corporations' calculation of their taxable income. In general, only the positive profits of profitable firms, or **gross profits,** are subject to tax. If a corporation's taxable income is negative (that is, if the firm loses money), its loss (within limits) may be carried backward or forward to be netted against previous or future taxable income and thus reduce its taxes in those other years.

A statutory tax rate is applied to the corporation's taxable income to determine its tax liability. A number of credits may pare that liability. The ratio of total corporate taxes to total corporate income (including negative income) is the **average tax rate.** The average tax rate that is calculated using economic profits is discussed in Box 4-2 on page 95.

rates on ordinary income will rise, the child tax credit will be reduced, and tax brackets and standard deductions for joint filers will contract in size to less than twice those for single taxpayers, among other changes. Of the projected increase in revenues relative to GDP of 2.4 percentage points from 2008 through 2018, changes in tax law account for about 1.5 percentage points, CBO estimates; about one-third of that increase results from the reduction in the AMT exemption after 2007, and the remainder from the expiration of EGTRRA and JGTRRA.

Characteristics of the Tax System. Effective tax rates will steadily rise over the next 10 years, according to CBO's baseline projections, thereby increasing the receipts generated by the economy. That increase occurs in part because of real bracket creep, as the overall growth of real income causes more income to be taxed in higher tax brackets. In the projections, real bracket creep causes revenues relative to GDP to climb by 0.6 percentage points of GDP over the next 10 years.

In addition, because the AMT is not indexed for inflation, it will claim a growing share of rising nominal income. That trend would occur even without the reduction in the AMT exemption amount in 2008, which, if left unchanged, is expected to boost receipts sharply in 2009. In its baseline, CBO projects that receipts from the AMT will rise from 2.6 percent of total individual income tax receipts in 2008 to 5.3 percent by 2018. The rising share of income subject to the AMT, absent changes in law, will cause revenues relative to GDP to increase by 0.4 percentage points from 2008 to 2018.

Without changes in law, the number of taxpayers affected by the AMT is expected to climb from 4.2 million in 2007 to over 26 million this year and nearly 44 million in 2018 (see Figure 4-4). The number is expected to temporarily dip in 2011 because of increases in regular tax rates and other changes resulting from the expiration of provisions originally enacted in EGTRRA and JGTRRA. In dollar terms, AMT receipts are expected to climb from $32 billion in 2008 to $111 billion in 2010, fall to $55 billion by 2012, and then resume growing and reach $130 billion by 2018.

Taxable distributions from certain tax-deferred retirement accounts such as traditional individual retirement accounts (IRAs) and 401(k) plans, which are expected to increase as the population ages, also raise effective rates in CBO's projections. Those contributions were exempt from taxation when they were initially made, which reduced taxable income reported to the IRS in earlier years. As retirees take distributions from those accounts, the money becomes taxable, thereby increasing tax receipts relative to GDP by about 0.4 percentage points over the next 10 years, CBO estimates.

Capital Gains Realizations. In CBO's projections, realizations of capital gains generally grow more slowly than GDP after 2007. Although capital gains plunged between 2000 and 2002, they rebounded strongly from 2003 to 2006. On the basis of recent economic growth and activity in the stock and housing markets, CBO estimates that capital gains realizations increased by 8 percent in calendar year 2007, a bit faster than GDP growth (see Table 4-3).

The strong upturn in capital gains realizations since 2002 has raised them to a level that, relative to the size of the economy, is well above that implied by their past historical relationship to GDP, with the rate at which they are taxed taken into account (see Figure 4-5). In the past, the ratio of gains realizations to GDP has tended to return to its average level relative to the size of the economy (adjusted for the tax rate on gains), although the speed of the reversion has been irregular. At times, it has been very fast, as in 2001, and at other times, it has been more delayed. The decline in stock prices so far in January 2008 suggests some reversion this year, although it is too early to draw any conclusions about the extent of such reversion for the whole year.

Consequently, CBO anticipates that capital gains will gradually return to their long-run average level (adjusted for tax rates) relative to the economy beyond 2007. Gains are also affected by the changes in tax rates scheduled to take effect in 2011 following the expiration of the lower rates originally enacted in JGTRRA. Higher tax rates reduce the long-run average amount of gains relative to the size of the economy because taxpayers tend to realize fewer gains at higher tax rates; however, CBO estimates that the effect of higher rates on realizations only partially offsets the increase in revenues from those higher rates. In other words, the estimated net effect of an increase in capital gains tax rates is an increase in revenues from that source despite a somewhat lower level of realizations.

Compared with the 4.6 percent average rate of growth expected for GDP between 2007 and 2018, capital gains realizations are projected to decline at an average annual

Table 4-3.

Actual and Projected Capital Gains Realizations and Taxes

	Capital Gains Realizations[a]		Capital Gains Tax Liabilities[a]		Capital Gains Tax Receipts[b]		Capital Gains Tax Receipts as a Percentage of Individual Income Tax Receipts
	Billions of Dollars	Percentage Change From Previous Year	Billions of Dollars	Percentage Change From Previous Year	Billions of Dollars	Percentage Change From Previous Year	
1990	124	-20	28	-21	32	-14	6.8
1991	112	-10	25	-11	27	-17	5.7
1992	127	14	29	16	27	1	5.6
1993	152	20	36	25	32	20	6.3
1994	153	*	36	*	36	12	6.7
1995	180	18	44	22	40	10	6.8
1996	261	45	66	50	54	36	8.3
1997	365	40	79	19	72	33	9.8
1998	455	25	89	12	84	16	10.1
1999	553	21	112	26	99	19	11.3
2000	644	17	127	14	119	20	11.8
2001	349	-46	66	-48	100	-16	10.0
2002	269	-23	49	-25	58	-42	6.8
2003	323	20	51	5	50	-14	6.3
2004	499	54	74	43	61	22	7.6
2005	690	38	101	37	86	40	9.3
2006	798	16	117	16	108	26	10.4
2007	863	8	127	8	122	12	10.5
2008	822	-5	117	-8	123	1	10.1
2009	800	-3	113	-3	115	-6	8.6
2010	899	12	128	13	115	*	8.3
2011	611	-32	112	-13	131	14	8.1
2012	717	17	133	18	115	-12	6.6
2013	722	1	133	*	133	15	7.1
2014	731	1	133	1	133	*	6.8
2015	744	2	135	1	134	1	6.5
2016	760	2	138	2	136	1	6.2
2017	780	3	141	2	139	2	6.0
2018	803	3	145	3	142	3	5.8

Source: Congressional Budget Office.

Note: * = between zero and 0.5 percent.

   Capital gains realizations are the sum of net capital gains from tax returns reporting a net gain. Data for realizations and liabilities after 2004 and data for tax receipts in all years are estimated or projected by CBO. Data on realizations and liabilities before 2005 are estimated by the Treasury Department.

a.   Calendar year basis.

b.   Fiscal year basis. This measure is CBO's estimate of when tax liabilities are paid to the Treasury.

Figure 4-5.

Capital Gains Realizations as a Share of Gross Domestic Product, Calendar Years 1954 to 2018

(Percent)

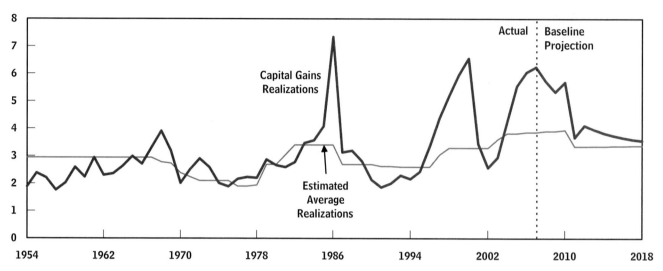

Source: Congressional Budget Office.

a. Estimated average realizations are the average ratio of realizations to gross domestic product adjusted for differences between each year's tax rate and the average tax rate over the period. The spike in realizations in 1986, caused by the pending tax increase in 1987, has been removed from the estimated average ratio.

rate of 0.7 percent. The declines in gains are concentrated in the early years of the 10-year projection period; gains rise during the last six years of the period, albeit more slowly than GDP.

The scheduled return to higher capital gains tax rates in 2011 also will alter the timing of realizations by encouraging taxpayers to speed up, from that year to late 2010, the sale of assets that will generate gains. Therefore, realizations are projected to rise by 12 percent in tax year 2010, decline by 32 percent in 2011, and rise by 17 percent in 2012 (when they rebound after the one-time speedup). After 2012, realizations are projected to rise by 1 percent to 3 percent annually through 2018.

Receipts from capital gains taxes are expected to grow in step with realizations, except when the tax rates change in 2011. Over the 2008–2018 period, receipts from capital gains taxes are projected to climb at an annual rate of 1.4 percent—even though realizations are projected to decline as a result of the increased tax rate after 2010. Receipts from capital gains taxes are projected to contribute a declining share of overall individual income tax receipts over the projection period, falling from 10.5 per-

cent of receipts in 2007 to 5.8 percent by 2018. CBO estimates that, without the changes in law scheduled to take effect in 2011, a decline in capital gains realizations and revenues relative to the economy would reduce individual income tax receipts by 0.4 percentage points of GDP over the next 10 years. That effect would offset a projected increase in those receipts relative to GDP of 2.9 percentage points resulting from scheduled changes in tax law and other factors that boost effective tax rates.

Social Insurance Taxes

In CBO's baseline, revenues from social insurance taxes decline slightly as a share of GDP, from 6.4 percent in 2008 to 6.3 percent in 2015 and thereafter (see Table 4-4). Such revenues are also projected to decline slightly in relation to wages and salaries—the approximate tax base for those payroll taxes—from 13.9 percent in 2008 to 13.8 percent in 2013 and thereafter. That pattern for social insurance taxes stems from modest declines in the share of earnings below the taxable maximum amount for Social Security and slower growth in the receipts from unemployment taxes and from federal retirement programs.

Table 4-4.

CBO's Projections of Social Insurance Tax Receipts and the Social Insurance Tax Base

	Actual 2007	2008	2009	2010	2011	2012	2013	2014	2015	2016	2017	2018	Total, 2009-2013[a]	Total, 2009-2018[a]
Social Insurance Tax Receipts														
In billions of dollars	870	910	947	997	1,049	1,101	1,149	1,199	1,249	1,301	1,355	1,411	5,244	11,758
As a percentage of GDP	6.4	6.4	6.4	6.4	6.4	6.4	6.4	6.4	6.3	6.3	6.3	6.3	6.4	6.4
Annual growth rate	3.8	4.6	4.1	5.3	5.2	5.0	4.4	4.3	4.2	4.1	4.1	4.1	4.8	4.5
Wages and Salaries														
In billions of dollars	6,290	6,555	6,828	7,186	7,573	7,947	8,309	8,682	9,056	9,437	9,834	10,248	37,844	85,101
As a percentage of GDP	46.0	46.2	46.1	46.1	46.1	46.1	46.0	46.0	46.0	45.9	45.9	45.8	46.1	46.0
Annual growth rate	6.2	4.2	4.2	5.2	5.4	4.9	4.6	4.5	4.3	4.2	4.2	4.2	4.9	4.6
Social Insurance Tax Receipts as a Percentage of Wages and Salaries	13.8	13.9	13.9	13.9	13.9	13.9	13.8	13.8	13.8	13.8	13.8	13.8	13.9	13.8

Source: Congressional Budget Office.

Notes: GDP = gross domestic product.

The tax base in this table (wages and salaries) reflects income as measured by the national income and product accounts rather than as reported on tax returns.

a. Measures expressed in billions of dollars are the cumulative amounts over the period. Measures expressed as a percentage of GDP or wages and salaries are averages over the period. Measures expressed as annual growth rates are the average rates compounded annually over the period, including growth in 2009.

The largest sources of payroll tax receipts are taxes for Social Security (called Old-Age, Survivors, and Disability Insurance, or OASDI) and Medicare's Hospital Insurance (HI). A small share of social insurance tax revenues comes from unemployment insurance taxes and contributions to federal retirement programs (see Table 4-5). The premiums for Medicare Part B (the Supplementary Medical Insurance program) and Part D (the prescription drug program) are considered offsets to spending and do not appear on the revenue side of the budget.

Social Security and Medicare taxes are calculated as a percentage of covered wages—15.3 percent for the two taxes combined. Unlike the Medicare tax, which applies to all wages, the Social Security tax of 12.4 percent applies only up to a taxable maximum, which is indexed to the growth of the average wages over time. (The taxable maximum is set at $102,000 for 2008.) Consequently, receipts from OASDI taxes tend to remain fairly stable as a proportion of wages as long as covered wages are a stable percentage of GDP and the distribution of wages remains relatively unchanged. The share of wages earned above the taxable

maximum has risen significantly over the past two decades, however, which has reduced the share of wages that is subject to the OASDI tax.

Social insurance tax receipts between 2008 and 2018 are expected to decline slightly as a share of GDP and wages for three reasons. First, receipts from payroll taxes for unemployment insurance—most of which are imposed by the states but yield amounts that are considered to be federal revenues—are projected to decline as a share of wages and GDP after 2012. At the close of fiscal year 2007, all states had replenished their unemployment trust funds, which were depleted by the 2001 recession and natural disasters that occurred after that. The economic slowdown in CBO's projection for 2008 puts some pressure on those trust funds, which in CBO's projection delays for a few years the reduction in those receipts relative to GDP. Second, revenues associated with federal retirement programs are projected to decline over time as a share of GDP and wages because the number of workers covered by the Railroad Retirement system and the Civil Service Retirement System is expected to decline. Third,

Table 4-5.

CBO's Projections of Social Insurance Tax Receipts, by Source

(Billions of dollars)

	Actual 2007	2008	2009	2010	2011	2012	2013	2014	2015	2016	2017	2018	Total, 2009-2013	Total, 2009-2018
Social Security	635	665	694	730	768	806	842	880	918	957	997	1,039	3,839	8,629
Medicare	185	194	202	213	224	235	246	257	269	280	292	305	1,121	2,524
Unemployment Insurance	41	42	43	46	49	52	53	54	55	56	58	60	242	524
Railroad Retirement	4	4	4	4	4	5	5	5	5	5	5	5	22	47
Other Retirement	4	4	4	4	4	4	4	3	3	3	3	3	19	35
Total	**870**	**910**	**947**	**997**	**1,049**	**1,101**	**1,149**	**1,199**	**1,249**	**1,301**	**1,355**	**1,411**	**5,244**	**11,758**

Source: Congressional Budget Office.

the share of wages subject to the Social Security tax is projected to decrease as a slightly higher fraction of total wage and salary income occurs above the taxable maximum. (That final effect of higher income concentration on social insurance tax receipts is more than offset for receipts as a whole, because individual income taxes rise when a greater share of income is in higher income tax brackets.)

Corporate Income Taxes

Receipts from corporate income taxes in 2007 grew by almost 5 percent, which is relatively slow compared with growth in the three prior years. Between 2005 and 2006, for instance, corporate income tax receipts grew by 27 percent. As a share of GDP in 2007, receipts from corporate income taxes remained at 2.7 percent, a level last seen in the 1970s. CBO projects that corporate tax revenues will decline slightly in dollar terms in 2008, falling to $364 billion (see Table 4-6). Because profits are expected to grow more slowly than GDP after 2008, receipts as a share of GDP are expected to decline from the high levels of the past two years. Receipts will remain within about 10 percent of the 2008 amount through 2018 in dollar terms, CBO projects, but will fall to 1.7 percent of GDP by 2018, levels similar to those in the early 1990s.

Receipts in Recent Years. Receipts from corporate income taxes—like those from individual income taxes—rose relative to the size of the economy in the 1990s, fell sharply between 2000 and 2003, and rebounded strongly in recent years (see Figure 4-3 on page 82). Relative to economic profits, a measure of profits that is not affected by changes in law regarding depreciation and other

accounting methods, corporate receipts also fell sharply over the 2002–2003 period before rebounding in the past four years. (See Box 4-2 for a discussion of movements in the average tax rate over time.)

Several factors have contributed to the movements in corporate receipts since 2000. The recession in 2001 reduced profits and tax revenues substantially. Business tax incentives enacted in the Job Creation and Worker Assistance Act of 2002 and JGTRRA further reduced revenues. Those incentives allowed firms to expense (immediately deduct from their taxable income) a portion of any investment made in equipment between September 11, 2001, and December 31, 2004. Before they expired, those partial-expensing provisions, combined with economic conditions, reduced corporate tax receipts. Corporate receipts as a share of GDP fell to 1.2 percent by 2003, their lowest share since 1983. Especially strong profit growth since 2003, combined with the expiration of the tax incentives and increases in average tax rates, caused corporate receipts to rise to 2.7 percent of GDP in 2006 and 2007, their highest share since 1978.

Projected Receipts. CBO's projection of corporate tax receipts largely follows its estimates of taxable profits. CBO uses economic profits as measured in the national income and product accounts as the most accurate measure over recent history.[4] Making several adjustments, the agency estimates taxable corporate profits, which more

---

4. In these projections, CBO has deemphasized the use of book profits, an alternative measure of profits in the NIPAs that is theoretically closer to the corporate tax base, because of difficulties in accurately estimating tax depreciation for recent years.

Table 4-6.

CBO's Projections of Corporate Income Tax Receipts and Tax Bases

	Actual 2007	2008	2009	2010	2011	2012	2013	2014	2015	2016	2017	2018	Total, 2009-2013[a]	Total, 2009-2018[a]
Corporate Income Tax Receipts														
In billions of dollars	370	364	356	334	333	357	327	342	350	361	374	388	1,707	3,522
As a percentage of GDP	2.7	2.6	2.4	2.1	2.0	2.1	1.8	1.8	1.8	1.8	1.7	1.7	2.1	1.9
Annual growth rate	4.6	-1.7	-2.2	-6.2	-0.2	7.0	-8.5	4.6	2.6	3.2	3.5	3.7	-2.2	0.6
Corporate Economic Profits														
In billions of dollars	1,586	1,604	1,648	1,667	1,717	1,776	1,830	1,888	1,969	2,065	2,172	2,289	8,637	19,020
As a percentage of GDP	11.6	11.3	11.1	10.7	10.4	10.3	10.1	10.0	10.0	10.1	10.1	10.2	10.5	10.3
Annual growth rate	4.1	1.1	2.7	1.2	2.9	3.4	3.0	3.2	4.3	4.9	5.2	5.4	2.7	3.6
Taxable Corporate Profits[b]														
In billions of dollars	1,279	1,224	1,217	1,197	1,202	1,211	1,219	1,238	1,272	1,316	1,366	1,422	6,046	12,660
As a percentage of GDP	9.4	8.6	8.2	7.7	7.3	7.0	6.8	6.6	6.5	6.4	6.4	6.4	7.4	6.8
Annual growth rate	-2.1	-4.3	-0.6	-1.6	0.4	0.7	0.7	1.5	2.8	3.5	3.8	4.1	-0.1	1.5
Corporate Receipts as a Percentage of Taxable Profits	28.9	29.7	29.3	27.9	27.7	29.5	26.8	27.6	27.5	27.5	27.4	27.3	28.2	27.8

Source: Congressional Budget Office.

Notes: GDP = gross domestic product.

The tax bases in this table (corporate economic profits and taxable corporate profits) reflect income as measured in the national income and product accounts rather than as reported on tax returns.

a. Measures expressed in billions of dollars are the cumulative amounts over the period. Measures expressed as a percentage of GDP or taxable profits are averages over the period. Measures expressed as annual growth rates are the average rates compounded annually over the period, including growth in 2009.

b. Taxable corporate profits are defined as economic profits plus economic depreciation minus book depreciation; minus profits earned by the Federal Reserve System, transnational corporations, and S corporations; and minus deductible payments of state and local corporate taxes. They include capital gains realized by corporations and profits from inventory revaluation.

closely approximate the tax base (see Box 4-1). Those adjustments include substituting CBO's estimates of past and future tax depreciation for economic depreciation; subtracting profits of S corporations, which are not taxed at the corporate level; subtracting "rest-of-world" profits earned by U.S. corporations; and adding realizations of capital gains.

In CBO's projections, taxable profits decline through 2010 and then begin to grow, albeit more slowly than GDP. The growth in taxable profits differs from that of economic profits, which grow in every year; many of the differences between the two grow at rates than are different from the rate for economic profits. CBO projects that tax depreciation, profits of S corporations, and rest-of-

world profits will all grow more quickly than economic profits. Subtracting those relatively rapidly growing components from economic profits reduces the growth rate of taxable profits, in some years causing it to be negative.

CBO projects that corporate income tax receipts will fall by less than taxable profits in 2008. Taxable profits are expected to decline by more in 2008 than they did in 2007, but some of the additional weakness in taxable profits will not affect receipts in 2008. (A portion will affect tax receipts in 2009, when firms file their income tax returns for the 2008 tax year and make the necessary final payments.) In addition, collections were relatively high in December 2007 (which is a part of fiscal year 2008). CBO expects payments to be slightly below the

Box 4-2.

Factors Affecting the Average Corporate Tax Rate

The average corporate tax rate measures corporate income tax receipts relative to corporate profits (see the figure to the right). Corporate tax receipts are adjusted for legislated timing shifts that move corporate estimated tax payments between fiscal years. To calculate the average tax rate, receipts are divided by economic profits, as measured in the national income and product accounts. Economic profits are net profits, the profits of profitable firms minus the losses of firms with losses. They are based solely on ongoing economic activities, excluding capital gains and losses. Compared with taxable profits, economic profits remove accelerated depreciation and inventory profits generated by inflation. They include the profits of so-called S corporations, whose profits are passed through to shareholders and taxed only under the individual income tax.

The dip in the average corporate tax rate in 2001 and 2002 and the rebound that followed have been notable. Those movements, along with a sharp drop and then rebound in corporate profits as a share of GDP, are reflected in the steep drop in corporate receipts from 2001 to 2003 and very strong growth in receipts since then. In the context of the period since 1960, the recent fluctuations in the average tax rate are not especially unusual.

The average corporate tax rate changes any time the tax liability as defined by law changes or any time the tax base changes relative to underlying economic profits. Over the past 47 years, the average corporate tax rate on economic profits has fluctuated from about 41 percent in 1961 to about 15 percent both in 1983 and in 2002 and 2003. Three factors have been primarily responsible for changes in the average tax rate: business cycles, revisions to tax law, and inflation.

Business Cycles

Business cycles affect the profitability of corporations and affect the average tax rate because they change

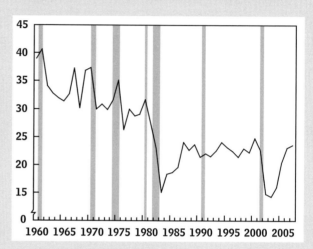

Adjusted Corporate Receipts as a Percentage of Economic Profits, Fiscal Years 1960 to 2007

Source: Congressional Budget Office.

the mix of profits and losses. Because only firms with positive profits in a year are potentially taxable, variations in net profits overstate the true effect on the tax base of business cycles. For example, during cyclical downturns, the tax base typically falls by less than indicated by the decrease in net profits, because some of the decline in net profits occurs in unprofitable firms; thus, the average tax rate rises because tax liability does not decline as much in percentage terms as net profits do. However, average tax rates tend to drop temporarily after recessions because tax law allows firms that experience losses during economic downturns to reduce their tax liability in future profitable years by deducting past losses in profitable years.

For example, the increase in the average tax rate during the 1973–1975 recession and then the decline in 1976 were caused in part by changes in the mix of profits and losses during the downturn and subsequent use of net operating losses carried forward during the recovery. That cyclical pattern cannot always be observed.

Box 4-2.
Continued

Changes to Tax Law

The average corporate tax rate is affected by legislation that changes either the corporate tax base or the tax liability due for any given level of profits. Legislation that changes the tax base typically acts either through changes to the definition of the base or changes to the deductions, such as depreciation, that firms can use to reduce taxable profits.

Numerous changes in law have affected the average tax rate since 1960. One of the most significant was the Economic Recovery Tax Act of 1981, which reduced the average corporate tax rate by significantly accelerating depreciation and by expanding the investment tax credit (ITC). The average tax rate fell from almost 32 percent in 1980 to about 15 percent in 1983. Legislation enacted during the rest of the 1980s reversed much of the decline in the average tax rate by scaling back or repealing several corporate tax preferences. In particular, the Tax Reform Act of 1986 (TRA-86) lengthened investment lifetimes for depreciation, repealed the ITC, and broadened the corporate tax base in other ways. Those effects on the average tax rate were only partially offset by a reduction in the statutory tax rates.

Changes in tax law have also encouraged many firms to become S corporations for tax purposes. Most significantly, TRA-86 reduced individual income tax rates relative to corporate income tax rates, thereby increasing the benefits of the S corporate form. Since then, shifts toward that corporate form have helped hold down the average tax rate.

Inflation

During periods of relatively high inflation, average tax rates rise because historical costs are used to measure deductions for tax depreciation and because inventories are valued at the new price level. The effect of inflation on average tax rates could be seen in 1975, when the high average tax rate was due to a spike in the value of inventory profits resulting from inflation. Inflation stabilized at a lower level after 1981, which contributed to the reduction in average corporate tax rates relative to what they were during most of the 1970s.

Average Tax Rates in Recent Years

Between 1987 and 2001, the average corporate tax rate remained relatively stable at between 20 percent and 25 percent. In 2002, it fell to under 15 percent and remained at about that level through 2004. Much of that decline can be attributed to the combined effects of legislation and the business cycle.

The Job Creation and Worker Assistance Act of 2002 allowed firms to partially expense (immediately deduct from taxable income) 30 percent of their investment in equipment made between September 11, 2001, and September 10, 2004, which was more generous depreciation than had been allowed before. The Jobs and Growth Tax Relief Reconciliation Act of 2003 increased the partial-expensing allowance from 30 percent to 50 percent and extended it until the end of calendar year 2004. CBO estimates that partial expensing alone lowered the average corporate tax rate by about 2 percentage points between 2002 and 2004. Other provisions in the legislation lowered effective tax rates to a lesser degree.

Net operating losses carried forward from the 2001 recession and from years when partial expensing caused some firms to incur losses also held down average tax rates in 2004 and 2005. Without the effects of partial expensing and the use of losses carried forward from the cyclical downturn, the recent dip in the average corporate tax rate would be less notable. Indeed, with the expiration of partial expensing in 2005 and with waning effects of the recession, the average tax rate rebounded in 2006 to the level seen in the 1990s.

Table 4-7.

CBO's Projections of Excise Tax Receipts, by Category

(Billions of dollars)

	Actual 2007	2008	2009	2010	2011	2012	2013	2014	2015	2016	2017	2018	Total, 2009-2013	Total, 2009-2018
Highway Taxes	35.8	34.7	33.9	34.2	39.7	41.9	42.5	43.0	43.4	43.6	43.9	44.0	192.2	410.1
Airport Taxes	11.3	12.1	12.7	13.4	14.2	15.0	15.7	16.5	17.2	18.1	18.9	19.8	70.9	161.4
Alcohol Taxes	9.1	9.3	9.6	9.8	10.1	10.3	10.6	10.9	11.2	11.4	11.7	12.0	50.4	107.6
Tobacco Taxes	8.5	8.3	8.2	8.1	8.0	7.9	7.9	7.8	7.7	7.6	7.5	7.4	40.1	78.1
Other Excise Taxes	0.3	4.0	3.7	3.5	3.5	3.5	3.6	3.6	3.7	3.7	3.8	3.8	17.9	36.6
Total	**65.1**	**68.4**	**68.0**	**69.1**	**75.5**	**78.7**	**80.2**	**81.7**	**83.1**	**84.5**	**85.8**	**87.1**	**371.5**	**793.8**

Source: Congressional Budget Office.

level of the comparable payments in 2007, on average, for the remaining three quarters of 2008, which is consistent with the agency's forecast of profits for those quarters. Finally, expirations of tax provisions such as the research and experimentation tax credit under current law contribute to a slight increase in the average tax rate in 2008.

CBO expects that corporate tax receipts will decline in 2009 and 2010 largely because of the assumption that the recent strength in collections that is not explained by available data on profits and other measures used in forecasting receipts will steadily diminish through 2010. That assumption causes receipts to grow more slowly than profits in those years. That effect is reinforced by CBO's projected decline in corporate profits.

In CBO's projections, taxable profits start to increase in dollar terms in 2011, although receipts remain low in that year in part because of the normal lag in the payment of taxes on profits. Legislated shifts in the timing of corporate estimated tax payments that will move about $3 billion out of 2011 and into other years also contribute to the low receipts in 2011.

CBO expects receipts in 2012 to increase because of multiple pieces of legislation that shift $22 billion in corporate tax payments into 2012 from payments that otherwise would have been made both before and after 2012. Some of that shifting can be seen in 2013 receipts, which are reduced by almost $11 billion for that reason. CBO expects that after 2013, corporate tax receipts will move roughly in tandem with taxable corporate profits.

As a result of a projected decline in taxable profits as a share of the economy, corporate receipts relative to GDP weaken steadily in CBO's baseline, reaching 1.7 percent of the economy in 2017 and 2018. That expected share at the end of the projection period is more in line with the receipts recorded in the early 1990s than with the higher amounts recorded in the late 1990s and from 2005 through 2007.

Excise Taxes

Receipts from excise taxes are expected to continue their long-term decline as a share of GDP, falling from 0.5 percent in 2007 to 0.4 percent toward the end of the 10-year projection period. Most excise taxes—those generating about 80 percent of total excise revenues—are levied per unit of good or per transaction rather than as a percentage of value. Thus, excise receipts grow with real GDP, but they do not rise with inflation and therefore do not grow as fast as nominal GDP does.

Nearly all excise taxes fall into four major categories: highway, airport, alcohol, and tobacco (see Table 4-7). More than half of all excise receipts come from taxes dedicated to the Highway Trust Fund—primarily taxes on gasoline and diesel fuel, including blends of those fuels with ethanol. Receipts from highway taxes are projected to decline by between 2 percent and 3 percent in both 2008 and 2009 and to remain roughly stable in 2010. CBO projects that aggregate consumption of motor fuel—gasoline, ethanol, and diesel—will increase by about 0.6 percent annually over the next three years. That rate of growth is substantially diminished by the recent increases in fuel prices, which are expected to largely persist and cause people to drive less and to purchase more-fuel-efficient vehicles. In the projections, receipts fall while fuel use rises because the increase in fuel use is largely of ethanol-blended fuels, which face lower effective tax rates. Those lower rates expire at the end of 2010, after which projected receipts from highway taxes jump to a higher level and then gradually rise, reflecting further expected increases in the use of motor fuel. The amount of revenues transferred to the Highway Trust Fund per gallon of fuel used is not affected by the change in tax rates on ethanol-blended fuels.

The main components of the aviation excise taxes are levied as a percentage of dollar value, so aviation tax receipts grow at a faster rate than the other categories do. According to CBO's projections, those revenues will increase at an average annual rate of 5.2 percent from 2007 to 2018. Under current law, most of those taxes are scheduled to expire on February 29, but as specified in the Balanced Budget and Emergency Deficit Control Act of 1985, CBO's baseline assumes the expiring excise taxes are extended.[5]

Receipts from alcohol taxes are projected to rise by about 2.6 percent per year through 2018, which is about the rate of growth of real GDP over the period. Receipts from tobacco taxes are expected to decline by a little more than 1 percent per year as per capita consumption continues to trend downward.

Other excise taxes include a variety of charges. Until recently, telecommunications taxes were also one of the major sources of excise tax revenues. However, in May 2006, after several successful court cases challenging the tax's validity, the IRS ceased collecting a variety of telephone excise taxes. Furthermore, the IRS refunded, with interest, revenues collected under those taxes since March 2003. Taxpayers claimed less in refunds on their tax returns than CBO and the IRS expected, but the amounts still totaled about $4 billion in 2007. As a result, net receipts from telecommunications taxes were negative in 2007, and the cessation of those refunds explains much of the strong growth of 5 percent expected for all excise tax receipts in 2008.

---

5. Some taxes on aviation fuel continue after February 29, 2008. Although the provisions of the Balanced Budget and Emergency Deficit Control Act of 1985 that pertain to the baseline expired on September 30, 2006, CBO continues to follow that law's specifications in constructing its baseline.

Estate and Gift Taxes

Under an assumption that provisions of current law remain in place, CBO projects that receipts from estate and gift taxes will fall from 0.2 percent of GDP in 2007 to 0.1 percent in 2010 and 2011 and then jump to 0.3 percent of GDP in 2012 and about 0.4 percent by 2014. That pattern reflects the phaseout of the estate tax through 2010, as provided by EGTRRA, and the subsequent reinstatement of the tax in 2011 as well as changes in the gift tax over that period. Recent declines in housing wealth, which CBO expects to continue to some degree over the near term, have only a small downward effect on projected estate and gift tax revenues.

In the past, revenues from estate and gift taxes tended to grow more rapidly than income because the unified credit for the two taxes, which effectively exempted some assets from taxation, was not indexed for inflation. However, EGTRRA gradually increased the credit before eliminating the estate tax (albeit temporarily) in 2010. The gift tax remains in the tax code but in a modified form. EGTRRA effectively exempted $2.0 million of an estate from taxation in 2007. That amount is scheduled to increase to $3.5 million in 2009. Under EGTRRA, the highest tax rate on estates was reduced incrementally from 50 percent in 2002 to 45 percent in 2007; the tax itself is scheduled to be eliminated in 2010. That year, the gift tax rate is slated to be 35 percent, its lowest rate over the projection period. The law is currently set to reinstate the estate and gift tax at pre-EGTRRA levels in 2011, which include an effective exemption of $1 million and a top marginal tax rate of 55 percent.

Because estate tax liabilities are typically paid after a lag of almost a year and because the gift tax remains in the tax code, estate and gift tax receipts are projected to reach a trough in 2010 and 2011 but do not completely disappear from the projections (see Table 4-8). The expected receipts in 2011 result largely from taxable gifts that people bestow in 2010 because of the relatively low rate as well as the legislated reinstatement of the estate tax in 2011. CBO assumes that those gifts would otherwise have been given in years before and after 2011 and therefore affect the pattern of receipts over the 2008–2018 period. CBO estimates that after 2011, estate and gift tax receipts will return to roughly the same share of GDP as that seen in the early 1970s. Projected receipts as a share of GDP exceed the levels seen immediately before the enactment of EGTRRA mostly because the exemption levels are not indexed for inflation and individuals' wealth

Table 4-8.

CBO's Projections of Other Sources of Revenue

(Billions of dollars)

	Actual 2007	2008	2009	2010	2011	2012	2013	2014	2015	2016	2017	2018	Total, 2009-2013	Total, 2009-2018
Estate and Gift Taxes	26	27	27	22	21	55	63	70	76	83	90	97	188	604
Customs Duties	26	27	29	32	34	37	39	42	45	48	51	54	171	410
Miscellaneous Receipts														
Federal Reserve System earnings	32	32	34	37	41	43	45	48	50	52	54	56	200	460
Universal Service Fund[a]	8	8	8	8	8	9	9	9	9	9	9	9	42	88
Other	8	7	8	8	8	9	9	9	9	9	8	8	42	86
Subtotal	47	47	50	54	58	61	63	66	68	70	72	73	285	633
Total	**99**	**101**	**106**	**108**	**113**	**153**	**165**	**178**	**189**	**200**	**212**	**224**	**645**	**1,647**

Source: Congressional Budget Office.

a. Fees on certain telecommunications services finance the Universal Service Fund.

has been growing faster than GDP on average in recent years.

Other Sources of Revenue

Customs duties and miscellaneous receipts yielded only about 3 percent of total revenues in 2007, or about 0.5 percent of GDP. CBO estimates that receipts from those smaller sources will rise to about 0.6 percent of GDP in 2010 and remain fairly steady throughout the rest of the projection window.

CBO projects that customs duties will grow over time in tandem with imports. The value of imports on a census basis is projected to grow faster than GDP, from 14.0 percent of GDP in 2007 to 17.0 percent by 2018. The value of imports besides petroleum—a better measure of the tax base because duties on petroleum are small and levied per unit—is also projected to rise relative to GDP. As a result, for all years of the projection period, customs duties rise slightly relative to GDP but still measure 0.2 percent.

Profits of the Federal Reserve System—the largest component of miscellaneous receipts—are counted as revenues when they are remitted to the Treasury. The Federal Reserve prices services performed for financial institutions to recover the costs of them, and it earns interest on its holdings of U.S. Treasury securities, which it uses to implement monetary policy. Therefore, profits of the

Federal Reserve depend primarily on interest earned on the portfolio of securities, adjusted for any gains and losses from holdings of foreign-denominated assets, whose value changes as exchange rates change.

Largely as a result of the outlook for interest rates, CBO expects receipts from the Federal Reserve System to be flat in 2008 relative to 2007, with a resumption of growth in 2009. CBO expects that, on average, Treasury yields will be about 1 percentage point lower in the first two quarters of calendar year 2008 than they were in the third calendar quarter of 2007, with the decline being more pronounced for short-term rates and somewhat less for long-term rates. CBO projects interest rates to rise gradually from that point through 2009 and to remain relatively stable thereafter. In CBO's projections, the interest rate increases cause Federal Reserve earnings to rise for some period beyond 2009 as the Federal Reserve replaces maturing securities. Consequently, CBO expects receipts from the Federal Reserve System to grow at a slightly higher rate than GDP from 2009 to 2014 and at about the same rate as GDP thereafter. The size of the Federal Reserve's portfolio of securities largely grows with GDP over the projection period.

Other forms of miscellaneous receipts consist of certain fees and fines, most significantly fees on telecommunications services dedicated to the Universal Service Fund. CBO projects that those sources combined will remain relatively stable from 2008 to 2018, at about 0.1 percent of GDP.

The Effects of Expiring Tax Provisions

CBO's revenue projections are based on the assumption that current tax laws will remain unaltered. Thus, the projections assume that provisions currently scheduled to expire will do so. The one exception applies to the expiration of excise taxes that are dedicated to trust funds; under the rules governing the baseline, those taxes are assumed to continue regardless of whether they are scheduled to expire.

The expiration of tax provisions has a substantial impact on CBO's projections, especially beyond 2010, when a number of revenue-reducing tax provisions enacted in the early part of this decade are slated to expire. Some of the provisions were enacted many years ago and have been routinely extended. Almost all of the expiring provisions reduce revenues. If the expiring provisions were extended rather than allowed to expire, future revenues would be significantly lower than they are under the baseline projections. This section provides a list of the various tax provisions whose expiration is reflected in CBO's baseline, along with estimates of the revenue effects of extending those provisions (see Table 4-9 on page 101). Most of the revenue effects are based on estimates supplied by the Joint Committee on Taxation (JCT).[6] This section also identifies a number of expiring provisions that, under rules for the baseline, are assumed to be extended.

The revenue estimates associated with the extensions cited in this section do not include the provisions' potential effects on the economy. In many instances, macroeconomic feedback would be too small to have a substantial effect on the estimates. However, some expiring

provisions influence the supply of labor and economic growth in CBO's baseline economic projections. The full "dynamic" effect on revenues from extending various tax provisions would differ from the estimates presented here.

Provisions That Expire in CBO's Baseline Projections

From a budgetary perspective, the most significant expiring provisions are the tax provisions originally enacted in EGTRRA and JGTRRA, as amended by several laws enacted since 2003. In particular, an increased exemption level designed to mitigate the effect of the AMT expired at the end of 2007. The deduction for tuition and other higher-education expenses also expired at the end of 2007. At the end of 2010, several provisions that collectively have the most significant budgetary effects are set to expire: reduced tax rates on dividends, capital gains, and ordinary income; a higher child tax credit; the elimination of the estate tax; and an expanded standard deduction and size of the 15 percent tax bracket for married couples. Assuming that those expiring provisions originally enacted in EGTRRA and JGTRRA are extended, CBO and JCT estimate that the baseline budget deficits would be increased or surpluses would be reduced by about $3.4 trillion from 2008 through 2018 (excluding the effects on debt service). (That amount includes about $3.3 trillion in lower revenues and more than $100 billion in higher outlays).[7] About 95 percent of that reduction would occur between 2011 and 2018.

Those estimates of the effects of extending expiring provisions incorporate the assumption that the temporarily higher exemption levels for the AMT are extended at their 2007 levels. Therefore, the exemption levels would not rise with inflation, so a growing number of taxpayers would still become subject to the AMT over time—albeit fewer than if the higher exemption levels were not extended. (See Table 1-5 on page 12 for the budgetary effects of selected policy alternatives not included in CBO's baseline, including the effects of reforming the AMT by indexing its higher exemptions and its tax brackets for inflation. That policy change would reduce the number of taxpayers that might become subject to

---

6. When this report went to press, JCT's estimates based on the new economic projections were unavailable for certain provisions, including extending various individual income tax provisions of EGTRRA and JGTRRA that are scheduled to expire at the end of 2010 and changes to the exemption amount under the AMT that expired at the end of 2007. CBO has adjusted JCT's estimates (which are based on CBO's baseline projections from a year ago) to take into account the effects of CBO's updated economic projections. Those adjustments by CBO increased the estimated loss in revenues from extending the EGTRRA provisions by about 0.2 percent and from extending the AMT exemption by about 5 percent over the projection period. CBO will make JCT's updated estimates available when they are completed.

---

7. The effects on outlays result from refundable tax credits. Such credits reduce a taxpayer's overall tax liability; if the credit exceeds that liability, the excess may be refunded, in which case it is classified as an outlay in the federal budget.

the AMT over time by more than extending the AMT's exemptions at their 2007 levels would.)

Another 87 provisions not initially enacted in EGTRRA or JGTRRA are also scheduled to expire between 2008 and 2018. Of those, all but three would reduce revenues if extended. Extending the 84 revenue-reducing provisions would decrease receipts by about $430 billion between 2008 and 2018. The provision with the largest effect is the research and experimentation tax credit, which was enacted in 1981 and extended (for the 11th time) through the end of 2007 in the Tax Relief and Health Care Act of 2006. Continuing the credit would reduce revenues by about $115 billion over the 2009–2018 period, JCT estimates. Income and excise tax credits for alcohol fuels expire at the end of 2010; JCT estimates that extending those credits would reduce revenues by about $58 billion from 2008 through 2018. The exemption of certain active financing income from the Subpart F rules of the tax law expires at the end of 2008; extending that provision would reduce revenues by an estimated $56 billion through 2018. According to JCT, continuing the deduction for state and local general sales taxes, which expired at the end of 2007, would reduce revenues by over $37 billion through 2018.

Conversely, three expiring provisions would increase revenues (or decrease outlays) if they were extended. The provision with the largest effect is the Federal Unemployment Tax Act surcharge, which was recently extended by the Tax Increase Prevention Act of 2007 through December 31, 2008. Extending it further would increase revenues by about $8.5 billion over the next 10 years, CBO estimates. The other provisions include allowing the disclosure of tax return information for the administration of veterans' programs (which CBO estimates would reduce outlays) and allowing employers to transfer excess assets in defined-benefit pension plans to a special account for retirees' health benefits. Each of those provisions, if extended, would reduce projected deficits or increase surpluses by about $180 million through 2018.

Expiring Provisions That Are Extended in CBO's Baseline

Rules in the Balanced Budget and Emergency Deficit Control Act of 1985, as amended, require CBO to include in its projections excise tax receipts earmarked for trust funds, even if those taxes are scheduled to expire. In 2018, those expiring provisions account for about two-

thirds of that year's total excise taxes. The largest such taxes that are scheduled to expire over the next 10 years finance the Highway Trust Fund. Some of the taxes for that fund are permanent, but most of them end on September 30, 2011. Extending those taxes contributes about $38 billion to CBO's revenue projections in 2018, or almost 45 percent of that year's total excise taxes.

Extending other expiring taxes dedicated to trust funds contributes smaller amounts of revenue to CBO's baseline projections in 2018. Taxes dedicated to the Airport and Airway Trust Fund, which are scheduled to expire at the end of February 2008, contribute about $19 billion to CBO's baseline revenue projection in 2018. Taxes for the Leaking Underground Storage Tank Trust Fund, set to end in 2011, add about $240 million to revenues in 2018. The assessment on tobacco manufacturers enacted in the American Jobs Creation Act of 2004 expires on September 30, 2014. Because the receipts from that assessment are dedicated to the Tobacco Trust Fund, rules for the baseline require CBO to assume that the assessment is extended, which adds almost $1 billion to revenues in 2018. The tax on domestic and imported petroleum that is dedicated to the Oil Spill Liability Trust Fund, which was suspended in the early 1990s and then reinstated in the Energy Policy Act of 2005, is set to expire on December 31, 2014. Extending the tax increases baseline revenues by about $375 million in 2018. Finally, a temporary tax on coal production that is dedicated to the Black Lung Disability Trust Fund is set to expire on January 1, 2014, and, if extended, would increase revenues by about $360 million in 2018. No other expiring tax provisions are automatically extended in CBO's baseline.

Potential Effect of Extending All Expiring Provisions on the CBO Baseline

If all of the tax provisions that are scheduled to expire were extended, projected revenues would be lower than in the baseline by about $12 billion in 2008 and $91 billion in 2009. That loss would grow to $100 billion in 2010, before jumping to $385 billion in 2012 and then reaching $575 billion in 2018. For the entire period from 2009 to 2018, revenues would be reduced by about $3.8 trillion. That estimate includes interactions between extending the higher exemption levels for the AMT and the provisions of EGTRRA and JGTRRA that affect individual income taxes. (All of those amounts include the effects that refundable tax credits have on outlays.)

Table 4-9.

Effects of Extending Tax Provisions Scheduled to Expire Before 2018

(Billions of dollars)

Tax Provision	Expiration Date	2008	2009	2010	2011	2012	2013	2014	2015	2016	2017	2018	Total, 2009-2013	Total, 2009-2018
						Provisions That Expired in 2007								
American Samoa Economic Development Credit	12/31/07	*	*	*	*	*	*	*	*	*	*	*	-0.1	-0.2
Archer Medical Savings Accounts	12/31/07	*	*	*	*	*	*	*	*	*	*	*	*	*
Basis Adjustment of S Corporate Stock for Donations	12/31/07	*	*	*	*	-0.1	-0.1	-0.1	-0.1	-0.1	-0.1	-0.1	-0.2	-0.6
Brownfields Remediation Expensing	12/31/07	-0.2	-0.4	-0.4	-0.3	-0.3	-0.3	-0.3	-0.3	-0.2	-0.2	-0.2	-1.6	-2.9
Combat Pay in Earned Income for Refundable Credits	12/31/07	*	*	*	*	*	*	*	*	*	*	*	-0.1	-0.1
Contributions of Book Inventory	12/31/07	0	*	*	*	*	*	*	*	*	-0.1	-0.1	-0.2	-0.4
Contributions of Food Inventory	12/31/07	*	-0.1	-0.1	-0.1	-0.1	-0.1	-0.1	-0.1	-0.1	-0.1	-0.1	-0.4	-0.9
Contributions of Real Property for Conservation Purposes	12/31/07	*	*	-0.1	-0.1	-0.1	-0.1	-0.1	-0.1	-0.1	-0.1	-0.1	-0.3	-0.9
Corporate Contributions of Computers to Schools	12/31/07	-0.1	-0.2	-0.2	-0.2	-0.2	-0.2	-0.2	-0.2	-0.3	-0.3	-0.3	-1.0	-2.3
Credit for Certain Nonbusiness Energy Property	12/31/07	-0.1	-0.4	-0.4	-0.4	-0.4	-0.4	-0.4	-0.4	-0.4	-0.4	-0.4	-1.9	-4.1
Credit for Energy Efficient Appliances	12/31/07	*	*	0	0	0	0	0	0	0	0	0	*	*
Credit for Maintaining Railroad Tracks	12/31/07	-0.1	-0.2	-0.2	-0.2	-0.2	-0.2	-0.2	-0.2	-0.2	-0.2	-0.2	-0.8	-1.7
Credit for Research and Experimentation	12/31/07	-3.0	-5.4	-6.8	-8.3	-10.0	-11.4	-12.5	-13.5	-14.6	-15.8	-17.1	-41.8	-115.3
Deduction for Domestic Production in Puerto Rico	12/31/07	-0.1	-0.1	-0.2	-0.2	-0.2	-0.2	-0.2	-0.2	-0.3	-0.3	-0.3	-0.9	-2.1
Deduction for Qualified Education Expenses	12/31/07	-0.3	-1.4	-1.3	-1.3	-1.2	-1.2	-1.1	-1.0	-0.9	-0.8	-0.8	-6.4	-11.0
Deduction for Teachers' Classroom Expenses	12/31/07	*	-0.2	-0.2	-0.2	-0.2	-0.2	-0.2	-0.2	-0.2	-0.2	-0.2	-1.0	-2.1
Deduction for State and Local Sales Taxes	12/31/07	-0.4	-3.0	-3.4	-3.5	-3.7	-3.8	-3.8	-3.9	-4.0	-4.0	-4.0	-17.4	-37.1

Continued

Table 4-9.

Continued

- -

(Billions of dollars)

Tax Provision	Expiration Date	2008	2009	2010	2011	2012	2013	2014	2015	2016	2017	2018	Total, 2009-2013	Total, 2009-2018
					Provisions That Expired in 2007 (Continued)									
Depreciation for Business Property on Indian Reservations	12/31/07	-0.1	-0.4	-0.4	-0.4	-0.4	-0.3	-0.2	-0.2	-0.2	-0.2	-0.2	-1.9	-3.1
Depreciation of Leasehold and Restaurant Equipment	12/31/07	-0.1	-0.4	-0.8	-1.3	-1.7	-2.1	-2.5	-3.0	-3.4	-3.9	-4.3	-6.3	-23.4
Depreciation Period for Motor Tracks	12/31/07	*	*	*	-0.1	-0.1	-0.1	-0.1	-0.1	-0.1	-0.1	-0.1	-0.3	-0.6
Dispositions of Electric Transmission Property	12/31/07	-0.2	-0.3	-0.3	-0.2	-0.2	-0.2	-0.2	-0.1	-0.1	-0.1	-0.1	-1.1	-1.8
Dividends of Mutual Funds	12/31/07	*	-0.1	-0.1	-0.1	-0.1	-0.1	-0.1	-0.1	-0.1	-0.1	-0.1	-0.4	-0.9
Increased AMT Exemption Amount	12/31/07	-5.5	-73.3	-71.1	-65.7	-38.1	-44.9	-52.3	-60.2	-69.5	-79.8	-91.4	-293.0	-646.2
Indian Employment Tax Credit	12/31/07	*	*	-0.1	-0.1	-0.1	-0.1	-0.1	-0.1	-0.1	-0.1	-0.1	-0.3	-0.6
Net Income Limitation for Marginal Oil and Gas Wells	12/31/07	-0.1	-0.1	-0.1	-0.1	-0.1	-0.1	-0.1	-0.1	-0.1	-0.1	-0.1	-0.6	-1.3
Parity in Mental Health Benefits	12/31/07	*	*	*	*	*	*	*	*	-0.1	-0.1	-0.1	-0.2	-0.4
Payments to Controlling Exempt Organizations	12/31/07	*	*	*	*	*	*	*	*	*	*	-0.1	-0.1	-0.3
Qualified Mortgage Bonds for Veterans' Residences	12/31/07	*	*	*	*	-0.1	-0.1	-0.1	-0.1	-0.1	-0.1	-0.1	-0.2	-0.8
Qualified Zone Academy Bonds	12/31/07	*	*	*	*	-0.1	-0.1	-0.1	-0.1	-0.1	-0.2	-0.2	-0.2	-0.9
Rum Excise Tax Revenue to Puerto Rico and the Virgin Islands	12/31/07	-0.1	-0.1	-0.1	-0.1	-0.1	-0.1	-0.1	-0.1	-0.1	-0.1	-0.1	-0.5	-1.0
Synthetic or Biomass Fuels	12/31/07	*	*	*	*	*	*	*	*	*	*	*	*	-0.1
Tax Incentives for Investment in the District of Columbia	12/31/07	*	-0.1	-0.1	-0.1	-0.1	-0.1	-0.1	-0.2	-0.2	-0.2	-0.2	-0.6	-1.4
Tax-Free Distributions from Retirement Plans for Donations	12/31/07	-0.1	-0.2	-0.2	-0.2	-0.3	-0.3	-0.3	-0.4	-0.4	-0.4	-0.4	-1.3	-3.2
Treatment of Nonrefundable Personal Credits Under the AMT	12/31/07	-0.2	-0.6	-0.7	-0.8	-0.6	-0.8	-0.9	-1.1	-1.4	-1.7	-2.1	-3.5	-10.7
Withdrawals From Retirement Plans for Military Personnel	12/31/07	*	*	*	*	*	*	*	*	*	*	*	*	*
Temporary Disaster Relief	Various[a]	-0.6	-1.2	-1.5	-2.0	-2.4	-2.7	-2.9	-3.2	-3.4	-3.6	-3.8	-9.9	-26.7

- -

Continued

Table 4-9.

Continued

- -

(Billions of dollars)

Tax Provision	Expiration Date	2008	2009	2010	2011	2012	2013	2014	2015	2016	2017	2018	Total, 2009-2013	Total, 2009-2018
							Provisions That Expire Between 2008 and 2018							
Andean Trade Preference Initiative	2/29/08	-0.1	-0.1	-0.2	-0.2	-0.2	-0.2	-0.2	-0.2	-0.2	-0.2	-0.3	-0.8	-2.0
Reporting Certain Insurance Contract Information	8/17/08	*	*	*	*	*	*	*	*	*	*	*	*	*
Caribbean Basin Trade Partnership Act	9/30/08	n.a.	*	*	*	*	*	*	*	*	*	*	-0.1	-0.3
Information for Administration of Veterans' Programs	9/30/08	n.a.	**	**	**	**	**	**	**	**	**	**	0.1	0.2
Biodiesel Credits	12/31/08	n.a.	-0.1	-0.1	-0.1	-0.2	-0.2	-0.2	-0.2	-0.2	-0.2	-0.3	-0.7	-1.8
Carryback Period for Electric Utility Companies	12/31/08	n.a.	0	-0.1	*	*	*	*	*	*	*	*	-0.2	-0.4
Credit for Business Solar Energy Property	12/31/08	n.a.	*	-0.1	-0.1	-0.1	-0.1	-0.1	-0.1	-0.1	-0.1	-0.1	-0.3	-0.6
Credit for Electricity Produced From Renewable Resources	12/31/08	n.a.	-0.1	-0.3	-0.6	-0.9	-1.3	-1.7	-2.1	-2.7	-3.4	-3.9	-3.2	-16.9
Credit for Energy-Efficient Homes	12/31/08	n.a.	*	*	*	*	*	*	-0.1	-0.1	-0.1	-0.1	-0.2	-0.5
Credit for Residential Solar and Fuel Cells	12/31/08	n.a.	*	*	*	*	*	*	*	*	*	*	-0.1	-0.2
Deduction for Energy-Efficient Commercial Buildings	12/31/08	n.a.	-0.1	-0.2	-0.2	-0.2	-0.2	-0.2	-0.2	-0.2	-0.2	-0.2	-0.9	-1.9
Expensing of Advanced Mine Safety Equipment	12/31/08	n.a.	*	*	*	*	*	*	*	**	**	**	-0.1	*
Expensing of Film and TV Productions	12/31/08	n.a.	*	-0.1	-0.1	-0.1	-0.1	*	*	*	*	*	-0.4	-0.5
FUTA Surtax of 0.2 Percentage Points	12/31/08	n.a.	1.1	1.5	1.5	1.3	1.0	0.7	0.5	0.3	0.1	0.4	6.4	8.5
Generalized System of Preferences	12/31/08	n.a.	-0.6	-0.9	-0.9	-1.0	-1.0	-1.1	-1.2	-1.2	-1.3	-1.4	-4.4	-10.6
Mine Rescue Team Training Credit	12/31/08	n.a.	*	*	*	*	*	*	*	*	*	*	*	*
New Markets Tax Credit	12/31/08	n.a.	-0.1	-0.3	-0.4	-0.6	-0.8	-1.0	-1.2	-1.3	-1.4	-1.6	-2.3	-8.9
Payments Between Related Controlled Foreign Corporations	12/31/08	n.a.	-0.1	-0.6	-0.7	-0.8	-0.9	-1.1	-1.2	-1.3	-1.5	-1.6	-3.3	-9.9
Qualified Methanol or Ethanol Fuel From Coal	12/31/08	n.a.	*	*	*	*	*	*	*	*	*	*	*	*
Renewable Energy Bonds	12/31/08	n.a.	*	*	*	*	*	*	*	*	*	*	*	*

- -

Continued

Table 4-9.

Continued

- -

(Billions of dollars)

Tax Provision	Expiration Date	2008	2009	2010	2011	2012	2013	2014	2015	2016	2017	2018	Total, 2009-2013	Total, 2009-2018
					Provisions That Expire Between 2008 and 2018 (Continued)									
Subpart F for Active Financing Income	12/31/08	n.a.	-1.0	-4.0	-4.6	-5.1	-5.6	-6.1	-6.8	-7.2	-7.7	-8.3	-20.3	-56.4
Tax Incentives for Diesel Fuel Production	12/31/08	n.a.	-0.1	-0.3	-0.4	-0.5	-0.5	-0.5	-0.5	-0.6	-0.6	-0.6	-1.8	-4.6
Trade Preferences for Haitian Woven Apparel	12/19/09	n.a.	n.a.	*	*	*	*	*	*	*	*	*	*	*
Additional IRA Contributions in Bankruptcy	12/31/09	n.a.	n.a.	*	*	*	*	*	*	*	*	*	*	-0.1
Alternative-Fuel Vehicle Refueling Property	12/31/09	n.a.	n.a.	*	-0.1	-0.1	-0.1	-0.1	-0.1	-0.1	-0.1	-0.1	-0.3	-0.6
Credit for Certain Diesel Fuel Production	12/31/09	n.a.	n.a.	*	*	*	*	*	**	**	**	**	*	*
Credit for Coke Production	12/31/09	n.a.	n.a.	*	*	*	*	*	*	*	*	*	*	-0.1
Empowerment and Community Renewal Zone Incentives	12/31/09	n.a.	n.a.	-0.3	-1.0	-1.1	-1.2	-1.2	-1.3	-1.4	-1.5	-1.6	-3.5	-10.4
Exclusion of Gain on Brownfield Transactions	12/31/09	n.a.	**	**	**	**	*	*	-0.1	-0.1	-0.1	-0.1	*	-0.3
Exclusion of Mortgage Debt Forgiveness	12/31/09	n.a.	n.a.	*	-0.1	-0.1	-0.1	-0.1	-0.1	-0.1	-0.1	-0.1	-0.3	-0.8
Hybrid Heavy Truck Credit	12/31/09	n.a.	n.a.	*	-0.2	-0.2	-0.2	-0.2	-0.2	-0.2	-0.2	-0.2	-0.5	-1.4
Qualified Green Building Bonds	12/31/09	n.a.	n.a.	*	*	*	*	*	*	*	*	*	*	*
Tax Incentives for Alternative Fuels	12/31/09	n.a.	n.a.	-0.3	-0.3	-0.3	-0.6	-0.7	-0.8	-0.9	-1.0	-1.1	-1.5	-5.9
Alcohol Fuel Tax Credit	12/31/10	n.a.	n.a.	n.a.	-3.6	-5.3	-6.0	-6.7	-7.5	-8.4	-9.4	-10.5	-14.9	-57.5
Alternative Motor Vehicle Credit	12/31/10	n.a.	n.a.	n.a.	*	-0.1	-0.1	-0.1	-0.1	-0.1	-0.1	-0.1	-0.2	-0.7
Credit for Lean Burn and Qualified Hybrid Vehicles	12/31/10	n.a.	n.a.	n.a.	*	-0.1	-0.1	-0.2	-0.2	-0.2	-0.1	-0.1	-0.2	-1.0
Deduction for Private Mortgage Insurance	12/31/10	n.a.	n.a.	n.a.	*	-0.2	-0.2	-0.2	-0.2	-0.1	*	**	-0.5	-0.9
Estate and Gift Tax Changes	12/31/10	n.a.	-1.5	-3.2	-33.4	-66.7	-75.9	-83.3	-90.1	-96.9	-104.5	-112.3	-180.7	-667.8
Exclusion of Benefits to Volunteer Firefighters and EMRs	12/31/10	n.a.	n.a.	n.a.	*	-0.1	-0.1	-0.1	-0.1	-0.1	-0.1	-0.1	-0.2	-0.9
Exclusion of Gain on Sale of Certain Residences	12/31/10	n.a.	n.a.	n.a.	*	*	*	*	*	*	*	*	*	*
Five-Year Amortization of Music Copyrights	12/31/10	n.a.	n.a.	n.a.	*	*	*	*	*	*	*	*	*	*

- -

Continued

Table 4-9.

Continued

- -

(Billions of dollars)

Tax Provision	Expiration Date	2008	2009	2010	2011	2012	2013	2014	2015	2016	2017	2018	Total, 2009-2013	Total, 2009-2018
						Provisions That Expire Between 2008 and 2018 (Continued)								
Natural Gas Distribution Lines Treated as 15-Year Property	12/31/10	n.a.	n.a.	n.a.	*	-0.1	-0.1	-0.1	-0.2	-0.2	-0.2	-0.3	-0.2	-1.1
Income Tax Provisions of EGTRRA	12/31/10	n.a.	n.a.	n.a.	-93.2	-166.6	-168.3	-171.3	-174.9	-178.8	-183.4	-188.5	-428.2	-1325.0
Reduced Tax Rates on Capital Gains	12/31/10	n.a.	n.a.	-2.1	-11.3	3.1	-10.4	-10.5	-10.7	-10.9	-11.1	-11.4	-20.7	-75.3
Reduced Tax Rates on Dividends	12/31/10	n.a.	0.2	0.2	-5.0	-17.3	-21.8	-23.3	-25.1	-26.7	-28.5	-30.5	-43.7	-177.8
Section 179 Expensing	12/31/10	n.a.	n.a.	n.a.	-3.2	-5.4	-3.8	-2.7	-2.0	-1.4	-1.1	-0.9	-12.3	-20.4
Work Opportunity and Welfare-to-Work Credit	8/31/11	n.a.	n.a.	n.a.	-0.1	-0.4	-0.7	-0.8	-0.9	-1.0	-1.0	-1.1	-1.1	-5.9
Haiti Trade Preferences	12/19/11	n.a.	n.a.	n.a.	n.a.	*	*	*	*	*	*	*	*	-0.1
Expensing of Refinery Property	12/31/11	n.a.	n.a.	n.a.	n.a.	-0.6	-0.9	-0.7	-0.7	-0.6	-0.5	-0.5	-1.4	-4.4
African Growth Opportunity Act (Least Developed Countries)	9/30/12	n.a.	n.a.	n.a.	n.a.	n.a.	*	*	*	*	*	-0.1	*	-0.3
Credit for Past Minimum Tax Liability	12/31/12	n.a.	n.a.	n.a.	n.a.	n.a.	-0.2	-0.3	-0.2	-0.2	-0.2	-0.2	-0.2	-1.3
Depreciation of Certain Ethanol Plant Property	12/31/12	n.a.	n.a.	n.a.	n.a.	n.a.	*	*	*	*	*	*	*	-0.1
Transfer of Excess Assets in Defined-Benefit Plans	12/31/13	n.a.	n.a.	n.a.	n.a.	n.a.	n.a.	**	**	**	**	**	n.a.	0.2
Liquefied Hydrogen Fuel Incentives	9/30/14	n.a.	n.a.	n.a.	n.a.	n.a.	n.a.	n.a.	*	*	*	*	n.a.	*
Automatic Amortization for Certain Pension Plans	12/31/14	n.a.	n.a.	n.a.	n.a.	n.a.	n.a.	n.a.	*	*	*	*	n.a.	-0.1
Credit for Motor Vehicles With a Fuel Cell	12/31/14	n.a.	n.a.	n.a.	n.a.	n.a.	n.a.	n.a.	*	*	*	*	n.a.	*
Hydrogen Refueling Property	12/31/14	n.a.	n.a.	n.a.	n.a.	n.a.	n.a.	n.a.	*	*	*	*	n.a.	*
African Growth Opportunity Act	9/30/15	n.a.	n.a.	n.a.	n.a.	n.a.	n.a.	n.a.	n.a.	-0.2	-0.2	-0.2	n.a.	-0.5

- -

Continued

Table 4-9.

Continued

- -

(Billions of dollars)

Tax Provision	Expiration Date	2008	2009	2010	2011	2012	2013	2014	2015	2016	2017	2018	Total, 2009-2013	Total, 2009-2018
						All Expiring Provisions								
Interaction From Extending the EGTRRA and AMT Provisions Together		0	0	0	-16.0	-53.9	-58.0	-61.3	-64.2	-66.4	-68.3	-69.7	-127.9	-457.8
Total		**-11.6**	**-91.0**	**-100.2**	**-260.5**	**-384.9**	**-428.9**	**-455.4**	**-482.3**	**-510.5**	**-541.8**	**-575.1**	**-1,265.4**	**-3,830.4**

Source: Congressional Budget Office; Joint Committee on Taxation (JCT).

Notes: * = between -$50 million and zero; ** = between zero and $50 million; n.a. = not applicable; AMT = alternative minimum tax; FUTA = Federal Unemployment Tax Act; IRA = individual retirement account; EMRs = emergency medical responders; EGTRRA = Economic Growth and Tax Relief Reconciliation Act of 2001. These estimates assume that the expiring provisions are extended immediately rather than when they are about to expire. The provisions are assumed to be extended at the rates or levels existing at the time of expiration. The estimates include some effects on outlays for refundable tax credits. These estimates do not include debt-service costs.

When this report went to press, JCT's estimates based on the new economic projections were unavailable for certain provisions, including extending various individual income tax provisions of EGTRRA and the Jobs and Growth Tax Relief Reconciliation Act of 2003 that are scheduled to expire at the end of 2010 and changes to the exemption amount under the alternative minimum tax that expired at the end of 2007. CBO has adjusted JCT's estimates (which are based on CBO's baseline projections from a year ago) to take into account the effects of CBO's updated economic projection. Those adjustments by CBO increased the estimated loss in revenues from the extending the EGTRRA provisions by about 0.2 percent and from extending the AMT exemption by about 5 percent over the projection period. CBO will make JCT's updated estimates available when they are completed.

a. Disaster relief provisions expire at various times between 2007 and 2011.

Changes in CBO's Baseline Since August 2007

The Congressional Budget Office (CBO) projects that—absent further changes to legislation affecting spending and revenues—the deficit for fiscal year 2008 will reach $219 billion, $64 billion more than the shortfall of $155 billion that the agency projected last August (see Table A-1).[1] Relative to its previous estimates, CBO has reduced projected revenues for 2008 by $116 billion; however, that reduction is partially offset by a drop of $52 billion in projected outlays. (Because CBO's budget projections generally do not include the effects of prospective legislation, the current baseline omits some spending that is likely to occur in 2008 to finance ongoing military operations in Iraq and Afghanistan. As a result, the decrease in outlays that is currently projected will probably be offset by additional spending later this year. Other potential legislative changes, such as the passage of an economic stimulus package, also could increase the 2008 deficit.)

For the 2009–2017 period, CBO has lowered the cumulative deficit projected in its budget baseline. The major contributor to that apparent improvement in the budgetary outlook is the use of partial-year funding for military operations in Iraq and Afghanistan rather than changes in the underlying budgetary and economic environment. If the changes in outlays for activities in Iraq and Afghanistan and for the war on terrorism were excluded, CBO's current baseline would show an increase in the cumulative deficit for 2008 through 2017 of more than $850 billion.

When CBO updates its 10-year baseline projections, it divides the changes into three categories: enacted legislation; changes to CBO's economic forecast; and other, so-called technical factors.[2] The largest change in CBO's baseline for 2008 results from the enactment of new legislation, which has added an estimated $59 billion to the deficit projection for this year; that total reflects an estimated decline in revenues of $69 billion, which is offset by a projected decrease in outlays of $10 billion. Within the 5- and 10-year budget windows, the greatest adjustments to CBO's baseline projections comprise legislative and economic changes, but with opposite effects on the deficit. The impact attributable to recent legislation improves the 10-year bottom line by $502 billion, but less-favorable economic projections offset most of that improvement, increasing the cumulative deficit by $486 billion. Technical adjustments (those not directly related to changes in law or in CBO's economic outlook) have a comparatively small impact on the bottom line, decreasing the projected deficit by $12 billion in 2008 and by $159 billion over the 2008–2017 period.

---

1. In accordance with long-standing procedures, CBO's projections assume that current laws and policies remain in place. The baseline, therefore, is not intended to predict future budgetary outcomes; instead, it is meant to serve as a neutral benchmark against which lawmakers can measure the effects of proposed changes to spending and taxes.

   CBO's previous estimate of the 2008 deficit, as well as other baseline projections, was published in Congressional Budget Office, *The Budget and Economic Outlook: An Update* (August 2007).

2. The categorization of such changes should be viewed with caution. For example, legislative changes represent CBO's best estimates of the future effects of laws enacted since the previous baseline was prepared. If a new law proves to have effects different from those that CBO initially estimated, the difference will appear as a technical change in later versions of the baseline. The distinction between economic and technical changes is similarly imprecise. CBO classifies as economic changes those that result directly from alterations in the components of its economic forecast (including interest rates, inflation, and the growth of gross domestic product). Changes in other factors related to the economy (such as capital gains realizations) are shown as technical adjustments.

Table A-1.

Changes in CBO's Baseline Projections of the Deficit or Surplus Since August 2007

(Billions of dollars)

	2008	2009	2010	2011	2012	2013	2014	2015	2016	2017	Total, 2008-2012	Total, 2008-2017
Total Deficit (-) or Surplus as Projected in August 2007	-155	-215	-255	-134	62	36	65	85	58	109	-696	-343
Changes to Revenue Projections												
Legislative	-69	20	*	1	3	-1	1	1	*	*	-46	-44
Economic	-33	-60	-63	-55	-45	-44	-44	-45	-45	-45	-256	-479
Technical	-14	2	19	10	7	10	7	4	2	1	25	51
Total Revenue Changes	**-116**	**-38**	**-43**	**-44**	**-35**	**-35**	**-36**	**-40**	**-42**	**-44**	**-276**	**-472**
Changes to Outlay Projections												
Legislative												
Mandatory outlays												
Terrorism risk insurance	*	1	1	1	1	1	1	1	1	*	3	7
Medicare	4	1	-2	-3	-2	2	1	-1	-1	-1	-2	-2
Education programs	-1	*	1	2	2	*	-3	*	*	*	4	1
Other	1	1	*	*	*	*	*	-1	*	*	2	*
Subtotal, mandatory	4	3	-1	-1	1	3	-1	-1	-1	-1	7	6
Discretionary outlays												
Defense	-20	-40	-51	-56	-56	-57	-58	-60	-62	-62	-222	-521
Nondefense	5	7	7	6	5	5	4	5	4	4	29	51
Subtotal, discretionary	-15	-33	-44	-50	-51	-53	-54	-55	-57	-58	-193	-470
Net interest outlays (Debt service)	1	1	-1	-3	-6	-8	-11	-15	-18	-22	-7	-82
Subtotal, legislative	**-10**	**-29**	**-45**	**-54**	**-56**	**-58**	**-66**	**-71**	**-77**	**-81**	**-194**	**-546**
Economic												
Mandatory outlays												
Medicare	-1	-3	-4	-5	-6	-6	-7	-7	-9	-10	-19	-58
Social Security	-1	2	4	4	3	3	2	1	-1	-2	13	15
Unemployment compensation	4	7	3	-2	-2	-2	-1	-1	-1	-1	10	4
Other	-2	1	2	3	2	2	2	2	2	2	5	14
Subtotal, mandatory	*	7	5	-1	-2	-3	-4	-6	-9	-11	9	-25
Discretionary outlays	0	1	*	*	-1	*	*	1	2	3	*	7
Net interest outlays												
Debt service	*	2	4	7	9	11	14	16	19	22	22	104
Rate effect/inflation	-17	-24	-14	-8	-6	-5	-2	-1	-1	-1	-69	-80
Subtotal, net interest	-16	-22	-10	-1	3	7	12	15	18	21	-47	25
Subtotal, economic	**-16**	**-14**	**-5**	**-2**	*****	**3**	**8**	**10**	**11**	**13**	**-37**	**8**

Continued

Table A-1.

Continued

(Billions of dollars)

	2008	2009	2010	2011	2012	2013	2014	2015	2016	2017	Total, 2008-2012	Total, 2008-2017
Changes to Outlay Projections (Continued)												
Technical												
Mandatory outlays												
Medicare	-9	-4	-3	-3	-3	-4	-4	-4	-4	-6	-21	-44
Medicaid	-2	-2	-1	-1	-1	-1	-2	-2	-3	-4	-6	-19
Food Stamps	2	2	3	3	3	2	2	1	1	1	12	19
Other	1	7	4	3	3	3	2	2	2	1	19	31
Subtotal, mandatory	-7	4	3	2	2	*	-2	-3	-4	-7	4	-12
Discretionary outlays	-16	-12	-6	-3	-2	-2	-3	-3	-4	-4	-38	-53
Net interest outlays												
Debt service	-1	-2	-3	-5	-5	-6	-7	-7	-8	-9	-16	-53
Other	-2	-2	-1	1	1	2	2	2	3	3	-3	10
Subtotal, net interest	-3	-5	-4	-4	-4	-3	-4	-5	-5	-6	-19	-43
Subtotal, technical	**-26**	**-12**	**-7**	**-4**	**-4**	**-5**	**-9**	**-11**	**-13**	**-17**	**-53**	**-108**
Total Outlay Changes	**-52**	**-55**	**-57**	**-61**	**-59**	**-60**	**-67**	**-72**	**-79**	**-85**	**-284**	**-647**
Total Impact on the Deficit or Surplus[a]	**-64**	**17**	**14**	**17**	**25**	**25**	**32**	**32**	**36**	**42**	**8**	**175**
Total Deficit (-) or Surplus as Projected in January 2008	-219	-198	-241	-117	87	61	96	117	95	151	-688	-168
Memorandum:[a]												
Total Legislative Changes	-59	49	45	54	59	57	67	71	77	81	148	502
Total Economic Changes	-17	-46	-58	-52	-45	-47	-52	-55	-56	-58	-218	-486
Total Technical Changes	12	15	26	15	11	15	16	16	16	18	79	159

Source: Congressional Budget Office.

Note: * = between -$500 million and $500 million.

a.   Positive numbers indicate a decrease in the deficit or an increase in the surplus.

Changes in the Budgetary Outlook for Fiscal Year 2008

CBO's projection of the baseline deficit for 2008 has risen from the $155 billion estimated last August to $219 billion, primarily because of legislative actions. The Tax Increase Prevention Act of 2007 (Public Law 110-166) modified certain provisions of the alternative minimum tax (AMT) in an effort to reduce the number of people who would otherwise be subject to that tax. Those modifications added $70 billion to the deficit and repre-

sent the largest factor in the deficit increase for this year. The enacted appropriations for 2008 also changed the budgetary outlook. CBO's previous baseline projections were based on appropriations for 2007, as adjusted for inflation in subsequent years. Appropriations for 2008 (other than those for activities in Iraq and Afghanistan and for the war on terrorism) are projected to be about 3 percent higher than the amount indicated in the previous baseline, adding $16 billion to outlays for 2008. However, funding for activities in Iraq and Afghanistan and for the war on terrorism has been provided for only part of the year, so estimated outlays for those activities are currently $31 billion less than the amounts shown in the August baseline. (Assuming that additional funding for those activities is provided later in the year, the difference in estimated outlays will decline or disappear.) Other legislation boosted the estimated deficit for 2008 by about $4 billion.

The revised economic outlook added $33 billion to the projected deficit because tax revenues are likely to be lower than CBO previously anticipated; savings in outlays resulting from lower interest rates offset about half of the revenue loss. By contrast, technical changes in CBO's estimates reduced the projected deficit by $12 billion, mostly because CBO now estimates lower outlays for Medicare and a number of discretionary programs.

The Effects of Recent Legislation Over the 2008–2017 Period

CBO's baseline projections have been greatly affected by funding provided in 2007 and 2008 for operations in Iraq and Afghanistan. The extrapolation of such spending—and of differences in regular appropriations—accounts for most of the $502 billion in cumulative improvement in the baseline deficit projection that is attributable to legislation. By contrast, legislation involving revenues and mandatory spending has had comparatively smaller effects on CBO's updated projections for the 2008–2017 period.

Discretionary Spending

Since August, CBO's baseline projection of discretionary spending has declined by $15 billion for 2008 and by $470 billion over the 2008–2017 period as a result of legislative changes. The guidelines for projecting discretionary spending state that all appropriations provided in the most recent year should be extended and inflated throughout the 10-year baseline-projection period. Thus, the current estimates of discretionary spending through 2017 are based on funding provided to date for 2008.

Defense. The $470 billion reduction in discretionary outlays consists of two offsetting components: a large decrease in defense discretionary spending ($521 billion) and a modest increase in nondefense discretionary spending ($51 billion). The decrease in defense discretionary

outlays is largely a result of the current partial-year funding for military operations in Iraq and Afghanistan. So far this year, the Congress and the President have provided $87 billion for military operations in those countries and for other defense activities related to the war on terrorism; last year, lawmakers provided $165 billion for such purposes, most of which went to the Department of Defense (DoD). Extrapolating the lower funding appropriated thus far in 2008 for such activities reduces projected outlays in the baseline by $30 billion in the current fiscal year and by an average of $85 billion a year from 2009 to 2017 (see Table A-2). (Additional appropriations for that purpose are expected later this year, which would eliminate some or all of the difference in subsequent baselines.)

Defense appropriations for 2008, other than those related to activities in Iraq and Afghanistan and for the war on terrorism, total $500 billion, which is about $29 billion—or about 6 percent—more than the amount projected in CBO's August baseline. When extrapolated to future years, that increase adds $275 billion in outlays for defense during the 10-year period (see Table A-2).

Nondefense. As a result of recently enacted legislation, nondefense discretionary spending is showing a net increase over the previous baseline projection. Extrapolating the lower amount of funding provided for nondefense activities in Iraq and Afghanistan and for the war on terrorism reduces projected nondefense outlays by $38 billion between 2008 and 2017; however, extrapolating higher levels of funding for other nondefense appropriations provided in 2008 boosts outlays by $89 billion over the 10-year period.

The increase in other nondefense appropriations for 2008 totals about $3 billion. Among the areas that received more funding in this year's appropriations than was projected in CBO's August baseline were the Department of Veterans Affairs ($4 billion for veterans' programs, primarily for medical care); the Department of Housing and Urban Development's Community Development Fund ($3 billion for the Louisiana Road Home program, which provides grants for homeowners affected by the 2005 Gulf Coast hurricanes); federal law enforcement ($2 billion); and energy efficiency and renewable energy programs ($1 billion).

Table A-2.

Changes in CBO's Baseline Projections of Discretionary Outlays Since August 2007

(Billions of dollars)

	2008	2009	2010	2011	2012	2013	2014	2015	2016	2017	Total, 2008-2012	Total, 2008-2017
Total Discretionary Outlays as Projected in August 2007	1,120	1,165	1,195	1,223	1,239	1,271	1,300	1,330	1,366	1,392	5,942	12,601
Changes to Outlay Projections												
Legislative												
Defense												
Iraq and Afghanistan	-30	-60	-76	-84	-85	-88	-90	-92	-95	-96	-335	-796
Other appropriations	10	20	26	28	30	31	32	33	33	34	113	275
Subtotal, defense	-20	-40	-51	-56	-56	-57	-58	-60	-62	-62	-222	-521
Nondefense												
Iraq and Afghanistan	-1	-2	-3	-4	-4	-5	-5	-5	-5	-5	-14	-38
Other appropriations	6	9	10	9	9	9	9	9	9	9	43	89
Subtotal, nondefense	5	7	7	6	5	5	4	5	4	4	29	51
Subtotal, legislative	**-15**	**-33**	**-44**	**-50**	**-51**	**-53**	**-54**	**-55**	**-57**	**-58**	**-193**	**-470**
Economic												
Defense	0	*	*	*	*	*	*	1	1	2	*	5
Nondefense	0	1	*	*	*	*	*	*	1	2	*	3
Subtotal, economic	**0**	**1**	*****	*****	**-1**	*****	*****	**1**	**2**	**3**	*****	**7**
Technical												
Defense	-7	-5	-2	-2	-2	-2	-2	-2	-3	-3	-18	-30
Nondefense	-8	-7	-3	-1	*	*	-1	-1	-1	-1	-20	-22
Subtotal, technical	**-16**	**-12**	**-6**	**-3**	**-2**	**-2**	**-3**	**-3**	**-4**	**-4**	**-38**	**-53**
Total Changes to Discretionary Outlays	**-31**	**-44**	**-49**	**-53**	**-53**	**-55**	**-56**	**-57**	**-59**	**-58**	**-230**	**-515**
Total Discretionary Outlays as Projected in January 2008	1,089	1,121	1,145	1,170	1,186	1,216	1,243	1,272	1,307	1,335	5,711	12,085
Memorandum:												
Total Defense Discretionary Changes	-27	-44	-53	-58	-58	-59	-60	-61	-63	-63	-239	-547
Total Nondefense Discretionary Changes	-3	*	3	5	4	5	4	4	5	5	9	32

Source: Congressional Budget Office.

Note: * = between -$500 million and $500 million.

Other sources of discretionary funding also increased. Transportation funding (which is subject to obligation limitations set in appropriation acts) has increased by $1.5 billion for 2008 relative to the August 2007 projection.[3] Further, additional advance appropriations for 2009 were provided for certain programs; those programs received $2 billion above the amount projected in the August baseline for that year.

Agencies receiving less funding in 2008 include the Army Corps of Engineers ($1 billion less because of a reduction in funding for Gulf Coast hurricane relief and recovery) and the Federal Housing Administration ($1 billion less because of lower estimated subsidy costs). In addition, across-the-board cuts totaling $3 billion were specified in the Consolidated Appropriations Act of 2008 (P.L. 110-161) and have been extrapolated throughout the baseline period.

Mandatory Spending

Recent legislative changes that affect mandatory spending—funding determined by laws other than annual appropriation acts—have had a small net effect on CBO's baseline projections, increasing estimated spending during the years 2008 to 2017 by $6 billion. Most of that change is seen in the terrorism risk insurance and Medicare programs.

Terrorism Risk Insurance. A seven-year extension of the terrorism risk insurance program—which was originally slated to expire on December 31, 2007—was signed into law on December 26, 2007 (in the Terrorism Risk Insurance Program Reauthorization Act of 2007, P.L. 110-160). That extension resulted in a projected increase of $7 billion in spending over the 2008–2017 period. However, this program will also generate an estimated $7 billion in revenues over the same period (for further discussion of this topic, see the Revenues section below).

Medicare and SCHIP. The Transitional Medical Assistance, Abstinence Education, and Qualifying Individuals Programs Extension Act of 2007 (P.L. 110-90), as well as the Medicare, Medicaid, and SCHIP [State Children's Health Insurance Program] Extension Act of 2007

(P.L. 110-173), modified Medicare's payment systems for various providers, including inpatient hospitals, physicians, and Medicare Advantage plans. Those two laws added $4 billion to CBO's estimate of Medicare outlays in 2008 and reduced projected outlays by $6 billion from 2009 through 2017, for a total 10-year decrease in outlays of $2 billion. By extending SCHIP, Public Law 110-173 also added $1 billion in outlays for that program in 2008.

Education Programs. The College Cost Reduction and Access Act of 2007 (P.L. 110-84) made significant changes to federal financial assistance programs related to postsecondary education. It reduced the government's payments to lenders in the Federal Family Education Loan Program and to guaranty agencies and modified fees for lenders; much of those savings were used to reduce the cost of federal loans for certain types of borrowers and to increase funding for the Pell Grant Program. As a result, the overall net impact of those changes on the federal budget was minimal over the 10-year period.

Revenues

Legislation enacted since August has had a modest effect on CBO's revenue projection—reducing receipts by $44 billion from 2008 through 2017. That change is dominated by a $69 billion decline in revenues in 2008 that is partially offset by a $20 billion increase in 2009. Nearly all of that adjustment—about $50 billion, in the estimation of CBO and the Joint Committee on Taxation—derives from the enactment of the Tax Increase Prevention Act of 2007. That act raised the amount of income exempted from the AMT in 2007. CBO estimates that, as a result, individual income tax receipts will decline by $70 billion in 2008 and increase by almost $19 billion in 2009.[4]

The Terrorism Risk Insurance Program Reauthorization Act of 2007 increased revenues by an estimated $7 billion between 2008 and 2017. In addition to extending the

---

3. An obligation limitation is a provision of a law that restricts the use of budget authority that would otherwise be available for obligation. Typically, an obligation limitation is included in an appropriation act and affects budget authority that has been provided in an authorization act.

4. In CBO's baseline, a one-year increase in the AMT exemption causes revenues to rise in the year following the largest downward effect. In the August baseline, taxpayers affected by the AMT were assumed to increase their estimated payments most significantly in 2008 in response to their higher tax liability for 2007. With the higher exemption amount now in effect for tax liabilities in 2007—but not for subsequent years—CBO projects that an increase in estimated payments will occur in 2009.

program, that act increased receipts expected over the next 10 years by raising the assessments to be paid in the event of a covered act of terrorism and accelerating the payment of those premiums to the government.

On net, the Energy Independence and Security Act of 2007 (P.L. 110-140) had a negligible impact on revenues—reducing excise tax receipts by an estimated $2 billion and increasing receipts from unemployment taxes by an estimated $2 billion between 2008 and 2017. The decline in excise tax receipts is attributable primarily to lower revenues from the gasoline tax, a result of increased Corporate Average Fuel Economy standards. In addition, the act's requirement for the use of renewable fuels will reduce revenues for the first few years because of higher excise tax credits for producers of ethanol; CBO estimates, however, that the requirement will cause revenues to increase after 2011 because the lower energy content of ethanol relative to gasoline will result in the sale of more fuel. The legislation also increased projected receipts from unemployment taxes, mainly in 2008, by extending the Federal Unemployment Tax Act surtax of 0.2 percent through 2008.

Net Interest
In all, legislative changes reduced CBO's projection of the cumulative deficit for the 2008–2017 period by an estimated $420 billion. That decrease, in turn, shrinks projected debt-service costs over the 10-year period by $82 billion.

The Effects of Economic Changes Over the 2008–2017 Period
Changes to CBO's economic assumptions increase the estimated deficit for 2008 by $17 billion relative to the previous baseline and boost the cumulative deficit for 2008 through 2017 by $486 billion. Those changes are largely attributable to reductions in projected revenues.

Revenues
CBO's current outlook for the economy incorporates a slowdown in economic growth in the final quarter of 2007 and in 2008 and a slight reduction in the economy's potential rate of growth over the next 10 years. The revised economic outlook reduces revenue projections in 2008 and 2009 by $33 billion and $60 billion, respectively, and lowers revenue projections between 2010 and 2017 by $385 billion. Over the entire 10-year budget period, the net result of changes in the economic outlook

is a reduction of $479 billion in projected receipts, most of which stems from lower projections of corporate income tax receipts.

Corporate Income Taxes. Changes in CBO's projections of corporate profits account for most of the $313 billion change in CBO's projection of corporate income tax receipts over the 2008–2017 period. Currently, CBO projects lower economic profits than it projected in August, which has the effect of lowering taxable profits. Taxable profits also decline because CBO increased its projection of the share of profits that U.S. firms earn abroad—often termed "rest-of-world profits"—which are taxed at a very low effective U.S. tax rate. The effects of lower taxable profits on receipts were only partially offset by a reduction in CBO's projection of profits earned by S corporations (which are subject to the individual income tax) and lower corporate tax payments to state and local governments (which are deducted from profits before taxes are calculated).[5]

Individual Income Taxes. For 2008 and beyond, CBO's projected pattern of revenues from the individual income tax reflects steady growth in personal income, punctuated by scheduled changes to tax law in specific years. Lower anticipated wages and salaries in the near term continue to cause estimated receipts to be lower in 2009. Beyond 2009, wages and salaries in CBO's forecast continue to be below levels projected in August, but interest income is higher. Those factors result in a $39 billion decline in receipts from individual income taxes over the 2008–2017 period, virtually all of which occurs between 2008 and 2011. (After 2011, the effects largely offset one another).

Social Insurance Taxes. As a result of lowered projections for wages and salaries over the 10-year budget window, CBO now projects $84 billion less in social insurance tax receipts than it did in the August baseline.

Excise Taxes. According to CBO's estimates, changes to economic projections that have been made since the

---

5. An S corporation is a domestically owned corporation with no more than 100 owners who have elected to pay taxes under Subchapter S of the Internal Revenue Code. Specifically, an S corporation is taxed like a partnership: It is exempt from the corporate income tax, but its owners pay individual income taxes on all of the firm's income, even if some of the earnings are retained by the firm.

August baseline reduce excise tax revenues by $14 billion between 2008 and 2017. A rise in energy prices as well as a lower forecast of gross domestic product (GDP) result in a drop in the projections of motor fuel consumption and excise taxes on that fuel.

Estate and Gift Taxes. Slowing growth in wealth that is attributable largely to slower economic growth over the next few years reduces CBO's estimate of receipts from estate and gift taxes by about $10 billion over the 10-year period.

Other Receipts. Because of changes to CBO's economic forecast, the agency lowered its projection of profits earned by the Federal Reserve System by almost $25 billion over the 2008–2017 period as compared with its August baseline. That change stems from CBO's projection of less currency in circulation, relative to GDP, in 2009 (which reduces the value of the Federal Reserve's portfolio of securities) and lower interest rates (which reduce the return on the Federal Reserve's portfolio of Treasury securities). Projections of customs duties are about $6 billion higher for the 2008–2017 period compared with CBO's August projections. That change is largely attributable to anticipated increases in non-petroleum-based imports and partially offset by a decrease in CBO's projection of oil imports (which are taxed on the basis of volume rather than price).

Mandatory Spending

On balance, changes to CBO's economic outlook have had a relatively small effect on its current projections of mandatory spending. Such changes—consisting of several offsetting adjustments—reduce projected spending by a net of $25 billion over the 2008–2017 period.

Medicare. A decrease in the projected growth in wages and other labor costs has led to a reduction of $58 billion in projected spending for Medicare relative to the August baseline. Growth in wages and other labor costs affects the formulas used to calculate payments under Medicare's fee schedules for physicians and inpatient hospitals, among other payment systems. As a result, lower growth in labor costs translates directly into lower fees paid to providers and thus less spending on Medicare.

Social Security. Economic changes increase projected spending for Social Security by $15 billion from 2008 through 2017. The cost-of-living adjustment (COLA) that Social Security beneficiaries received in January 2008

is slightly lower (0.2 percentage points) than the increase CBO projected last August; as a result, CBO expects outlays for 2008 to be nearly $1 billion less than previously projected. However, CBO now anticipates that the COLA in January 2009 will be 0.8 percentage points above its August estimate, which will increase the projected growth of benefit payments in the baseline beginning in 2009. Over the 2009–2017 period, changes in the COLA will raise baseline Social Security outlays by $36 billion, CBO estimates. However, revisions to CBO's projections of the growth of wages and salaries reduce projected growth in benefit payments from 2008 to 2017, shaving a little more than $20 billion from estimated benefits during that period.

Unemployment Compensation. Projected outlays for unemployment compensation are up by $10 billion over CBO's August projections for the 2008–2012 period and up by $4 billion over the entire 10-year projection period. In the short term, an anticipated increase in the unemployment rate leads to higher payments for unemployment compensation. Those increased costs are mitigated somewhat by CBO's forecast of wage growth, which is lower in the short term than it was in August, thereby resulting in lower average benefits over the entire baseline period.

Other Programs. Average Food Stamp benefits are projected to increase from 2008 to 2017, boosting outlays by $10 billion over the 10-year baseline period. The maximum benefit under the Food Stamp program automatically rises each year, based on the June-over-June increase in the cost of the Department of Agriculture's Thrifty Food Plan. To estimate that annual change, CBO uses the consumer price index for the cost of food purchased for consumption at home. Relative to its August projections, CBO now projects that the index will be higher over the 2008–2010 period, leading to higher estimated per-person benefits. A small portion of the economic change is also attributable to a forecast of higher unemployment.

In addition, CBO has reduced its projection of spending for Medicaid over the 2008–2017 period by $6 billion for economic reasons. On the basis of lowered projections for wage growth and hospital costs, CBO reduced its projection of Medicaid spending by a total of $20 billion. Those reductions were offset by slightly higher projections for inflation and medical cost growth over the 10-year period, and higher projections of unemployment between 2008 and 2011, which have the effect of increasing projected Medicaid spending by $14 billion.

Discretionary Spending
CBO projects discretionary budget authority by using two measures of inflation: the GDP price index (which covers changes in price for all goods and services that contribute to GDP) and the employment cost index (ECI) for wages and salaries. Since its August baseline was published, CBO has decreased its estimate of the ECI by 0.6 percentage points for 2009 and 0.5 percentage points for 2010. The resulting decreases in projected spending are more than offset by a small increase in the GDP price index and adjustments to certain other calculations used to extrapolate discretionary spending. In total, revisions attributed to economic factors add $7 billion to projected discretionary outlays over the 2008–2017 period.

Net Interest
Economic revisions to CBO's projections of spending on net interest have two components: the effects of changes in the agency's economic outlook related to interest rates and inflation and the effects of changes in debt-service costs resulting from the impact of all other economic changes on deficits in the baseline. Although the first factor has reduced projected outlays for net interest, the second factor has increased them—resulting in a net increase of $25 billion between 2008 and 2017.

In CBO's current economic outlook, the interest rates on 3-month Treasury bills and 10-year Treasury notes are lower in 2008 and 2009 than they were in last August's forecast. For those years, the rate projected for 3-month Treasury bills has dropped by about 160 basis points and 90 basis points, respectively (a basis point is one one-hundredth of a percentage point). The rate on 10-year notes has fallen by 100 basis points and 50 basis points for those years. As a result, CBO anticipates that net interest will total $41 billion less during those two years than it projected in its previous baseline. In the other direction, CBO has boosted its estimate of inflation by 0.5 percentage points for 2008, which causes projected outlays for the Treasury's inflation-protected securities to increase by $3 billion that same year. Overall, revisions to interest rates and estimates of inflation reduce outlays for net interest in the baseline by $80 billion over the 2008–2017 period.

Changes in the economic outlook—primarily those leading to estimates of lower revenues—have increased the

government's projected borrowing needs, thereby raising estimated debt-service costs between 2008 and 2017 by $104 billion.

The Effects of Technical Changes Over the 2008–2017 Period
Technical changes cause revisions to the baseline that are not directly attributable to newly enacted laws or changes in CBO's economic forecast. Since August, such revisions have generally raised projections of revenues and lowered estimates of outlays over the 2008–2017 period, thereby reducing this year's estimated deficit by $12 billion and the 10-year cumulative deficit by $159 billion.

Mandatory Spending
Technical revisions have reduced CBO's estimate of mandatory outlays in its current baseline by $7 billion in 2008 and by a total of $12 billion through 2017. The largest changes involve Medicare, Medicaid, and the Food Stamp program.

Medicare. Changes in mandatory spending for Medicare that result from technical adjustments lower outlays by $44 billion (0.8 percent) over the 2008–2017 period as compared with the August 2007 baseline; the largest reduction ($9 billion) occurs in 2008. The most significant technical changes to projected spending for Medicare were made in spending for Part D, the prescription drug program, because bids from private plans to provide the prescription drug benefit came in lower than expected for 2008. Those results translated into reductions in projected spending throughout the baseline period. CBO also lowered its estimate for 2008 to reflect larger-than-expected refunds to such plans for payments made in 2006. (Initial payments to prescription drug plans are based on projected expenses, and adjustments are made to compensate for under- or overpayments; actual costs in 2006 were lower than projected.)

Medicaid. CBO has made technical changes that reduce its projection of Medicaid spending for the 2008–2017 period by $19 billion (or 0.6 percent). On the basis of lower-than-expected outlays in 2007 (about $2 billion lower than anticipated in the August baseline), updated information about the distribution of spending across service categories, and the issuance of final regulations related to Medicaid payment policy for government providers, CBO has reduced its projections of spending for Medicaid by a total of $52 billion over the 10-year period. Those changes were partially offset by projected increases in program enrollment and in payment rates to providers (which raised estimated outlays by $26 billion over the 10-year projection period) and other revisions that increased CBO's estimate of spending by a total of $7 billion between 2008 and 2017.

Food Stamps. Between 2008 and 2017, projected outlays for the Food Stamp program have grown by $19 billion relative to CBO's previous projections. That increase stems from a boost in CBO's estimate of participation in the program, which has been higher than expected for the past several years, despite falling unemployment rates.

Other Revisions. Other technical adjustments have increased CBO's estimate of mandatory spending in the baseline by $1 billion for 2008 and by a total of $31 billion through 2017. The largest of those increases in projected spending are attributable to the student loan program ($14 billion—largely because of changes to projections of loan volume through 2017) and the Civil Service Retirement Fund ($10 billion—stemming from an increase in the expected number of annuitants as well as an adjustment in the assumed average benefit at retirement).

Discretionary Spending

Technical changes to CBO's baseline projections for discretionary programs decreased outlays by $53 billion over the 2008–2017 period, with the majority of that reduction occurring in 2008 ($16 billion) and 2009 ($12 billion).

Defense. CBO has lowered its estimate of defense outlays by $7 billion in 2008 and by $30 billion over the 10-year period, reflecting a lower rate of spending in recent months than previously anticipated. That change also reflects smaller accruals for the TRICARE For Life program, offset by slight increases in military construction in 2009 and 2010 that result from adjustments in spending rates for base realignment and closure activities.

Nondefense. Estimated outlays for surface transportation are $18 billion lower over the 10-year baseline period than CBO projected in August; CBO has adjusted its projections because of overestimations of spending in the past several years. The remaining reduction in the nondefense discretionary category reflects smaller adjustments in many other areas of the federal budget.

Revenues

Adjustments to CBO's technical assumptions increase projected revenues by $51 billion from 2008 through 2017. Such changes lower projected receipts by almost $14 billion in 2008 but increase receipts by an average of $7 billion a year thereafter. Higher estimates of receipts from individual income, social insurance, and estate and gift taxes are partially offset by lower estimates of corporate and excise taxes.

Individual Income Taxes. Technical changes to CBO's projection of individual income taxes increase revenues by a total of $18 billion over the 2008–2017 period. Most of the effect of those changes results from CBO's extending by one year, through 2009, its projection of increases in receipts that are attributable to a recent unexplained strength in collections. CBO assumes that the effect gradually diminishes over the next few years because of trends indicating that, over the long term, most forms of taxable income return to their historical relationship to GDP. Other technical changes, mostly affecting the timing of tax collections, affect receipts in specific years. These changes offset most of the effects of the technical change in 2009 that arises from the adjustment for unexplained collections.

Corporate Income Taxes. Technical changes account for $18 billion of CBO's projected decline in corporate tax revenues since August. Much of that decrease results from updated data about historical interest payments on back taxes that are lower than CBO had estimated in August. In addition, CBO lowered its projections of receipts from 2008 through 2010 because of unexpectedly low collections in the final quarter of 2007. CBO assumes that the effect gradually diminishes over the subsequent several years. Those factors were partially offset by two other changes: an increase in the projection of profitable firms' earnings resulting from updated historical data as well as higher estimates of corporate capital gains realizations for 2006. CBO assumes that, over time, the increase will decline gradually as capital gains return to historical norms relative to GDP.

Social Insurance Taxes. Technical changes to CBO's projection of social insurance taxes increased receipts by almost $26 billion over the 2008–2017 period, mostly because of revised historical data on taxable wages for Social Security and projected increases in the amount of unemployment benefits to be paid. CBO assumes that such higher unemployment benefits would cause states to replenish their trust funds for unemployment insurance (those amounts are considered to be federal revenues).

Estate and Gift Taxes. CBO's current projection of estate and gift taxes is almost $29 billion higher than that indicated in its August baseline because of technical changes. That revision was caused partly by higher actual collections in 2007 than CBO originally projected. CBO assumes that such higher collections will continue throughout the projection period, adjusted for differences in tax liability arising from changes in rates and exemption levels. CBO also lowered its projection of the value of deductions taken by estates before the tax is calculated, which raised the projection of the value of taxable estates and the resulting tax receipts.

Other Receipts. Technical changes to CBO's projections of other tax sources lower the collective projection of receipts by $4 billion over the 2008–2017 period. CBO projects that excise taxes will be $6 billion lower than indicated in its August baseline primarily because of lower-than-expected collections of taxes on heavy trucks. Partially offsetting about $2 billion of that reduction are higher customs duties, based on larger-than-expected recent collections.

Net Interest
Because technical revisions increase revenues in the baseline by $51 billion from 2008 to 2017 and lower outlays by $55 billion for the same period, projected debt-service costs decline by $53 billion over those years. Other technical changes to net interest total $10 billion (0.3 percent) over the 10-year period.

Trust Funds and Measures of Debt

The federal government uses a number of accounting mechanisms to link earmarked receipts (money designated for a specific purpose) with the expenditure of those resources. Trust funds—for example, those for Social Security—are one such mechanism. Others include special funds (such as the Department of Defense's fund used to finance its health care program for military retirees) and revolving funds (for example, the federal employees' life insurance fund). Trust funds are simply those designated as such by law, and there is no substantive difference between trust funds and those other types of funds.

Trust funds and other government funds with receipts in excess of amounts needed for current expenditures are credited with nonmarketable Treasury debt known as government account series securities. Currently, about $3.9 trillion in such securities is outstanding, which is a measure of how much receipts have exceeded outlays over time for the programs financed through those funds. The value of outstanding government account securities—that is, debt held by government accounts—is combined with the amount of debt held by the public (described in Chapter 1) in two measures of the government's debt: gross federal debt and debt subject to limit.

Trust Funds

In total, the federal budget includes more than 200 trust funds, although fewer than a dozen account for most of the government's trust fund dollars. Among the largest are the two Social Security trust funds (the Old-Age and Survivors Insurance Trust Fund and the Disability Insurance Trust Fund) and the funds dedicated to civil service retirement, Medicare's Hospital Insurance program (Part A), and military retirement.

When a trust fund receives payroll taxes or other income that is not currently needed to pay benefits, the Treasury credits the fund and uses the excess cash for other purposes. As a result, the government borrows less from the public than it would in the absence of those excess funds. The process is reversed when revenues for a trust fund program fall short of expenses.

Including in the budget totals the cash receipts and expenditures of trust funds along with those of other federal programs is useful for assessing how federal activities affect the economy and capital markets. Therefore, the Congressional Budget Office (CBO), the Administration's Office of Management and Budget, and many other fiscal analysts focus on the total deficit or surplus rather than on the deficit or surplus with or without particular trust funds.

In CBO's current baseline, trust funds as a whole are projected to run a surplus of $262 billion in 2008 (see Table B-1). That balance is affected, however, by interest and other sums transferred from other parts of the budget. Such intragovernmental transfers, which are projected to total $544 billion in 2008, reallocate costs from one category of the budget to another but do not directly change the total deficit or the government's borrowing needs. If intragovernmental transfers are excluded and only income from sources outside the government is counted, the trust funds as a whole are projected to run annual deficits from 2008 through 2018 that grow from $281 billion to $700 billion; about two-thirds of those deficits is attributable to the Medicare trust funds.

Although the full budgetary impact of the aging of the baby-boom generation will not be felt during the 2008–2018 period, CBO's baseline provides an initial indication of those coming budgetary pressures. Examining the differences over the next 10 years between projected receipts and outlays for the Social Security trust funds reveals those strains. Receipts, excluding interest, are

Table B-1.

CBO's Baseline Projections of Trust Fund Surpluses

(Billions of dollars)

	Actual 2007	2008	2009	2010	2011	2012	2013	2014	2015	2016	2017	2018
Social Security	187	197	199	210	226	238	244	250	253	254	253	249
Medicare												
Hospital Insurance (Part A)	17	16	11	14	8	16	6	2	-5	-22	-25	-30
Supplementary Medical Insurance (Part B)	6	2	7	7	2	13	4	6	9	1	9	15
Subtotal, Medicare	23	18	19	21	9	28	10	8	4	-21	-17	-15
Military Retirement	8	19	26	29	32	35	39	43	47	51	56	61
Civilian Retirement[a]	12	28	27	26	26	26	26	26	26	26	27	27
Unemployment Insurance	9	4	-3	3	10	11	10	9	8	8	7	8
Highway and Mass Transit	1	-3	-5	-8	-9	-10	-11	-11	-12	-13	-14	-14
Airport and Airway	*	*	*	*	1	1	2	2	2	3	4	3
Other[b]	5	1	2	2	2	2	2	2	2	2	2	3
Total Trust Fund Surplus	**245**	**262**	**264**	**285**	**298**	**331**	**321**	**328**	**330**	**310**	**318**	**322**
Intragovernmental Transfers to Trust Funds[c]	505	544	578	611	657	687	740	790	843	912	970	1,022
Net Budgetary Impact of Trust Fund Programs[d]	**-260**	**-281**	**-314**	**-327**	**-359**	**-356**	**-418**	**-462**	**-513**	**-602**	**-652**	**-700**

Source: Congressional Budget Office.

Note: * = between -$500 million and $500 million.

a. Includes Civil Service Retirement, Foreign Service Retirement, and several smaller retirement trust funds.

b. Primarily trust funds for railroad workers' retirement, federal employees' health and life insurance, Superfund, and various insurance programs for veterans.

c. Includes interest paid to trust funds, payments from the Treasury's general fund to the Supplementary Medical Insurance program, the employer's share of payments for employees' retirement, lump-sum payments to the Civil Service and Military Retirement Trust Funds, taxes on Social Security benefits, and smaller miscellaneous payments.

d. Negative numbers indicate that the trust fund transactions add to total budget deficits or reduce total surpluses.

projected to exceed expenditures in each year of the period, but under current policies, the amount by which they do so will peak at $86 billion in 2012 and then decline steadily to about $13 billion in 2018 (see Figure B-1). The net surplus of the Social Security trust funds, including interest payments, will peak in 2016 and decline thereafter. As a result, the capacity of the Social Security system to offset some of the deficit in the rest of the budget will begin to dwindle.

Measures of Federal Debt

Debt held by the public (which is discussed in Chapter 1) is the most meaningful measure to use in assessing the relationship between federal debt and the economy because it represents the amount that the government has

borrowed in the financial markets to pay for its operations and activities; such borrowing competes with other participants in credit markets for financial resources. By contrast, debt held by trust funds and other government accounts represents internal transactions of the government and has no effect on credit markets. Combined, debt held by the public and debt held by government accounts are the basis of two other measures of debt: gross federal debt and debt subject to limit.

Gross Federal Debt

Gross federal debt comprises both debt held by the public and debt issued to government accounts. CBO projects that under current law, gross federal debt will increase in every year of the 2009–2018 period, reaching $12.7 trillion in 2018—roughly 40 percent more than its total of

Figure B-1.

CBO's Baseline Projections of Surpluses in Social Security's Trust Funds

(Billions of dollars)

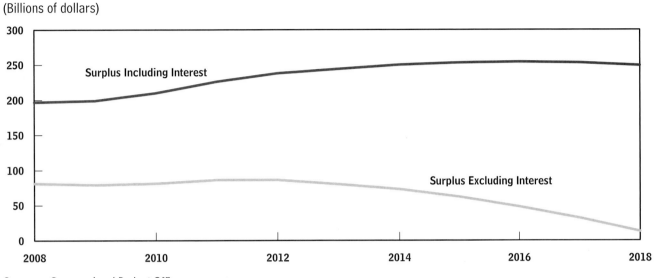

Source: Congressional Budget Office.

$9.0 trillion at the end of 2007 (see Table B-2). Nearly all of that increase reflects debt held by government accounts, which is projected to grow from $3.9 trillion in 2007 to $7.7 trillion in 2018.

Debt Subject to Limit

The Treasury's authority to issue debt is restricted by a statutory ceiling. Although that limit covers both debt held by the public and that held by government accounts, it does not include debt issued by agencies other than the Treasury (such as the $23 billion in debt issued by the Tennessee Valley Authority and the $14 billion issued by the Federal Financing Bank).[1] The current debt ceiling,

which was set in September 2007 in Public Law 110-91, is $9.815 trillion. By CBO's estimates, under current policies, that ceiling will be reached in the spring or summer of 2009 (see Figure B-2). That point will occur sooner if changes in law reduce projected revenues or increase spending over the next 18 months.

---

1.   The Federal Financing Bank is a government entity that was established to centralize and reduce the cost of federal borrowing. In 2004, the bank issued $14 billion in securities to the Civil Service Retirement and Disability Fund when the Treasury's borrowing reached the $7.384 trillion ceiling on debt.

Table B-2.

CBO's Baseline Projections of Federal Debt

(Billions of dollars)

	Actual 2007	2008	2009	2010	2011	2012	2013	2014	2015	2016	2017	2018
Debt Held by the Public	5,035	5,232	5,443	5,698	5,827	5,751	5,701	5,613	5,503	5,414	5,269	5,050
Debt Held by Government Accounts												
Social Security	2,181	2,378	2,577	2,788	3,014	3,252	3,496	3,746	4,000	4,254	4,506	4,755
Other government accounts[a]	1,735	1,822	1,910	2,009	2,109	2,233	2,343	2,457	2,573	2,673	2,781	2,899
Total	3,916	4,200	4,487	4,797	5,123	5,485	5,839	6,203	6,573	6,927	7,287	7,654
Gross Federal Debt	8,951	9,432	9,930	10,495	10,950	11,236	11,540	11,817	12,076	12,341	12,556	12,704
Debt Subject to Limit[b]	8,921	9,403	9,901	10,466	10,921	11,207	11,511	11,788	12,048	12,313	12,528	12,676

Source: Congressional Budget Office.

Note: Figures are as of the end of the year.

a. Mainly Civil Service Retirement and Disability, Military Retirement, Medicare, and Unemployment Insurance Trust Funds.

b. Differs from the gross federal debt primarily because debt issued by agencies other than the Treasury is excluded from the debt limit. The current debt limit is $9,815 billion.

Figure B-2.

CBO's Baseline Projection of Debt Subject to Limit, October 2006 to September 2009

(Trillions of dollars)

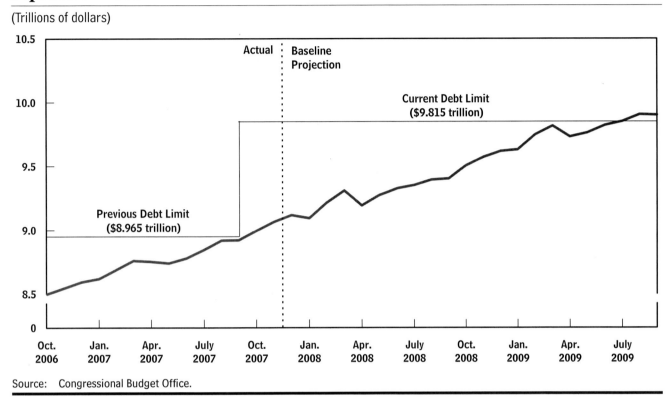

Source: Congressional Budget Office.

How Changes in Economic Assumptions Can Affect Budget Projections

The federal budget is highly sensitive to economic conditions. Revenues depend on the amount of taxable income, including wages and salaries, other (nonwage) income, and corporate profits. Those types of income generally rise or fall in tandem with overall economic activity. Spending for many mandatory programs is pegged to inflation, either directly (as with Social Security) or indirectly (as with Medicaid). In addition, the Treasury regularly refinances portions of the government's outstanding debt—and issues more debt to finance any new deficit spending—at market interest rates. Thus, the amount that the federal government spends for interest on its debt is directly tied to those rates.

To show how assumptions about the economy can affect projections of the federal budget, the Congressional Budget Office (CBO) has constructed simplified "rules of thumb." The rules provide rough orders of magnitude for gauging how changes in individual economic variables, taken in isolation, would affect the budget totals. (The rules of thumb are not intended to substitute for a full analysis of an alternative economic forecast.)

This illustration addresses four variables:

■ Real (inflation-adjusted) growth of the nation's gross domestic product (GDP),

■ Interest rates,

■ Inflation, and

■ Wages and salaries as a share of GDP.

For real growth, CBO's rule of thumb shows the effects of rates that are 0.1 percentage point lower each year, beginning in January 2008, than the rates assumed for the agency's baseline budget projections. (Those projections

are outlined in Chapter 1; the economic assumptions that underpin them are described in Chapter 2.) The rules of thumb for interest rates and inflation assume that those rates are 1 percentage point higher each year, also starting in January 2008, than the rates in the baseline. The final rule of thumb assumes that, beginning in January 2008, wages and salaries as a percentage of GDP are 1 percentage point larger each year than those projected in the baseline. Correspondingly, corporate profits are assumed to be 1 percentage point smaller each year relative to GDP. (The scenario incorporates no changes in projected levels of nominal or real GDP.)

Each rule of thumb is roughly symmetrical. Thus, if economic growth was higher or interest rates, inflation, or wages and salaries as a percentage of GDP were lower than CBO projects, the effects would be about the same as those shown here, but with the opposite sign.

The calculations that appear in this appendix merely illustrate the impact that such changes can have. CBO chose the variations of 0.1 percentage point or 1 percentage point solely for the sake of simplicity. Those changes do not necessarily indicate the extent to which actual economic performance might differ from CBO's assumptions. For example, although the rule of thumb for real GDP shows the effects of a 0.1 percentage point change in the average rate of growth over the next 10 years, the standard deviation for growth rates of real GDP over 10-year periods is roughly five times larger, or about 0.5 percentage points.[1] Extrapolating from small, incremental rule-of-thumb calculations to much larger changes would

---

1. A conventional way to measure past variability is to use the standard deviation. In the case of GDP growth, CBO calculates the extent to which actual growth over 10-year periods differs from the post–World War II average. The standard deviation is the size of the difference that is exceeded about one-third of the time.

be inadvisable, however, because the size of the effect of a larger change is not necessarily a multiple of a smaller change.

The other rules of thumb—each of which considers an average change of 1 percentage point from the assumption used for the baseline projection—are much closer to historical deviations for those variables. The standard deviation for the 10-year average of real interest rates is about 1.3 percentage points. Standard deviations for inflation and for wages and salaries as a percentage of GDP are each about 2 percentage points, slightly less than twice the change incorporated in CBO's rules of thumb.

Lower Real Growth

Stronger economic growth improves the budget's bottom line, and weaker economic growth worsens it. The first rule of thumb illustrates the impact of slightly weaker-than-expected economic growth on federal revenues and outlays.[2]

CBO's baseline reflects an assumption that real GDP grows by 1.7 percent in calendar year 2008, by 2.8 percent in 2009, and by an average of 2.7 percent annually from 2010 to 2018. Subtracting 0.1 percentage point from each of those growth rates implies that by 2018, GDP would be roughly 1 percent smaller than in CBO's baseline.

Slower growth of GDP would have several budgetary implications. For example, it would imply less growth in taxable income and thus a smaller amount of tax revenues—$1 billion less in 2008 and $51 billion less in 2018 (see Table C-1). With a smaller amount of revenues, the federal government would have to borrow more and incur higher interest costs. Payments to service federal debt would be slightly larger during the first few years of the 10-year projection period but substantially larger in later years, with the increase reaching $13 billion by 2018. Mandatory spending, however, would be only minimally affected by slower economic growth: Medicare outlays would be slightly lower, but that decrease would be mostly offset by higher outlays for the refundable portions of the earned income and child tax credits.[3]

All told, if growth in real GDP each year was 0.1 percentage point lower than the rates assumed in CBO's baseline, annual deficits would be larger or surpluses smaller by amounts that would climb to $63 billion in 2018. The cumulative surplus for the 2009–2018 period would fall by $297 billion. Those effects differ from the effects of a cyclical change in economic growth, such as a recession, which are usually larger but of much shorter duration. (For a discussion of the possible budgetary effects of a recession, see Box C-1.)

Higher Interest Rates

The second rule of thumb illustrates the sensitivity of the budget to changes in interest rates, which affect the flow of interest payments to and from the federal government. When the budget is in deficit, the Treasury must borrow additional funds from the public—by selling bonds and other securities—to cover any shortfall. (The Treasury currently issues 1-, 3-, and 6-month bills; 2-, 5-, and 10-year notes; 5-, 10-, and 20-year inflation-protected securities; and 30-year bonds.) When the budget is in surplus, the Treasury uses some of its income to reduce federal debt held by the public. In either case, the Treasury refinances a portion of the nation's debt at market interest rates. Those rates also determine how much the Federal Reserve earns on its holdings of securities, which in turn affects federal revenues.

If interest rates on all types of Treasury securities were 1 percentage point higher each year through 2018, compared with the interest rates underlying the baseline, and all other economic variables were unchanged, the government's interest costs would be approximately $9 billion greater in 2008 (see Table C-1). That jump would be fueled largely by the extra costs of refinancing Treasury bills, which make up about 22 percent of the government's marketable debt. Roughly $1 trillion in Treasury bills are currently outstanding, all of which mature within the next six months. However, most marketable government debt is in the form of coupon securities, which consist of medium-term notes, inflation-protected securities, and long-term bonds. As Treasury securities mature, they are replaced with new issues. Therefore, the budgetary

---

2. A change in the rate of real growth could affect other economic variables, such as inflation and unemployment; however, CBO's rule of thumb does not include such effects.

3. Medicare's payment rates for physicians' services are computed using a formula that compares annual spending with a target amount that partly reflects the growth of GDP. The impact of lower real growth would not affect those payment rates until 2017.

Table C-1.

How Selected Economic Changes Might Affect CBO's Baseline Budget Projections

(Billions of dollars)

	2008	2009	2010	2011	2012	2013	2014	2015	2016	2017	2018	Total, 2009-2013	Total, 2009-2018
Growth Rate of Real GDP Is 0.1 Percentage Point Lower Each Year													
Change in Revenues	-1	-4	-7	-11	-16	-21	-26	-32	-38	-45	-51	-59	-250
Change in Outlays													
Mandatory spending	*	*	*	*	*	*	*	*	*	*	-1	1	1
Debt service	*	*	*	1	2	3	4	6	7	10	13	6	45
Total	*	*	1	1	2	3	4	6	8	10	12	6	46
Change in Deficit or Surplus[a]	**-1**	**-4**	**-8**	**-12**	**-18**	**-23**	**-30**	**-38**	**-46**	**-55**	**-63**	**-65**	**-297**
Interest Rates Are 1 Percentage Point Higher Each Year													
Change in Revenues	2	4	6	7	8	8	9	9	10	10	11	33	82
Change in Outlays													
Higher rates	9	23	31	36	39	41	41	42	42	43	41	170	379
Debt service	*	1	2	4	6	8	11	13	16	19	22	22	103
Total	10	24	33	40	45	49	52	55	58	61	63	191	482
Change in Deficit or Surplus[a]	**-8**	**-19**	**-28**	**-33**	**-37**	**-41**	**-43**	**-46**	**-49**	**-51**	**-52**	**-158**	**-399**
Inflation Is 1 Percentage Point Higher Each Year													
Change in Revenues	14	41	74	112	156	201	250	306	367	433	505	584	2,445
Change in Outlays													
Discretionary spending	0	6	16	27	39	52	66	80	95	111	128	139	619
Mandatory spending	4	14	29	47	67	90	115	143	175	208	245	247	1,133
Higher rates[b]	12	28	37	42	45	47	48	48	49	49	48	198	439
Debt service	*	*	1	1	1	1	*	-2	-5	-8	-13	4	-25
Total	15	48	82	117	152	189	228	268	314	361	409	588	2,167
Change in Deficit or Surplus[a]	**-2**	**-7**	**-8**	**-4**	**4**	**12**	**22**	**38**	**53**	**72**	**96**	**-4**	**278**
Wages and Salaries' Share of GDP Is 1 Percentage Point Higher Each Year													
Change in Revenues	10	8	10	13	12	14	15	16	17	19	21	58	146
Change in Outlays (Debt service)	*	-1	-1	-2	-2	-3	-4	-5	-6	-7	-9	-9	-40
Change in Deficit or Surplus[a]	**10**	**9**	**11**	**15**	**15**	**17**	**19**	**21**	**24**	**26**	**29**	**66**	**186**
Memorandum:													
Deficit (-) or Surplus in CBO's January 2008 Baseline	-219	-198	-241	-117	87	61	96	117	95	151	223	-408	274

Source: Congressional Budget Office.

Notes: GDP = gross domestic product; * = between -$500 million and $500 million.

a.   Negative amounts indicate an increase in the deficit or a decrease in the surplus.

b.   The change in outlays attributable to higher rates in this scenario is different from the estimate in the rule of thumb for interest rates because the principal on the Treasury's inflation-protected securities grows with inflation.

Box C-1.

The Potential Budgetary Impact of a Recession

The Congressional Budget Office (CBO), in its current economic outlook, does not forecast a recession for this year, but it does assume that growth will be very slow. That slowdown will increase the deficit even without a recession, just as periods of sluggish growth have increased it in the past. If the economy were to slide into a recession, however, the outcome for the budget during the period covered by CBO's economic forecast—2008 and 2009—would be worse than CBO now projects. A recession's overall effect on the budget would depend not only on the downturn's depth and length but also on other factors that might accompany it, such as a further drop in the stock market.

CBO's estimate of movements in the cyclical component of the budget deficit (relative to potential gross domestic product, or GDP) over the two-year periods associated with each of the past six recessions help illustrate the potential impact of such an event (see the table to the right).[1] The cyclical component— also known as the automatic stabilizers—is the drop in revenues that automatically occurs when GDP and incomes decline, plus the increase in benefit pay-

ments for programs such as unemployment insurance that accompanies a rise in the unemployment rate.[2]

During the past six recessions, the cyclical component of the deficit rose by amounts ranging from 1.1 percent of potential GDP to 2.5 percent. (CBO estimates that in 2008, GDP will be about $14 trillion.) The largest change was in the 1973–1975 period, which experienced the biggest jump in the gap between actual and potential GDP. By contrast, the largest increase in the actual deficit occurred during the most recent recession, which included a sizable loss of revenues associated with the bursting of the stock market bubble. The estimated increase in the cyclical component of the deficit during that downturn was the same as the average for the past six recessions as a group.

It is unclear to what extent a recession this year would resemble those of the past. The post-World War II period has recorded 10 recessions, and the two most recent ones have been relatively mild. The combination of problems in the subprime mortgage market, falling house values, and high oil prices could lead to weaker growth than CBO anticipates. However, without the addition of a further drop in the stock market similar to that beginning in 2000, a recession this year would probably not have as big an impact on the actual budget deficit as the effects felt during and following the recession in 2001.

---

1. By contrast with the rule-of-thumb estimates for the current-law effects on the budget of persisting changes in real growth, inflation, interest rates, and the wages and salaries share of GDP (shown in Table C-1), CBO's estimates of changes in the cyclical component of the deficit during the past six recessions reflect the short-term effects of the economy's movements away from its potential level—that is, potential GDP. (Potential GDP is the level of real output corresponding to a high rate of resource—labor and capital—use.)

2. For further discussion, see Congressional Budget Office, *The Cyclically Adjusted and Standardized Budget Measures: An Update* (August 2007).

---

effects of higher interest rates would mount each year, peaking under this scenario at an additional $43 billion in 2017. (In 2018, the budget surplus projected in CBO's baseline and the effect of projected surpluses in prior years would reduce projected federal borrowing, thereby slightly lessening the effect of higher interest rates.)

As part of its conduct of monetary policy, the Federal Reserve buys and sells Treasury securities in the open

market. The interest that it earns on its securities portfolio helps determine its profits, which are counted as revenues when they are turned over to the Treasury. If interest rates each year were 1 percentage point higher than CBO projects, annual earnings on those securities—and thus revenues—would increase by amounts growing from $2 billion in 2008 to $11 billion in 2018.

Box C-1.
Continued

Budgetary Effects of the Past Six Recessions

Year Before the Peak to the Trough[a]	Change as a Percentage of Potential GDP[b]		GDP Gap[d]
	Actual Deficit	Cyclical Component[c]	
1969 to 1971	-2.5	-1.9	4.5
1973 to 1975	-2.1	-2.5	6.6
1979 to 1981	-0.9	-1.1	2.7
1981 to 1983	-3.1	-1.7	4.6
1990 to 1992	-0.7	-1.1	2.9
2000 to 2002	-4.0	-1.6	4.2
Average, all periods	**-2.2**	**-1.6**	**4.3**

Source: Congressional Budget Office.

a. In this table, the period before the peak is the fiscal year preceding the onset of a recession, and the trough is either the fiscal year containing the last quarter in which the economy was in recession or the fiscal year following that last quarter.

b. Potential GDP is the level of gross domestic product that corresponds to a high rate of resource (labor and capital) use.

c. The cyclical component—also known as the automatic stabilizers—is the decline in revenues that automatically occurs when GDP and incomes decline, plus the increase in benefit payments for programs such as unemployment insurance that occurs when the rate of unemployment rises. For further discussion, see Congressional Budget Office, *The Cyclically Adjusted and Standardized Budget Measures: An Update* (August 2007).

d. The GDP gap equals the difference between potential and actual GDP as a percentage of potential GDP.

In addition, the larger deficits or smaller surpluses that would accompany higher interest rates would require the Treasury to raise more cash than the amounts assumed in the baseline. The resulting increase in annual debt-service costs would be as much as $22 billion by 2018.

All told, if interest rates were a full percentage point higher than the rates assumed in CBO's baseline, the budget's bottom line would worsen by increasing amounts over the projection period: by $8 billion in 2008, up to $52 billion in 2018. The cumulative surplus over the 2009–2018 period would drop by $399 billion.

Higher Inflation
The third rule of thumb shows the budgetary impact of inflation that is 1 percentage point higher than the rates assumed in the baseline. That change has a bigger effect on federal revenues and outlays than do the other rules of thumb. For the most part, the effects of inflation on revenues and outlays offset each other, although after a few

years, the impact on revenues is the larger of the two effects.

On the one hand, higher inflation leads to increases in wages and other income, which translate directly into more income and payroll taxes being withheld from people's paychecks. The resulting impact on revenues is dampened (with a lag) because the thresholds for various tax rate brackets are indexed to rise with inflation. In addition, the faster growth of prices boosts corporate profits, which quickly leads to greater federal receipts from firms' quarterly estimated tax payments.

On the other hand, higher inflation increases spending for many federal benefit programs and, because of the statutory rules governing the baseline, drives growth in projections of discretionary spending. Many mandatory programs automatically adjust their benefit levels each year to reflect price increases. Social Security, federal employees' retirement programs, Supplemental Security Income, veterans' disability compensation, Food Stamps, and child nutrition programs, among others, are adjusted (with a lag) for changes in the consumer price index or one of its components. Many Medicare payment rates are also adjusted annually for inflation. Other programs, such as Medicaid, are not formally indexed but grow with inflation nonetheless. In addition, to the extent that initial benefit payments to participants in retirement and disability programs are related to wages, changes in nominal wages as a result of inflation will be reflected in future outlays for those programs—because the initial payments are the basis for future cost-of-living adjustments. Finally, future spending for discretionary programs is projected on the basis of assumed rates of wage and price growth.

Inflation also has an impact on federal net interest outlays because it is one component of nominal long-term interest rates (the other being a real rate of return). For example, if real rates of return remain constant but inflation rises, interest rates will climb, and new federal borrowing will incur higher interest costs. For this rule of thumb, CBO assumed that nominal interest rates would rise in step with inflation, thus increasing the cost of financing the government's debt.

If inflation each year was 1 percentage point higher than the rate assumed in CBO's baseline, total revenues over the 2009–2018 period would be about 7 percent and outlays about 6 percent larger compared with projections. The effects of higher inflation on outlays and revenues in the near term, from 2008 to 2011, would basically offset each other, mainly because CBO assumed that interest rates would rise with inflation and thus drive up federal interest payments relatively quickly. Higher inflation would also boost mandatory spending in the short run. As a consequence, over the 2008–2011 period, the increase in outlays would slightly exceed the rise in revenues projected under this scenario (see Table C-1).

By 2012, however, the growth in revenues associated with higher inflation would outdistance the growth in outlays; the gap between the two would widen thereafter, reaching $83 billion (plus $13 billion in additional debt-service costs) by 2018. As a result, the cumulative surplus for the 10-year projection period (including debt-service costs) would be $278 billion larger than in CBO's baseline.

Wages and Salaries as a Larger Share of GDP

Because different types of income are taxed at different rates, changes over time in the share of total income that each type represents have contributed to changes in federal tax receipts measured as a percentage of GDP. However, considerable uncertainty surrounds projections of those income shares.

Two of the most important categories of income for projecting federal revenues are wages and salaries and corporate profits. Wages and salaries are the most highly taxed form of income because they are subject to the individual income tax as well as to payroll taxes for Social Security (up to a maximum annual amount) and for Medicare. Consequently, an additional dollar of wages and salaries will produce more revenues than will an additional dollar of corporate profits, CBO estimates. Larger projections of wages and salaries and correspondingly smaller projections of profits will thus result in larger projected federal revenues.

CBO's baseline incorporates the assumption that total wages and salaries will equal about 46 percent of GDP between 2008 and 2018 and that taxable corporate profits will range from 6.4 percent to 8.6 percent of GDP (see Chapter 4). If, instead, wages and salaries each year were 1 percentage point larger relative to GDP and corporate profits were 1 percentage point smaller, annual revenues would be $10 billion greater in 2008 and $21 billion greater by 2018 (see Table C-1).

Two years stand out in what is basically a pattern of steadily increasing revenues under this scenario. The first is 2009, when revenues are higher by $8 billion, which is less than the $10 billion increase in 2008. That relatively small drop results from CBO's assumption that corporations pay the taxes they owe on profits more slowly than individuals pay the taxes they owe on their wages (which are subject to automatic withholding). Those slower payments delay the fall in corporate receipts—from the 1 percentage point cut in corporate profits—from 2008 to 2009. In addition, firms can carry forward any losses they incur in earlier years to help reduce their tax liability in subsequent years—specifically, in 2009 and beyond. Those effects make the decline in corporate receipts larger in 2008 than in 2009.

The net effect on revenues also dips slightly in 2012 before resuming an upward trend over the rest of the 10-year period. That drop is primarily attributable to legislation that shifts estimated corporate tax payments from 2013 into 2012. The shift thereby magnifies the effect that lower profits under the rule of thumb have on changes in corporate receipts in 2012 and offsets some of the impact of increased individual and payroll taxes.

The larger amount of revenues that would result from an increase in wages and salaries as a share of GDP would further improve the budget's bottom line by reducing the borrowing costs assumed in the baseline in each year of the projection period. That decrease in interest payments would gradually reach $9 billion by 2018. Overall, under this scenario, the cumulative 10-year surplus would be $186 billion larger than the surplus in CBO's baseline.

The Treatment of Federal Receipts and Expenditures in the National Income and Product Accounts

The fiscal transactions of the federal government are recorded in two major sets of accounts that are conceptually quite different. The presentation generally used by executive branch agencies and the Congress and typically discussed in the press (and followed in this report) is the *Budget of the United States Government,* as reported by the Office of Management and Budget. The budget focuses on cash flows—revenues and outlays, or the collection of taxes and fees and the disbursement of cash for the various federal functions. The objectives of the budget are to provide information that can assist lawmakers in their policy deliberations, facilitate the management and control of federal activities, and help the Treasury manage its cash balances and determine its borrowing needs.

The national income and product accounts (NIPAs) also record the federal government's transactions, but with different objectives. The NIPAs, which are produced by the Bureau of Economic Analysis (BEA), an agency within the Department of Commerce, are intended to provide a comprehensive measure of current production and related income generated by the U.S. economy.[1] A well-known measure of current production in the NIPAs is gross domestic product (GDP). The accounts, which are used extensively in macroeconomic analysis, divide the economy into four major sectors—business, government, household, and the rest of the world (the foreign sector), each with its own set of accounts.[2] The federal sector, which is the focus of this report, is one component of the government sector (the state and local sector is the other component).[3] Because the aims of the NIPAs differ from those of the budget, the two accounting systems treat some government transactions very differently. On average, the differences cause receipts and expenditures in the NIPAs, as projected by the Congressional Budget Office (CBO), to be about 2 percent and 3 percent higher, respectively, than the corresponding budget totals for the 2009–2018 period.

Conceptual Differences Between the NIPAs' Federal Sector and the Federal Budget

The budget of the federal government is best understood as an information and management tool. It focuses primarily on cash flows, recording for each fiscal period the inflow of revenues and the outflow of spending. The period of foremost interest in the budget is the federal fiscal year, which runs from October 1 through September 30. There are a few exceptions to the general rule of recording transactions on a cash basis, but they are designed to improve the usefulness of the budget as a decisionmaking tool. For example, when the federal

---

1. The discussion of the national income and product accounts in this report generally refers to Table 3.2 in the accounts, "Federal Government Current Receipts and Expenditures," which most closely resembles the presentation in the budget. For other discussions of the NIPAs, see Department of Commerce, Bureau of Economic Analysis, "Federal Budget Estimates for Fiscal Year 2008," *Survey of Current Business* (March 2007); and *Budget of the United States Government, Fiscal Year 2008: Analytical Perspectives.*

2. Some accounts in the NIPAs, such as the domestic capital account (which shows saving and investment), focus on components of gross domestic product or income rather than on a specific sector, and they bring together relevant information from all four sectors.

3. More formally, BEA regards the federal government and state and local governments as subsectors. The treatment of state and local governments' transactions in the NIPAs closely resembles that of the federal government's transactions.

government makes direct loans or provides loan guarantees (as with student loans), tracking cash flows gives a misleading view of current costs; therefore, under what is termed credit reform, the budget records the estimated subsidy costs at the time the loans are made.

The federal sector of the NIPAs has none of the planning and management goals of the budget. Instead, it focuses on displaying how the federal government fits into a general economic framework that describes current production and income within specific periods, the major sources of that production, and recipients of income by type. The main periods of interest for the NIPAs are calendar years and calendar quarters, although approximate totals for fiscal years can be derived from the quarterly estimates. (The tables in this appendix show fiscal year numbers.)

From the perspective of the NIPAs, the federal government is both a producer and a consumer. Its workforce uses purchased goods and services and government-owned capital (buildings, equipment, and software) to produce services for the public at large; because those services are consumed by the public, that consumption, by convention, is regarded as a federal consumption expenditure in the NIPAs. In addition, through its taxes and transfers, the federal government affects the resources available to the private sector. The purpose of the NIPAs is to record all of those activities consistently.

The federal sector of the NIPAs tracks how much the government spends on its consumption of goods and services, and it records the transfer of resources that occurs through taxes, payments to beneficiaries of federal programs, and federal interest payments. The federal sector's contribution to GDP is presented elsewhere in the NIPAs (Table 1.1.5 in the accounts).

Differences in Accounting for Major Transactions

The accounting differences between the NIPAs and the federal budget stem from the conceptual differences discussed above. In attempting to properly incorporate federal transactions into the framework used to determine GDP, the NIPAs reflect judgments about the best treatment of such transactions as government investment,

sales and purchases of existing assets, federal credit, and federal activities that resemble those of businesses, along with transactions involving U.S. territories. In some cases, the appropriate treatment may be to move a transaction from the federal sector to another place in the NIPAs or to exclude the transaction from the NIPAs entirely. In other cases, the appropriate treatment may involve recording as a receipt in the NIPAs an item that the federal budget reports as an offsetting (negative) budget outlay, or adjusting the timing of a federal transaction to better match the timing of related production or income flow.[4]

The Measurement of National Saving

Several conventions in the NIPAs are intended to show the federal government's contribution to the NIPAs' measure of national saving—net federal government saving (current receipts minus current expenditures). Two major departures from the budget are the treatment of federal investment spending (for such things as ships, computers, and office buildings) and the treatment of federal employees' retirement programs. As a result of such differences, the concept of net federal saving in the NIPAs is akin to but not the same as the federal budget surplus.

Federal Investment. In the federal budget, outlays for investment purchases are treated like other cash outlays and thus are subtracted from budget revenues in determining the size of the federal deficit or surplus. By contrast, in the NIPAs, federal investment is not counted as federal spending for the purpose of measuring net federal government saving, because new purchases of federal capital (investments) do not measure the current inputs from the existing stock of capital that are used to provide government services.[5] To approximate the cost of those

---

4. The resulting differences between the numbers in the NIPAs and the budget are sometimes divided into three groups: coverage, timing, and netting. Although all three types of differences can affect total revenues or outlays, netting differences have no effect on the federal deficit or surplus because they affect revenues and outlays equally.

5. Federal investment, along with private investment spending, is shown in the NIPAs in the domestic capital account, which displays saving and investment (Table 5.1 in the accounts; see also Table 3.9.5, which shows both federal investment and consumption).

capital inputs, the NIPAs include in current federal expenditures an estimate of the depreciation (consumption of fixed capital) of the stock of federal capital. The treatment is conceptually similar to that applied to the corporate business sector, which uses depreciation rather than investment purchases to compute net corporate saving (retained earnings). In the federal budget, depreciation is not tracked. Table D-1, which provides a crosswalk between the budget and the NIPAs, shows that difference in coverage in the row labeled "Treatment of investment and depreciation."[6]

Federal Retirement. The transactions of federal employees' retirement programs are also handled differently in the budget and in the NIPAs. In the budget, federal employees' contributions for their retirement are recorded as revenues, whereas agencies' contributions on behalf of their employees (as well as interest payments from the Treasury to trust funds) have no overall budgetary effect because they are simply transfers of funds between two government accounts.[7] Benefit payments to federal retirees are recorded as outlays in the budget. By contrast, in the NIPAs, the aim is to make the measurement of saving by the federal government consistent with that of the private sector. Therefore, the NIPAs treat some of the transactions of federal retirement plans as part of the household sector.[8] The receipts from federal employers' retirement contributions (and the interest earned by retirement accounts) are considered part of workers' personal income and thus are not recorded as federal

transactions (receipts or negative expenditures). Employees' contributions are not recorded as income in either the federal or the household sector but are considered transfers within the household sector.

On the outlay side, pension benefit payments to retirees are not recorded as federal expenditures in the NIPAs because they are treated as transfers from pension funds within the household sector. Some transactions, however, are treated as part of federal expenditures even though the corresponding receipts are recorded in the household sector. The government's contributions to its workers' retirement are counted as federal expenditures (as part of employees' compensation), as is the interest paid to federal retirement accounts.[9] The different treatment of retirement contributions by federal employees is shown in the top section of Table D-1 under "Receipts"; the different treatment of contributions by federal employers, interest earnings, and benefit payments is shown below that, under "Expenditures."

Capital Transfers and Exchanges of Existing Assets

The NIPAs' measure of current production and income is not affected by transactions that involve existing assets. Therefore, the NIPAs do not count capital transfers or asset exchanges as part of current federal receipts or expenditures, although the budget generally does include those transactions. The NIPAs define as capital transfers—and thus exclude—estate and gift taxes (which are taxes on private-capital transfers) and investment grants to state and local governments (for air transportation,

---

6. The estimates and the presentation of the reconciliation between the budget and the NIPAs in Table D-1 are based on CBO's interpretation of the methodology for the accounts as detailed in Department of Commerce, Bureau of Economic Analysis, *Survey of Current Business* (June 2003), and in BEA's reconciliation of the Administration's budget for fiscal year 2008 and the accounts, published in the *Survey of Current Business* (March 2007).

7. In the budget, contributions by an agency for its employees' retirement are considered outlays for that agency and offsetting receipts (negative outlays) elsewhere within the budget. Thus, those intragovernmental transfers result in no net outlays or receipts for the total budget. That treatment is the same as the treatment of the federal government's contributions for Social Security and Medicare for its employees.

8. Transactions of the National Railroad Retirement Investment Trust are part of the federal sector in the NIPAs. In addition, Social Security contributions and benefit payments for private and government employees alike are recorded in the federal sector as receipts and expenditures rather than moved to the household sector.

9. However, in the future BEA may consider recording the annual lump-sum payments to amortize the unfunded liabilities of the military and civilian service retirement funds as a capital transfer rather than as employees' compensation. That treatment would reflect the view that such payments are not related to current production; see www.bea.gov, "Frequently Asked Questions," Answer ID 480.

Table D-1.

Relationship of the Budget to the Federal Sector of the NIPAs

(Billions of dollars)

	Actual 2007	2008	2009	2010	2011	2012	2013	2014	2015	2016	2017	2018
						Receipts						
Revenues (Budget)[a]	2,568	2,654	2,817	2,907	3,182	3,442	3,585	3,763	3,941	4,131	4,334	4,548
Differences												
Coverage												
Contributions for government employees' retirement	-4	-4	-4	-4	-4	-4	-4	-3	-3	-3	-3	-3
Estate and gift taxes	-26	-27	-27	-22	-21	-55	-63	-70	-76	-83	-90	-97
Geographic adjustments	-5	-5	-5	-5	-6	-6	-6	-6	-7	-7	-7	-7
Universal Service Fund receipts	-7	-8	-8	-8	-8	-9	-9	-9	-9	-9	-9	-9
Subtotal, coverage	-42	-44	-45	-39	-39	-74	-81	-89	-95	-102	-109	-116
Netting												
Medicare premiums	51	54	58	61	65	69	74	79	85	92	99	107
Deposit insurance premiums	1	1	1	1	1	1	1	2	2	2	2	2
Government contributions for OASDI and HI for employees	16	17	18	19	20	21	22	23	24	25	26	28
Income receipts on assets	18	19	17	17	18	18	19	19	19	19	19	19
Government enterprises' surpluses	-3	-4	-5	-7	-8	-10	-10	-10	-11	-11	-11	-12
Other	30	33	32	33	34	35	35	36	34	34	35	36
Subtotal, netting	112	119	121	125	130	134	142	149	154	161	169	180
Timing shift of corporate estimated tax payments	3	0	0	8	3	-22	11	*	0	0	0	0
Other adjustments[b]	-5	-2	-9	-2	-6	-2	-4	3	1	3	2	3
Total Differences	67	73	67	91	88	37	67	63	60	62	62	66
Receipts in the NIPAs	2,635	2,727	2,884	2,998	3,270	3,479	3,652	3,826	4,001	4,193	4,396	4,614
						Expenditures						
Outlays (Budget)[a]	2,731	2,873	3,015	3,148	3,299	3,355	3,524	3,666	3,824	4,037	4,183	4,325
Differences												
Coverage												
Treatment of investment and depreciation	-18	-23	-27	-28	-30	-30	-31	-31	-31	-32	-32	-33
Contributions for government employees' retirement	33	55	56	59	61	64	68	72	76	81	86	91
Capital transfers[c]	-51	-53	-55	-58	-59	-61	-62	-63	-64	-65	-66	-66
Lending and financial adjustments	24	21	10	9	10	9	9	9	10	10	11	11
Geographic adjustments	-16	-17	-18	-19	-20	-20	-21	-22	-23	-25	-26	-27
Universal Service Fund payments	-7	-8	-8	-8	-8	-8	-8	-9	-9	-9	-9	-6
Subtotal, coverage[c]	-34	-26	-42	-45	-46	-46	-46	-44	-42	-40	-36	-30
Netting												
Medicare premiums	51	54	58	61	65	69	74	79	85	92	99	107
Deposit insurance premiums	1	1	1	1	1	1	1	2	2	2	2	2

Continued

Table D-1.

Continued

(Billions of dollars)

	Actual 2007	2008	2009	2010	2011	2012	2013	2014	2015	2016	2017	2018
					Expenditures (Continued)							
Differences (Continued)												
Government contributions for OASDI and HI for employees	16	17	18	19	20	21	22	23	24	25	26	28
Income receipts on assets	18	19	17	17	18	18	19	19	19	19	19	19
Government enterprises' surpluses	-3	-4	-5	-7	-8	-10	-10	-10	-11	-11	-11	-12
Other	30	33	32	33	34	35	35	36	34	34	35	36
Subtotal, netting	112	119	121	125	130	134	142	149	154	161	169	180
Timing adjustments	7	*	0	0	-29	29	1	0	0	-40	-4	44
Other adjustments[d]	30	-1	-5	-4	-3	0	0	3	4	5	-3	-5
Total Differences[c]	**114**	**92**	**72**	**74**	**52**	**117**	**97**	**107**	**115**	**86**	**126**	**189**
Expenditures in the NIPAs[c]	2,845	2,966	3,087	3,222	3,350	3,473	3,621	3,773	3,939	4,122	4,309	4,514
					Net Federal Government Saving							
Budget Deficit (-) or Surplus[a]	-163	-219	-198	-241	-117	87	61	96	117	95	151	223
Differences												
Coverage												
Treatment of investment and depreciation	18	23	27	28	30	30	31	31	31	32	32	33
Contributions for government employees' retirement	-37	-59	-60	-63	-65	-68	-71	-75	-79	-84	-89	-94
Estate and gift taxes	-26	-27	-27	-22	-21	-55	-63	-70	-76	-83	-90	-97
Capital transfers[c]	51	53	55	58	59	61	62	63	64	65	66	66
Lending and financial adjustments	-24	-21	-10	-9	-10	-9	-9	-9	-10	-10	-11	-11
Geographic adjustments	11	12	13	14	14	14	15	16	17	18	19	20
Universal Service Fund	*	*	*	*	*	*	*	*	*	*	*	-3
Subtotal, coverage[c]	-8	-18	-3	6	7	-28	-36	-44	-53	-62	-73	-86
Timing adjustments	-4	*	0	8	32	-50	10	*	0	40	4	-44
Other adjustments[e]	-35	-2	-4	2	-3	-2	-5	0	-3	-2	5	7
Total Differences[c]	**-47**	**-19**	**-5**	**17**	**36**	**-80**	**-30**	**-44**	**-56**	**-24**	**-64**	**-123**
Net Federal Government Saving[c]	-210	-238	-203	-224	-81	7	31	52	62	71	87	100

Source: Congressional Budget Office.

Note: NIPAs = national income and product accounts; * = between -$500 million and $500 million; OASDI = Old-Age, Survivors, and Disability Insurance; HI = Hospital Insurance.

a.   Includes Social Security and the Postal Service.

b.   Includes timing differences not shown elsewhere in the table, plus discrepancies between figures in the NIPAs and in the budget that may diminish when BEA makes subsequent revisions.

c.   May change in the future if BEA decides to record as capital transfers rather than as employees' compensation the annual lump-sum payments, to amortize the unfunded liabilities of military and civilian service retirement funds.

d.   Includes coverage differences not shown elsewhere.

e.   On the receipts side, includes timing differences not shown elsewhere in the table, plus discrepancies between figures in the NIPAs and in the budget that may diminish when BEA makes subsequent revisions. On the expenditure side, numbers include coverage differences not shown elsewhere.

highways, transit, and water treatment plants).[10] Exchanges of existing assets include federal transactions for deposit insurance and sales and purchases of government assets (including assets that are not produced, such as land and licenses to use the radio spectrum). Those differences between the NIPAs' federal sector and the budget accounts appear on the revenue side in Table D-1 as estate and gift taxes and on the outlay side as capital transfers and lending and financial adjustments.

Credit Programs

For federal credit programs (loans and loan guarantees), only the estimated credit subsidy and administrative costs are included in outlays. Cash flows from loan disbursements, repayments, and interest, by contrast, are reported in what are termed financing accounts, which have no effect on outlays.

As in the budget, the NIPAs record administrative costs and generally exclude loan disbursements and repayments and other cash flows that are considered exchanges of existing assets or financial and lending transactions that are unrelated to current production. The NIPAs do not record subsidy costs. In another departure from the budget, the NIPAs include the interest receipts from credit programs (as part of federal receipts). Those differences in the treatment of credit programs are recorded in two places in Table D-1: Under the heading "Expenditures," the row labeled "Lending and financial adjustments" shows the differences in handling the loan subsidies; under "Receipts," the difference in the treatment of loan interest is captured as part of "Income receipts on assets."

Geographic Coverage

The NIPAs exclude all government transactions with Puerto Rico and the U.S. territories, whose current production, according to the NIPAs' definition, is not part of the nation's GDP. Because federal transfers dominate those transactions, their exclusion tends to increase the NIPAs' depiction of net federal government saving by comparison with the budget's measure of saving—the federal deficit or surplus. That difference in coverage is shown as geographic adjustments in Table D-1.

Universal Service Fund

The business activity of the Universal Service Fund, which provides resources to promote access to telecommunications, is recorded in the budget but not in the NIPAs' federal sector. The Universal Service Fund receives federally required payments from providers of interstate and international telecommunications services and disburses those funds to local providers that serve high-cost areas, low-income households, libraries, and schools, as well as to rural health care providers. The fund is administered by the Universal Service Administrative Company, an independent nonprofit corporation regulated by the Federal Communications Commission.

Although the Universal Service Fund's revenues and outlays appear in the federal budget, they have little net effect on the deficit or surplus. In the NIPAs, the fund's receipts and payments are classified as intracorporate transfers (from one business to another within the corporate sector). The difference in treatment of the Universal Service Fund is so labeled in Table D-1.

Interest Receipts

In the NIPAs, federal interest receipts are grouped with other types of federal receipts (in the category designated "Income receipts on assets") rather than netted against federal interest payments, as they are in the federal budget.[11] BEA's treatment is consistent with international accounting practices, under which interest receipts and payments are reported separately. That difference in the treatment of interest receipts in the NIPAs and in the federal budget raises the NIPAs' measure of government receipts relative to federal budget revenues and increases the NIPAs' measure of federal spending relative to budget outlays. However, because the difference in treatment affects receipts and expenditures in the NIPAs by exactly the same amount, it has no effect on the NIPAs' measurement of net federal government saving.

---

10. Another type of capital transfer that BEA does not include in the NIPAs is an annual lump-sum payment from the Treasury to the Department of Defense Medicare-Eligible Retiree Health Care Fund—a trust fund that in October 2002 began to pay for benefits received by retired members of the armed forces who are eligible for Medicare and by their dependents. Those payments to the trust fund are for accrued but unfunded liabilities for benefits attributable to work performed before 2003; BEA excludes those payments from federal expenditures because they are not related to current production. Those annual payments are made by the Treasury and recorded as outlays. However, the Treasury also records offsetting receipts (negative outlays) elsewhere within the budget. Because those annual payments have no net effect on federal spending either in the NIPAs or in the budget, there is no corresponding reconciliation item in Table D-1.

---

11. About half of the NIPAs' interest receipts, mainly from penalties on late tax payments, are recorded as revenues in the federal budget.

Surpluses of Government Enterprises

In the NIPAs, the surpluses (or deficits) of government enterprises, such as the Postal Service, are shown on a separate line as current receipts of the federal government. That treatment is in keeping with international accounting standards, which generally advocate reporting spending on a gross, rather than a net, basis. By contrast, surpluses of government enterprises are treated as offsetting receipts in the federal budget.

Military Sales and Assistance in Kind

The NIPAs attempt to identify contributions to GDP by sector. Therefore, they do not classify as part of federal consumption military purchases of equipment and services that are intended for sale or as gifts to foreign governments. Instead, those transactions are considered net exports in the NIPAs' foreign transactions account (Table 14.1 in the accounts). In the case of gifts, the transactions also are recorded in the federal sector of the NIPAs as a portion of transfers to the rest of the world—a classification that parallels their treatment as outlays in the federal budget. By contrast, although the cost of acquiring the military equipment sold to foreign governments is recorded in the federal budget as outlays, the proceeds from those sales are recorded as offsetting receipts.

Timing Differences

As much as is possible, the NIPAs attempt to measure income flows when income is earned (on an accrual basis) rather than when income is received (on a cash basis).[12] For example, BEA attributes corporate tax payments to the year in which the liabilities are incurred rather than to the time when the payments are actually made. That approach makes sense in an integrated system of accounts that tracks both production and income because, on an accrual basis, the value of what is produced in a given period should—measurement problems aside—match the total income generated. However, the NIPAs are not entirely consistent in that respect: Personal tax payments are counted as they are made and are not attributed retroactively to the year in which the liabilities were incurred. Because the budget is recorded mostly on a cash basis and

the NIPAs' federal sector is recorded largely on an accrual basis, there are differences in several areas in the timing of recorded transactions.

Corporate Taxes. Legislation sometimes temporarily shifts the timing of corporate tax payments (usually from the end of one fiscal year to the beginning of the next or vice versa). The NIPAs exclude such timing shifts, which are not consistent with accrual accounting. The timing adjustments for the net effects of enacted legislation are shown in Table D-1 under the heading "Receipts" in the row labeled "Timing shift of corporate estimated tax payments."

Although corporations make estimated tax payments throughout the year, any shortfalls (or overpayments) are corrected in the form of final payments (or refunds) in subsequent years. The NIPAs shift those final payments back to the year in which the corporate profits that gave rise to the tax liabilities were actually generated, whereas the budget records them on a cash basis. The results of that difference are difficult to identify for recent history and thus appear in the "Other adjustments" category under the heading "Receipts" in Table D-1.[13]

Personal Taxes. Although personal taxes are not recorded on an accrual basis in the NIPAs, BEA nevertheless attempts to avoid large, distorting upward or downward spikes in personal disposable income that result from timing quirks. Such quirks occur each year in April, for example, when most final settlements for the previous year's personal taxes are paid. In the NIPAs, therefore, those settlements are evenly spread over the four quarters of the calendar year in which they are paid. (As with accrual accounting, that treatment avoids spikes. Unlike accrual treatment, however, it does not move payments back to the year in which the liabilities were incurred.) Such "smoothing" can alter the relationship of the NIPAs and the budget accounts for various fiscal years because it shifts some receipts into the last quarter of the calendar year and thus into the following fiscal year.[14]

---

12. See United Nations, *System of National Accounts* (1993), paragraph 3.19, which emphasizes reporting transactions on an accrual basis. Many of the conceptual changes to the NIPAs have been based on guidelines from that U.N. document. See also Department of Commerce, Bureau of Economic Analysis, "The NIPAs and the System of National Accounts," *Survey of Current Business* (December 2004), pp. 17–32.

13. "Other adjustments" include timing differences not shown elsewhere in Table D-1, plus discrepancies between figures in the NIPAs and the budget that may diminish when BEA makes subsequent revisions.

14. A change in the relationship between receipts in the budget and in the NIPAs is projected to occur after certain changes in tax laws, such as the changes scheduled to take effect in 2011. CBO's baseline for revenues incorporates the assumption that those changes do, indeed, occur.

Again, those adjustments are difficult to identify for recent history and thus are not shown separately in Table D-1. They appear instead in the row labeled "Other adjustments" under "Receipts."

Transfers and Military Compensation. Timing adjustments are needed on the spending side of the NIPAs to align military compensation and government transfer payments—for example, veterans' benefits, Supplemental Security Income (SSI) payments, and Medicare's payments to providers—with income that is reported on an accrual basis in the NIPAs. Misalignments can occur because of accelerations in the timing of payments that result from quirks in the calendar or because of legislation designed to delay payments.

For example, although SSI payments are usually made on the first day of each month, if the first of the month falls on a weekend or holiday, payments are made a day or more in advance. If that occurs for the October benefits, payments are pushed into the previous fiscal year in the budget. In such cases, the NIPAs introduce a timing adjustment that effectively moves the payments back to the first day of the month. Hence, the NIPAs' adjustment always ensures that there are exactly 12 monthly SSI payments in a year, whereas in the budget, there may be 11 in some years and 13 in others.

For military compensation, which is normally paid at the beginning and middle of each month but may sometimes, like SSI, be paid early to avoid weekends, the adjustment in the NIPAs always ensures 24 payments in a year. In the budget, by contrast, there may be 23 payments in some years and 25 in others. The row labeled "Timing adjustments" under "Expenditures" in Table D-1 reflects that regularizing for transfers and for military pay.

In another contrast with the federal budget, the NIPAs record Medicare payments on an accrual basis rather than on a cash basis. That treatment better illustrates the link between the underlying economic activity (the medical services provided) and the associated federal transactions (payment for those services), which can be several months apart. The timing adjustment, however, has only a small effect on the NIPA measure of net federal government saving.

Business Activities
Both the federal budget and the NIPAs treat certain revenues as offsetting receipts when they result from voluntary transactions with the public that resemble business activities, such as proceeds from the sale of government publications. However, the NIPAs generally have a stricter view of what resembles a business transaction. In particular, Medicare premiums, deposit insurance premiums, rents, royalties, and regulatory or inspection fees are deemed equivalent to business transactions in the budget but not in the NIPAs. Consequently, those transactions (negative outlays in the budget) are treated in the NIPAs as government receipts (contributions for government social insurance, and current transfers from business—such as fines and fees, and taxes on production and imports). Those differences are recorded within the category "Netting" in Table D-1. Because they affect total current receipts and total current expenditures by exactly the same amounts, they have no effect on the NIPAs' measure of net federal government saving.

Presentation of the Federal Government's Receipts and Expenditures in the NIPAs
As in the budget, the federal sector of the NIPAs classifies receipts by type, but the categories differ (see Table D-2). The NIPAs' classifications help determine measures such as disposable income and corporate profits after taxes. There are five major categories of current receipts. The largest, current tax receipts, includes taxes on personal income, corporate income, and production and imports (excise taxes and customs duties), as well as taxes from the rest of the world. The next-largest category—contributions for government social insurance—consists of Social Security taxes, Medicare taxes and premiums, and unemployment insurance taxes. The remaining categories are current transfer receipts (fines and fees), income receipts on assets (interest, rents, and royalties), and current surpluses of government enterprises (such as the Postal Service).

Table D-2.

Baseline Receipts and Expenditures as Measured by the NIPAs

(Billions of dollars)

	Actual 2007	2008	2009	2010	2011	2012	2013	2014	2015	2016	2017	2018
						Receipts						
Current Tax Receipts												
Taxes on personal income	1,140	1,192	1,303	1,370	1,572	1,712	1,822	1,920	2,024	2,134	2,253	2,378
Taxes on corporate income	381	383	381	369	369	373	372	384	393	407	421	438
Taxes on production and imports	99	98	100	103	112	118	122	126	129	132	137	141
Taxes from the rest of the world	14	13	14	15	17	18	19	20	21	23	24	25
Subtotal	1,634	1,686	1,798	1,857	2,070	2,221	2,336	2,451	2,566	2,696	2,834	2,982
Contributions for Government												
Social Insurance[a]	941	977	1,022	1,076	1,133	1,190	1,245	1,301	1,358	1,418	1,480	1,546
Current Transfer Receipts	38	40	42	43	45	48	49	52	55	58	60	63
Income Receipts on Assets	25	29	28	28	29	30	32	32	33	33	33	34
Current Surpluses of Government Enterprises	-3	-4	-5	-7	-8	-10	-10	-10	-11	-11	-11	-12
Total current receipts	**2,635**	**2,727**	**2,884**	**2,998**	**3,270**	**3,479**	**3,652**	**3,826**	**4,001**	**4,193**	**4,396**	**4,614**
						Expenditures						
Consumption Expenditures												
Defense												
Consumption[b]	495	530	553	567	579	593	607	621	637	652	669	687
Consumption of fixed capital	75	76	76	78	80	83	87	90	93	96	100	103
Nondefense												
Consumption[c]	245	257	264	271	277	283	290	299	307	317	327	335
Consumption of fixed capital	28	29	29	30	30	31	32	32	33	33	34	34
Subtotal[b]	843	892	923	946	967	991	1,015	1,042	1,070	1,099	1,129	1,159
Current Transfer Payments												
Government social benefits												
To persons	1,252	1,311	1,381	1,447	1,517	1,587	1,683	1,778	1,886	2,006	2,129	2,270
To the rest of the world	4	4	4	4	4	5	5	5	6	6	6	7
Subtotal	1,255	1,314	1,385	1,451	1,522	1,591	1,688	1,783	1,892	2,012	2,135	2,277
Other transfer payments												
Grants-in-aid to state and local governments[c]	372	385	403	422	441	461	485	511	540	570	603	639
To the rest of the world	31	37	32	31	31	32	32	33	33	34	35	35
Subtotal	403	422	435	454	472	493	517	544	573	604	638	674
Interest Payments[c]	296	293	299	327	346	353	356	359	360	360	358	353
Subsidies	47	44	45	44	44	44	45	45	44	46	48	50
Total current expenditures[b]	**2,845**	**2,966**	**3,087**	**3,222**	**3,350**	**3,473**	**3,621**	**3,773**	**3,939**	**4,122**	**4,309**	**4,514**
						Net Federal Government Saving						
Net Federal Government Saving[b]	-210	-238	-203	-224	-81	7	31	52	62	71	87	100

Source: Congressional Budget Office.

Note: NIPAs = national income and product accounts.

a.   Includes Social Security taxes, Medicare taxes and premiums, and unemployment insurance taxes.

b.   May change in the future if BEA decides to exclude from consumption the increase in the annual lump-sum payment to amortize unfunded liabilities of the military and civilian service retirement funds.

c.   Includes Social Security and the Postal Service.

In the NIPAs, the government's expenditures are classified according to purpose. The major groups, which are fewer than in the federal budget, are consumption expenditures, or spending on goods and services, including costs of capital depreciation (with separate estimates for defense and nondefense spending); transfer payments (to individuals, state and local governments, and the rest of the world); interest payments; and subsidies to businesses and to government enterprises.

Consumption of goods and services (for defense and nondefense purposes) consists of spending by the government for its immediate use in production. (The largest portion of such consumption is the compensation of military and civilian federal employees.) Among the government's consumption expenditures, the consumption of fixed capital—depreciation—represents a partial measure of the services the government receives from its stock of fixed assets, such as buildings or equipment.

Transfer payments (cash payments made directly to individuals and the rest of the world, as well as grants to state and local governments or foreign nations) constitute another grouping. Social benefits make up most of the transfers to individuals. Grants-in-aid are payments the federal government makes to state or local governments, which generally use them for transfers (such as benefits provided by the Medicaid program) and consumption (such as the hiring of additional police officers). Current transfers to the rest of the world include federal purchases of military equipment for delivery to foreign governments.

The NIPAs' category for federal interest payments shows only payments and thus differs from the budget category labeled "Net interest." In the NIPAs, federal interest receipts are classified with other federal receipts.

The NIPAs' category labeled "Subsidies" primarily consists of payments by the federal government to businesses, including state and local government enterprises, such as public housing authorities. Federal housing and agricultural assistance have long dominated that category.

Net federal government saving in the NIPAs is the difference between the current receipts and the current expenditures of the federal sector.[15] It is a component of net national saving (which also includes net saving by the state and local government sector, personal saving, and corporate retained earnings) and thus is a partial measure of how much of the nation's income from current production is not consumed in the current period. Net federal saving (or dissaving) is akin to the federal surplus or deficit measured in the budget. However, net federal government saving is not a good indicator of federal borrowing requirements because, unlike the budget deficit or surplus, it is not a measure of cash flows.[16]

---

15. Gross federal saving—a component of gross national saving—equals net federal saving plus depreciation (consumption of fixed capital).

16. As an addendum to the NIPAs' Table 3.2, BEA publishes a measure labeled "Net lending or net borrowing," which is closer to a cash or financial measure in several ways. Like the budget, it includes investment purchases as expenditures because those purchases must be financed from current receipts or from federal borrowing. At the same time, it excludes consumption of fixed capital because those accounting charges are not a drain on current financial resources. In addition, it includes receipts from the sale of existing assets and capital transfer receipts (for example, estate and gift taxes) and capital transfer payments (for example, investment grants to state and local governments), which are not part of current receipts or expenditures in the NIPAs but do affect cash flows. Despite those adjustments, net federal lending or borrowing in the NIPAs differs from the budget deficit or surplus because of all of the other differences in timing and coverage that distinguish the NIPAs from the budget. BEA presents those differences in Table 3.18, which is similar to Table D-1 presented here.

CBO's Economic Projections for 2008 to 2018

The tables in this appendix expand on the information in Chapter 2 by showing the Congressional Budget Office's (CBO's) year-by-year economic projections for 2008 to 2018 (by calendar year in Table E-1 and by fiscal year in Table E-2). CBO does not forecast cyclical fluctuations in its projections for years after 2009. Instead, the projected values shown in the tables for 2010 through 2018 reflect CBO's assessment of average values for that period. That assessment takes into account economic and demographic trends but does not attempt to forecast the frequency and size of ups and downs in the business cycle.

Table E-1.

CBO's Year-by-Year Forecast and Projections for Calendar Years 2008 to 2018

	Estimated 2007	Forecast 2008	Forecast 2009	Projected 2010	Projected 2011	Projected 2012	Projected 2013	Projected 2014	Projected 2015	Projected 2016	Projected 2017	Projected 2018
Nominal GDP (Billions of dollars)	13,828	14,330	14,997	15,812	16,651	17,453	18,243	19,062	19,896	20,758	21,654	22,593
Nominal GDP (Percentage change)	4.8	3.6	4.7	5.4	5.3	4.8	4.5	4.5	4.4	4.3	4.3	4.3
Real GDP (Percentage change)	2.2	1.7	2.8	3.5	3.4	2.9	2.6	2.6	2.5	2.4	2.4	2.4
GDP Price Index (Percentage change)	2.5	1.9	1.8	1.8	1.8	1.9	1.9	1.9	1.9	1.9	1.9	1.9
PCE Price Index[a] (Percentage change)	2.5	2.6	1.8	1.9	1.9	1.9	1.9	1.9	1.9	1.9	1.9	1.9
Core PCE Price Index[b] (Percentage change)	2.1	1.9	1.9	1.8	1.9	1.9	1.9	1.9	1.9	1.9	1.9	1.9
Consumer Price Index[c] (Percentage change)	2.8	2.9	2.3	2.2	2.2	2.2	2.2	2.2	2.2	2.2	2.2	2.2
Core Consumer Price Index[d] (Percentage change)	2.3	2.2	2.2	2.2	2.2	2.2	2.2	2.2	2.2	2.2	2.2	2.2
Employment Cost Index[e] (Percentage change)	3.4	2.9	2.7	2.9	3.2	3.3	3.3	3.3	3.3	3.3	3.3	3.3
Unemployment Rate (Percent)	4.6	5.1	5.4	5.1	4.8	4.8	4.8	4.8	4.8	4.8	4.8	4.8
Three-Month Treasury Bill Rate (Percent)	4.4	3.2	4.2	4.6	4.7	4.7	4.7	4.7	4.7	4.7	4.7	4.7
Ten-Year Treasury Note Rate (Percent)	4.6	4.2	4.9	5.2	5.2	5.2	5.2	5.2	5.2	5.2	5.2	5.2
Tax Bases (Billions of dollars)												
Economic profits	1,599	1,620	1,649	1,678	1,731	1,791	1,842	1,905	1,993	2,091	2,200	2,320
Wages and salaries	6,368	6,615	6,913	7,318	7,633	8,037	8,401	8,778	9,149	9,535	9,936	10,354
Tax Bases (Percentage of GDP)												
Economic profits	11.6	11.3	11.0	10.6	10.4	10.3	10.1	10.0	10.0	10.1	10.2	10.3
Wages and salaries	46.0	46.2	46.1	46.3	45.8	46.1	46.0	46.0	46.0	45.9	45.9	45.8

Sources: Congressional Budget Office; Department of Commerce, Bureau of Economic Analysis; Department of Labor, Bureau of Labor Statistics; Federal Reserve Board.

Notes: GDP = gross domestic product; percentage changes are measured from one year to the next.

a. The personal consumption expenditure chained price index.

b. The personal consumption expenditure chained price index excluding prices for food and energy.

c. The consumer price index for all urban consumers.

d. The consumer price index for all urban consumers excluding prices for food and energy.

e. The employment cost index for wages and salaries of workers in private industry.

Table E-2.

CBO's Year-by-Year Forecast and Projections for Fiscal Years 2008 to 2018

	Actual 2007	Forecast 2008	Forecast 2009	Projected 2010	2011	2012	2013	2014	2015	2016	2017	2018
Nominal GDP (Billions of dollars)	13,670	14,201	14,812	15,600	16,445	17,256	18,043	18,856	19,685	20,540	21,426	22,355
Nominal GDP (Percentage change)	5.0	3.9	4.3	5.3	5.4	4.9	4.6	4.5	4.4	4.3	4.3	4.3
Real GDP (Percentage change)	2.2	2.0	2.3	3.4	3.5	3.0	2.6	2.6	2.5	2.4	2.4	2.4
GDP Price Index (Percentage change)	2.7	1.9	1.9	1.8	1.8	1.8	1.9	1.9	1.9	1.9	1.9	1.9
PCE Price Index[a] (Percentage change)	2.2	2.9	1.9	1.9	1.9	1.9	1.9	1.9	1.9	1.9	1.9	1.9
Core PCE Price Index[b] (Percentage change)	2.1	1.9	1.9	1.8	1.9	1.9	1.9	1.9	1.9	1.9	1.9	1.9
Consumer Price Index[c] (Percentage change)	2.3	3.2	2.3	2.2	2.2	2.2	2.2	2.2	2.2	2.2	2.2	2.2
Core Consumer Price Index[d] (Percentage change)	2.4	2.2	2.2	2.2	2.2	2.2	2.2	2.2	2.2	2.2	2.2	2.2
Employment Cost Index[e] (Percentage change)	3.4	3.0	2.7	2.8	3.1	3.3	3.3	3.3	3.3	3.3	3.3	3.3
Unemployment Rate (Percent)	4.5	4.9	5.3	5.2	4.9	4.8	4.8	4.8	4.8	4.8	4.8	4.8
Three-Month Treasury Bill Rate (Percent)	4.7	3.2	3.9	4.6	4.7	4.7	4.7	4.7	4.7	4.7	4.7	4.7
Ten-Year Treasury Note Rate (Percent)	4.7	4.2	4.7	5.2	5.2	5.2	5.2	5.2	5.2	5.2	5.2	5.2
Tax Bases (Billions of dollars)												
Economic profits	1,586	1,604	1,648	1,667	1,717	1,776	1,830	1,888	1,969	2,065	2,172	2,289
Wages and salaries	6,290	6,555	6,828	7,186	7,573	7,947	8,309	8,682	9,056	9,437	9,834	10,248
Tax Bases (Percentage of GDP)												
Economic profits	11.6	11.3	11.1	10.7	10.4	10.3	10.1	10.0	10.0	10.1	10.1	10.2
Wages and salaries	46.0	46.2	46.1	46.1	46.1	46.1	46.0	46.0	46.0	45.9	45.9	45.8

Sources: Congressional Budget Office; Department of Commerce, Bureau of Economic Analysis; Department of Labor, Bureau of Labor Statistics; Federal Reserve Board.

Notes: GDP = gross domestic product; percentage changes are measured from one year to the next.

a.   The personal consumption expenditure chained price index.

b.   The personal consumption expenditure chained price index excluding prices for food and energy.

c.   The consumer price index for all urban consumers.

d.   The consumer price index for all urban consumers excluding prices for food and energy.

e.   The employment cost index for wages and salaries of workers in private industry.

Historical Budget Data

This appendix provides historical data for revenues, outlays, and the deficit or surplus—in forms consistent with the projections in Chapters 1, 3, and 4—for fiscal years 1968 to 2007. The data are shown both in nominal dollars and as a percentage of gross domestic product. Data come from the Congressional Budget Office and the Office of Management and Budget. Some of the numbers have been revised since January 2007, the last time these tables were published.

Federal revenues, outlays, the deficit or surplus, and debt held by the public are shown in Tables F-1 and F-2. Revenues, outlays, and the deficit or surplus have both on-budget and off-budget components. Social Security's receipts and outlays were placed off-budget by the Balanced Budget and Emergency Deficit Control Act of 1985. For the sake of consistency, the tables show the budgetary components of Social Security as off-budget before that year. The Postal Service was moved off-budget by the Omnibus Reconciliation Act of 1989.

The major sources of federal revenues (including off-budget revenues) are presented in Tables F-3 and F-4. Social insurance taxes include payments by employers and employees for Social Security, Medicare, Railroad Retirement, and unemployment insurance, as well as pension contributions by federal workers. Excise taxes are levied on certain products and services, such as gasoline, alcoholic beverages, and air travel. Estate and gift taxes are levied on assets when they are transferred. Miscellaneous receipts consist of earnings of the Federal Reserve System and income from numerous fees and charges.

Total outlays for major categories of spending appear in Tables F-5 and F-6. (Those totals include on- and off-budget outlays.) Spending controlled by the appropriation process is classified as discretionary. Spending governed by permanent laws, such as those that set eligibility requirements for certain programs, is considered

mandatory. Offsetting receipts include the government's contributions to retirement programs for its employees, fees, charges (such as Medicare premiums), and receipts from the use of federally controlled land and offshore territory. Net interest (function 900 of the budget) comprises the interest paid by the government on federal debt offset by its interest income.

Tables F-7 and F-8 divide discretionary spending into its defense, international, and domestic components. Tables F-9 and F-10 classify mandatory spending by the three major entitlement programs—Social Security, Medicare, and Medicaid—and by other categories of mandatory spending. Income-security programs provide benefits to recipients with limited income and assets; those programs include unemployment compensation, Supplemental Security Income, and Food Stamps. Other federal retirement and disability programs provide benefits to federal civilian employees, members of the military, and veterans. The category of other mandatory programs includes the activities of the Commodity Credit Corporation, TRICARE For Life (which provides health care benefits to retirees of the uniformed services who are eligible for Medicare), the subsidy costs of federal student loan programs, the Universal Service Fund (which reduces the cost of telecommunications services for selected areas and individuals), the State Children's Health Insurance Program, and the Social Services Block Grant program.

The remaining tables, F-11 through F-13, show estimates of the standardized-budget deficit or surplus and its outlay and revenue components. The standardized-budget deficit or surplus attempts to filter out the effects that cyclical fluctuations in output and unemployment have on revenues and outlays; it also incorporates other adjustments. The change in that deficit or surplus is commonly used to measure the short-term impact of fiscal policy on total demand. Table F-11 also presents estimates of potential and actual gross domestic product.

Table F-1.

Revenues, Outlays, Deficits, Surpluses, and Debt Held by the Public, 1968 to 2007, in Billions of Dollars

| | Revenues | Outlays | Deficit (-) or Surplus | | | | Debt Held by the Public[a] |
			On-Budget	Social Security	Postal Service	Total	
1968	153.0	178.1	-27.7	2.6	n.a.	-25.2	289.5
1969	186.9	183.6	-0.5	3.7	n.a.	3.2	278.1
1970	192.8	195.6	-8.7	5.9	n.a.	-2.8	283.2
1971	187.1	210.2	-26.1	3.0	n.a.	-23.0	303.0
1972	207.3	230.7	-26.1	3.1	-0.4	-23.4	322.4
1973	230.8	245.7	-15.2	0.5	-0.2	-14.9	340.9
1974	263.2	269.4	-7.2	1.8	-0.8	-6.1	343.7
1975	279.1	332.3	-54.1	2.0	-1.1	-53.2	394.7
1976	298.1	371.8	-69.4	-3.2	-1.1	-73.7	477.4
1977	355.6	409.2	-49.9	-3.9	0.2	-53.7	549.1
1978	399.6	458.7	-55.4	-4.3	0.5	-59.2	607.1
1979	463.3	504.0	-39.6	-2.0	0.9	-40.7	640.3
1980	517.1	590.9	-73.1	-1.1	0.4	-73.8	711.9
1981	599.3	678.2	-73.9	-5.0	-0.1	-79.0	789.4
1982	617.8	745.7	-120.6	-7.9	0.6	-128.0	924.6
1983	600.6	808.4	-207.7	0.2	-0.3	-207.8	1,137.3
1984	666.5	851.9	-185.3	0.3	-0.4	-185.4	1,307.0
1985	734.1	946.4	-221.5	9.4	-0.1	-212.3	1,507.3
1986	769.2	990.4	-237.9	16.7	*	-221.2	1,740.6
1987	854.4	1,004.1	-168.4	19.6	-0.9	-149.7	1,889.8
1988	909.3	1,064.5	-192.3	38.8	-1.7	-155.2	2,051.6
1989	991.2	1,143.8	-205.4	52.4	0.3	-152.6	2,190.7
1990	1,032.1	1,253.1	-277.6	58.2	-1.6	-221.0	2,411.6
1991	1,055.1	1,324.3	-321.4	53.5	-1.3	-269.2	2,689.0
1992	1,091.3	1,381.6	-340.4	50.7	-0.7	-290.3	2,999.7
1993	1,154.5	1,409.5	-300.4	46.8	-1.4	-255.1	3,248.4
1994	1,258.7	1,461.9	-258.8	56.8	-1.1	-203.2	3,433.1
1995	1,351.9	1,515.9	-226.4	60.4	2.0	-164.0	3,604.4
1996	1,453.2	1,560.6	-174.0	66.4	0.2	-107.4	3,734.1
1997	1,579.4	1,601.3	-103.2	81.3	*	-21.9	3,772.3
1998	1,722.0	1,652.7	-29.9	99.4	-0.2	69.3	3,721.1
1999	1,827.6	1,702.0	1.9	124.7	-1.0	125.6	3,632.4
2000	2,025.5	1,789.2	86.4	151.8	-2.0	236.2	3,409.8
2001	1,991.4	1,863.2	-32.4	163.0	-2.3	128.2	3,319.6
2002	1,853.4	2,011.2	-317.4	159.0	0.7	-157.8	3,540.4
2003	1,782.5	2,160.1	-538.4	155.6	5.2	-377.6	3,913.4
2004	1,880.3	2,293.0	-568.0	151.1	4.1	-412.7	4,295.5
2005	2,153.9	2,472.2	-493.6	173.5	1.8	-318.3	4,592.2
2006	2,407.3	2,655.4	-434.5	185.2	1.1	-248.2	4,829.0
2007	2,567.7	2,730.5	-344.3	186.5	-5.1	-162.8	5,035.3

Sources: Congressional Budget Office; Office of Management and Budget.

Note: n.a. = not applicable; * = between -$50 million and $50 million.

a. End of year.

Table F-2.

Revenues, Outlays, Deficits, Surpluses, and Debt Held by the Public, 1968 to 2007, as a Percentage of Gross Domestic Product

			Deficit (-) or Surplus				Debt Held by the Public[a]
	Revenues	Outlays	On-Budget	Social Security	Postal Service	Total	
1968	17.6	20.5	-3.2	0.3	n.a.	-2.9	33.3
1969	19.7	19.4	-0.1	0.4	n.a.	0.3	29.3
1970	19.0	19.3	-0.9	0.6	n.a.	-0.3	28.0
1971	17.3	19.5	-2.4	0.3	n.a.	-2.1	28.1
1972	17.6	19.6	-2.2	0.3	*	-2.0	27.4
1973	17.6	18.7	-1.2	*	*	-1.1	26.0
1974	18.3	18.7	-0.5	0.1	-0.1	-0.4	23.9
1975	17.9	21.3	-3.5	0.1	-0.1	-3.4	25.3
1976	17.1	21.4	-4.0	-0.2	-0.1	-4.2	27.5
1977	18.0	20.7	-2.5	-0.2	*	-2.7	27.8
1978	18.0	20.7	-2.5	-0.2	*	-2.7	27.4
1979	18.5	20.1	-1.6	-0.1	*	-1.6	25.6
1980	19.0	21.7	-2.7	*	*	-2.7	26.1
1981	19.6	22.2	-2.4	-0.2	*	-2.6	25.8
1982	19.2	23.1	-3.7	-0.2	*	-4.0	28.7
1983	17.4	23.5	-6.0	*	*	-6.0	33.0
1984	17.3	22.1	-4.8	*	*	-4.8	34.0
1985	17.7	22.8	-5.3	0.2	*	-5.1	36.3
1986	17.5	22.5	-5.4	0.4	*	-5.0	39.5
1987	18.4	21.6	-3.6	0.4	*	-3.2	40.6
1988	18.1	21.2	-3.8	0.8	*	-3.1	40.9
1989	18.3	21.2	-3.8	1.0	*	-2.8	40.6
1990	18.0	21.8	-4.8	1.0	*	-3.9	42.0
1991	17.8	22.3	-5.4	0.9	*	-4.5	45.3
1992	17.5	22.1	-5.5	0.8	*	-4.7	48.1
1993	17.5	21.4	-4.6	0.7	*	-3.9	49.4
1994	18.1	21.0	-3.7	0.8	*	-2.9	49.3
1995	18.5	20.7	-3.1	0.8	*	-2.2	49.2
1996	18.9	20.3	-2.3	0.9	*	-1.4	48.5
1997	19.3	19.6	-1.3	1.0	*	-0.3	46.1
1998	20.0	19.2	-0.3	1.2	*	0.8	43.1
1999	20.0	18.6	*	1.4	*	1.4	39.8
2000	20.9	18.4	0.9	1.6	*	2.4	35.1
2001	19.8	18.5	-0.3	1.6	*	1.3	33.0
2002	17.9	19.4	-3.1	1.5	*	-1.5	34.1
2003	16.5	20.0	-5.0	1.4	*	-3.5	36.2
2004	16.3	19.9	-4.9	1.3	*	-3.6	37.3
2005	17.6	20.2	-4.0	1.4	*	-2.6	37.5
2006	18.5	20.4	-3.3	1.4	*	-1.9	37.1
2007	18.8	20.0	-2.5	1.4	*	-1.2	36.8

Sources: Congressional Budget Office; Office of Management and Budget.

Note: n.a. = not applicable; * = between -0.05 percent and 0.05 percent.

a.   End of year.

Table F-3.

Revenues by Major Source, 1968 to 2007, in Billions of Dollars

	Individual Income Taxes	Corporate Income Taxes	Social Insurance Taxes	Excise Taxes	Estate and Gift Taxes	Customs Duties	Miscellaneous Receipts	Total Revenues
1968	68.7	28.7	33.9	14.1	3.1	2.0	2.5	153.0
1969	87.2	36.7	39.0	15.2	3.5	2.3	2.9	186.9
1970	90.4	32.8	44.4	15.7	3.6	2.4	3.4	192.8
1971	86.2	26.8	47.3	16.6	3.7	2.6	3.9	187.1
1972	94.7	32.2	52.6	15.5	5.4	3.3	3.6	207.3
1973	103.2	36.2	63.1	16.3	4.9	3.2	3.9	230.8
1974	119.0	38.6	75.1	16.8	5.0	3.3	5.4	263.2
1975	122.4	40.6	84.5	16.6	4.6	3.7	6.7	279.1
1976	131.6	41.4	90.8	17.0	5.2	4.1	8.0	298.1
1977	157.6	54.9	106.5	17.5	7.3	5.2	6.5	355.6
1978	181.0	60.0	121.0	18.4	5.3	6.6	7.4	399.6
1979	217.8	65.7	138.9	18.7	5.4	7.4	9.3	463.3
1980	244.1	64.6	157.8	24.3	6.4	7.2	12.7	517.1
1981	285.9	61.1	182.7	40.8	6.8	8.1	13.8	599.3
1982	297.7	49.2	201.5	36.3	8.0	8.9	16.2	617.8
1983	288.9	37.0	209.0	35.3	6.1	8.7	15.6	600.6
1984	298.4	56.9	239.4	37.4	6.0	11.4	17.1	666.5
1985	334.5	61.3	265.2	36.0	6.4	12.1	18.6	734.1
1986	349.0	63.1	283.9	32.9	7.0	13.3	20.0	769.2
1987	392.6	83.9	303.3	32.5	7.5	15.1	19.5	854.4
1988	401.2	94.5	334.3	35.2	7.6	16.2	20.3	909.3
1989	445.7	103.3	359.4	34.4	8.7	16.3	23.3	991.2
1990	466.9	93.5	380.0	35.3	11.5	16.7	28.1	1,032.1
1991	467.8	98.1	396.0	42.4	11.1	15.9	23.7	1,055.1
1992	476.0	100.3	413.7	45.6	11.1	17.4	27.3	1,091.3
1993	509.7	117.5	428.3	48.1	12.6	18.8	19.5	1,154.5
1994	543.1	140.4	461.5	55.2	15.2	20.1	23.3	1,258.7
1995	590.2	157.0	484.5	57.5	14.8	19.3	28.7	1,351.9
1996	656.4	171.8	509.4	54.0	17.2	18.7	25.6	1,453.2
1997	737.5	182.3	539.4	56.9	19.8	17.9	25.6	1,579.4
1998	828.6	188.7	571.8	57.7	24.1	18.3	32.8	1,722.0
1999	879.5	184.7	611.8	70.4	27.8	18.3	35.1	1,827.6
2000	1,004.5	207.3	652.9	68.9	29.0	19.9	43.1	2,025.5
2001	994.3	151.1	694.0	66.2	28.4	19.4	38.0	1,991.4
2002	858.3	148.0	700.8	67.0	26.5	18.6	34.1	1,853.4
2003	793.7	131.8	713.0	67.5	22.0	19.9	34.7	1,782.5
2004	809.0	189.4	733.4	69.9	24.8	21.1	32.8	1,880.3
2005	927.2	278.3	794.1	73.1	24.8	23.4	33.0	2,153.9
2006	1,043.9	353.9	837.8	74.0	27.9	24.8	45.0	2,407.3
2007	1,163.5	370.2	869.6	65.1	26.0	26.0	47.2	2,567.7

Sources: Congressional Budget Office; Office of Management and Budget.

Table F-4.

Revenues by Major Source, 1968 to 2007, as a Percentage of Gross Domestic Product

	Individual Income Taxes	Corporate Income Taxes	Social Insurance Taxes	Excise Taxes	Estate and Gift Taxes	Customs Duties	Miscellaneous Receipts	Total Revenues
1968	7.9	3.3	3.9	1.6	0.4	0.2	0.3	17.6
1969	9.2	3.9	4.1	1.6	0.4	0.2	0.3	19.7
1970	8.9	3.2	4.4	1.6	0.4	0.2	0.3	19.0
1971	8.0	2.5	4.4	1.5	0.3	0.2	0.4	17.3
1972	8.0	2.7	4.5	1.3	0.5	0.3	0.3	17.6
1973	7.9	2.8	4.8	1.2	0.4	0.2	0.3	17.6
1974	8.3	2.7	5.2	1.2	0.3	0.2	0.4	18.3
1975	7.8	2.6	5.4	1.1	0.3	0.2	0.4	17.9
1976	7.6	2.4	5.2	1.0	0.3	0.2	0.5	17.1
1977	8.0	2.8	5.4	0.9	0.4	0.3	0.3	18.0
1978	8.2	2.7	5.5	0.8	0.2	0.3	0.3	18.0
1979	8.7	2.6	5.6	0.7	0.2	0.3	0.4	18.5
1980	9.0	2.4	5.8	0.9	0.2	0.3	0.5	19.0
1981	9.3	2.0	6.0	1.3	0.2	0.3	0.5	19.6
1982	9.2	1.5	6.2	1.1	0.2	0.3	0.5	19.2
1983	8.4	1.1	6.1	1.0	0.2	0.3	0.5	17.4
1984	7.8	1.5	6.2	1.0	0.2	0.3	0.4	17.3
1985	8.1	1.5	6.4	0.9	0.2	0.3	0.4	17.7
1986	7.9	1.4	6.4	0.7	0.2	0.3	0.5	17.5
1987	8.4	1.8	6.5	0.7	0.2	0.3	0.4	18.4
1988	8.0	1.9	6.7	0.7	0.2	0.3	0.4	18.1
1989	8.3	1.9	6.7	0.6	0.2	0.3	0.4	18.3
1990	8.1	1.6	6.6	0.6	0.2	0.3	0.5	18.0
1991	7.9	1.7	6.7	0.7	0.2	0.3	0.4	17.8
1992	7.6	1.6	6.6	0.7	0.2	0.3	0.4	17.5
1993	7.7	1.8	6.5	0.7	0.2	0.3	0.3	17.5
1994	7.8	2.0	6.6	0.8	0.2	0.3	0.3	18.1
1995	8.1	2.1	6.6	0.8	0.2	0.3	0.4	18.5
1996	8.5	2.2	6.6	0.7	0.2	0.2	0.3	18.9
1997	9.0	2.2	6.6	0.7	0.2	0.2	0.3	19.3
1998	9.6	2.2	6.6	0.7	0.3	0.2	0.4	20.0
1999	9.6	2.0	6.7	0.8	0.3	0.2	0.4	20.0
2000	10.3	2.1	6.7	0.7	0.3	0.2	0.4	20.9
2001	9.9	1.5	6.9	0.7	0.3	0.2	0.4	19.8
2002	8.3	1.4	6.8	0.6	0.3	0.2	0.3	17.9
2003	7.3	1.2	6.6	0.6	0.2	0.2	0.3	16.5
2004	7.0	1.6	6.4	0.6	0.2	0.2	0.3	16.3
2005	7.6	2.3	6.5	0.6	0.2	0.2	0.3	17.6
2006	8.0	2.7	6.4	0.6	0.2	0.2	0.3	18.5
2007	8.5	2.7	6.4	0.5	0.2	0.2	0.3	18.8

Sources: Congressional Budget Office; Office of Management and Budget.

Table F-5.

Outlays for Major Categories of Spending, 1968 to 2007, in Billions of Dollars

| | Discretionary Spending | Mandatory Spending | | Net Interest | Total Outlays |
		Programmatic Spending[a]	Offsetting Receipts		
1968	118.0	59.7	-10.6	11.1	178.1
1969	117.3	64.6	-11.0	12.7	183.6
1970	120.3	72.5	-11.5	14.4	195.6
1971	122.5	86.9	-14.1	14.8	210.2
1972	128.5	100.8	-14.1	15.5	230.7
1973	130.4	116.0	-18.0	17.3	245.7
1974	138.2	130.9	-21.2	21.4	269.4
1975	158.0	169.4	-18.3	23.2	332.3
1976	175.6	189.1	-19.6	26.7	371.8
1977	197.1	203.7	-21.5	29.9	409.2
1978	218.7	227.4	-22.8	35.5	458.7
1979	240.0	247.0	-25.6	42.6	504.0
1980	276.3	291.2	-29.2	52.5	590.9
1981	307.9	339.4	-37.9	68.8	678.2
1982	326.0	370.8	-36.0	85.0	745.7
1983	353.3	410.6	-45.3	89.8	808.4
1984	379.4	405.6	-44.2	111.1	851.9
1985	415.8	448.2	-47.1	129.5	946.4
1986	438.5	461.8	-45.9	136.0	990.4
1987	444.2	474.2	-52.9	138.6	1,004.1
1988	464.4	505.1	-56.8	151.8	1,064.5
1989	488.8	549.8	-63.8	169.0	1,143.8
1990	500.6	626.9	-58.7	184.3	1,253.1
1991	533.3	702.3	-105.7	194.4	1,324.3
1992	533.8	716.8	-68.4	199.3	1,381.6
1993	539.4	738.0	-66.6	198.7	1,409.5
1994	541.4	786.1	-68.5	202.9	1,461.9
1995	544.9	818.6	-79.7	232.1	1,515.9
1996	532.7	858.8	-71.9	241.1	1,560.6
1997	547.2	896.4	-86.3	244.0	1,601.3
1998	552.1	938.7	-79.2	241.1	1,652.7
1999	572.0	976.9	-76.6	229.8	1,702.0
2000	614.8	1,030.0	-78.6	222.9	1,789.2
2001	649.3	1,094.5	-86.8	206.2	1,863.2
2002	734.3	1,196.9	-91.0	170.9	2,011.2
2003	825.4	1,281.8	-100.2	153.1	2,160.1
2004	895.5	1,346.0	-108.7	160.2	2,293.0
2005	968.5	1,445.6	-125.8	184.0	2,472.2
2006	1,016.7	1,552.7	-140.6	226.6	2,655.4
2007	1,042.1	1,628.3	-177.8	238.0	2,730.5

Sources: Congressional Budget Office; Office of Management and Budget.

a. Excludes offsetting receipts.

Table F-6.

Outlays for Major Categories of Spending, 1968 to 2007, as a Percentage of Gross Domestic Product

| | Discretionary Spending | Mandatory Spending | | Net Interest | Total Outlays |
		Programmatic Spending[a]	Offsetting Receipts		
1968	13.6	6.9	-1.2	1.3	20.5
1969	12.4	6.8	-1.2	1.3	19.4
1970	11.9	7.2	-1.1	1.4	19.3
1971	11.3	8.0	-1.3	1.4	19.5
1972	10.9	8.6	-1.2	1.3	19.6
1973	9.9	8.8	-1.4	1.3	18.7
1974	9.6	9.1	-1.5	1.5	18.7
1975	10.1	10.9	-1.2	1.5	21.3
1976	10.1	10.9	-1.1	1.5	21.4
1977	10.0	10.3	-1.1	1.5	20.7
1978	9.9	10.3	-1.0	1.6	20.7
1979	9.6	9.9	-1.0	1.7	20.1
1980	10.1	10.7	-1.1	1.9	21.7
1981	10.1	11.1	-1.2	2.2	22.2
1982	10.1	11.5	-1.1	2.6	23.1
1983	10.3	11.9	-1.3	2.6	23.5
1984	9.9	10.5	-1.2	2.9	22.1
1985	10.0	10.8	-1.1	3.1	22.8
1986	10.0	10.5	-1.0	3.1	22.5
1987	9.5	10.2	-1.1	3.0	21.6
1988	9.3	10.1	-1.1	3.0	21.2
1989	9.0	10.2	-1.2	3.1	21.2
1990	8.7	10.9	-1.0	3.2	21.8
1991	9.0	11.8	-1.8	3.3	22.3
1992	8.6	11.5	-1.1	3.2	22.1
1993	8.2	11.2	-1.0	3.0	21.4
1994	7.8	11.3	-1.0	2.9	21.0
1995	7.4	11.2	-1.1	3.2	20.7
1996	6.9	11.2	-0.9	3.1	20.3
1997	6.7	10.9	-1.1	3.0	19.6
1998	6.4	10.9	-0.9	2.8	19.2
1999	6.3	10.7	-0.8	2.5	18.6
2000	6.3	10.6	-0.8	2.3	18.4
2001	6.5	10.9	-0.9	2.0	18.5
2002	7.1	11.5	-0.9	1.6	19.4
2003	7.6	11.9	-0.9	1.4	20.0
2004	7.8	11.7	-0.9	1.4	19.9
2005	7.9	11.8	-1.0	1.5	20.2
2006	7.8	11.9	-1.1	1.7	20.4
2007	7.6	11.9	-1.3	1.7	20.0

Sources: Congressional Budget Office; Office of Management and Budget.

a. Excludes offsetting receipts.

Table F-7.

Discretionary Outlays, 1968 to 2007, in Billions of Dollars

	Defense	International	Domestic	Total
1968	82.2	4.9	31.0	118.0
1969	82.7	4.1	30.5	117.3
1970	81.9	4.0	34.4	120.3
1971	79.0	3.8	39.8	122.5
1972	79.3	4.6	44.6	128.5
1973	77.1	4.8	48.5	130.4
1974	80.7	6.2	51.3	138.2
1975	87.6	8.2	62.2	158.0
1976	89.9	7.5	78.2	175.6
1977	97.5	8.0	91.5	197.1
1978	104.6	8.5	105.5	218.7
1979	116.8	9.1	114.1	240.0
1980	134.6	12.8	128.9	276.3
1981	158.0	13.6	136.3	307.9
1982	185.9	12.9	127.1	326.0
1983	209.9	13.6	129.8	353.3
1984	228.0	16.3	135.1	379.4
1985	253.1	17.4	145.3	415.8
1986	273.8	17.7	147.0	438.5
1987	282.5	15.2	146.5	444.2
1988	290.9	15.7	157.8	464.4
1989	304.0	16.6	168.2	488.8
1990	300.1	19.1	181.4	500.6
1991	319.7	19.7	193.9	533.3
1992	302.6	19.2	212.1	533.8
1993	292.4	21.6	225.4	539.4
1994	282.3	20.8	238.3	541.4
1995	273.6	20.1	251.2	544.9
1996	266.0	18.3	248.4	532.7
1997	271.7	19.0	256.6	547.2
1998	270.3	18.1	263.8	552.1
1999	275.5	19.5	277.0	572.0
2000	295.0	21.3	298.6	614.8
2001	306.1	22.5	320.8	649.3
2002	349.0	26.2	359.2	734.3
2003	405.0	27.9	392.5	825.4
2004	454.1	33.8	407.6	895.5
2005	493.6	39.0	435.8	968.5
2006	520.0	36.1	460.7	1,016.7
2007	548.6	34.5	458.9	1,042.1

Sources: Congressional Budget Office; Office of Management and Budget.

Table F-8.

Discretionary Outlays, 1968 to 2007, as a Percentage of Gross Domestic Product

	Defense	International	Domestic	Total
1968	9.5	0.6	3.6	13.6
1969	8.7	0.4	3.2	12.4
1970	8.1	0.4	3.4	11.9
1971	7.3	0.3	3.7	11.3
1972	6.7	0.4	3.8	10.9
1973	5.9	0.4	3.7	9.9
1974	5.6	0.4	3.6	9.6
1975	5.6	0.5	4.0	10.1
1976	5.2	0.4	4.5	10.1
1977	4.9	0.4	4.6	10.0
1978	4.7	0.4	4.8	9.9
1979	4.7	0.4	4.6	9.6
1980	4.9	0.5	4.7	10.1
1981	5.2	0.4	4.5	10.1
1982	5.8	0.4	3.9	10.1
1983	6.1	0.4	3.8	10.3
1984	5.9	0.4	3.5	9.9
1985	6.1	0.4	3.5	10.0
1986	6.2	0.4	3.3	10.0
1987	6.1	0.3	3.1	9.5
1988	5.8	0.3	3.1	9.3
1989	5.6	0.3	3.1	9.0
1990	5.2	0.3	3.2	8.7
1991	5.4	0.3	3.3	9.0
1992	4.8	0.3	3.4	8.6
1993	4.4	0.3	3.4	8.2
1994	4.1	0.3	3.4	7.8
1995	3.7	0.3	3.4	7.4
1996	3.5	0.2	3.2	6.9
1997	3.3	0.2	3.1	6.7
1998	3.1	0.2	3.1	6.4
1999	3.0	0.2	3.0	6.3
2000	3.0	0.2	3.1	6.3
2001	3.0	0.2	3.2	6.5
2002	3.4	0.3	3.5	7.1
2003	3.7	0.3	3.6	7.6
2004	3.9	0.3	3.5	7.8
2005	4.0	0.3	3.6	7.9
2006	4.0	0.3	3.5	7.8
2007	4.0	0.3	3.4	7.6

Sources: Congressional Budget Office; Office of Management and Budget.

Table F-9.

Outlays for Mandatory Spending, 1968 to 2007, in Billions of Dollars

	Social Security	Medicare	Medicaid	Income Security[a]	Other Retirement and Disability	Other Programs	Offsetting Receipts	Total
1968	23.3	5.1	1.8	5.9	10.1	13.4	-10.6	49.1
1969	26.7	6.3	2.3	6.5	11.1	11.8	-11.0	53.6
1970	29.6	6.8	2.7	8.2	12.4	12.8	-11.5	61.0
1971	35.1	7.5	3.4	13.4	14.5	13.0	-14.1	72.8
1972	39.4	8.4	4.6	16.4	16.2	15.8	-14.1	86.7
1973	48.2	9.0	4.6	14.5	18.5	21.3	-18.0	98.0
1974	55.0	10.7	5.8	17.4	20.9	21.1	-21.2	109.7
1975	63.6	14.1	6.8	28.9	26.4	29.6	-18.3	151.1
1976	72.7	16.9	8.6	37.6	27.7	25.6	-19.6	169.5
1977	83.7	20.8	9.9	34.6	31.2	23.6	-21.5	182.2
1978	92.4	24.3	10.7	32.1	33.9	34.0	-22.8	204.6
1979	102.6	28.2	12.4	32.2	38.7	32.9	-25.6	221.4
1980	117.1	34.0	14.0	44.3	44.4	37.5	-29.2	262.1
1981	137.9	41.3	16.8	49.9	50.8	42.6	-37.9	301.6
1982	153.9	49.2	17.4	53.2	55.0	42.1	-36.0	334.8
1983	168.5	55.5	19.0	64.0	58.0	45.5	-45.3	365.2
1984	176.1	61.1	20.1	51.7	59.8	36.8	-44.2	361.3
1985	186.4	69.7	22.7	52.3	61.0	56.3	-47.1	401.1
1986	196.5	74.2	25.0	54.2	63.4	48.4	-45.9	415.9
1987	205.1	79.9	27.4	55.0	66.5	40.2	-52.9	421.3
1988	216.8	85.7	30.5	57.3	71.1	43.7	-56.8	448.2
1989	230.4	93.2	34.6	60.8	74.6	56.2	-63.8	486.0
1990	246.5	107.0	41.1	68.4	76.1	87.7	-58.7	568.2
1991	266.8	114.2	52.5	86.6	82.2	100.0	-105.7	596.6
1992	285.2	129.4	67.8	110.0	84.8	39.6	-68.4	648.5
1993	302.0	143.2	75.8	116.1	87.2	13.8	-66.6	671.4
1994	316.9	159.6	82.0	115.3	93.2	19.0	-68.5	717.6
1995	333.3	177.1	89.1	116.0	95.5	7.7	-79.7	738.9
1996	347.1	191.3	92.0	121.0	96.9	10.5	-71.9	786.8
1997	362.3	207.9	95.6	121.9	102.3	6.5	-86.3	810.1
1998	376.1	211.0	101.2	121.6	105.0	23.7	-79.2	859.5
1999	387.0	209.3	108.0	128.6	105.1	38.9	-76.6	900.3
2000	406.0	216.0	117.9	133.5	113.8	42.7	-78.6	951.4
2001	429.4	237.9	129.4	142.7	116.3	38.9	-86.8	1,007.7
2002	452.1	253.7	147.5	179.9	124.9	38.8	-91.0	1,105.9
2003	470.5	274.2	160.7	196.2	129.4	51.0	-100.2	1,181.6
2004	491.5	297.0	176.2	190.7	135.0	55.5	-108.7	1,237.3
2005	518.7	332.6	181.7	195.9	147.6	69.0	-125.8	1,319.8
2006	543.9	373.8	180.6	199.2	149.4	105.8	-140.6	1,412.1
2007	581.5	436.3	190.6	202.3	158.7	58.9	-177.8	1,450.5

Sources: Congressional Budget Office; Office of Management and Budget.

a. Includes unemployment compensation, Supplemental Security Income, the refundable portion of the earned income and child tax credits, Food Stamps, family support, child nutrition, and foster care.

Table F-10.

Outlays for Mandatory Spending, 1968 to 2007, as a Percentage of Gross Domestic Product

	Social Security	Medicare	Medicaid	Income Security[a]	Other Retirement and Disability	Other Programs	Offsetting Receipts	Total
1968	2.7	0.6	0.2	0.7	1.2	1.5	-1.2	5.6
1969	2.8	0.7	0.2	0.7	1.2	1.2	-1.2	5.7
1970	2.9	0.7	0.3	0.8	1.2	1.3	-1.1	6.0
1971	3.3	0.7	0.3	1.2	1.3	1.2	-1.3	6.7
1972	3.3	0.7	0.4	1.4	1.4	1.3	-1.2	7.4
1973	3.7	0.7	0.4	1.1	1.4	1.6	-1.4	7.5
1974	3.8	0.7	0.4	1.2	1.4	1.5	-1.5	7.6
1975	4.1	0.9	0.4	1.9	1.7	1.9	-1.2	9.7
1976	4.2	1.0	0.5	2.2	1.6	1.5	-1.1	9.7
1977	4.2	1.1	0.5	1.8	1.6	1.2	-1.1	9.2
1978	4.2	1.1	0.5	1.4	1.5	1.5	-1.0	9.2
1979	4.1	1.1	0.5	1.3	1.5	1.3	-1.0	8.8
1980	4.3	1.2	0.5	1.6	1.6	1.4	-1.1	9.6
1981	4.5	1.4	0.6	1.6	1.7	1.4	-1.2	9.9
1982	4.8	1.5	0.5	1.6	1.7	1.3	-1.1	10.4
1983	4.9	1.6	0.6	1.9	1.7	1.3	-1.3	10.6
1984	4.6	1.6	0.5	1.3	1.6	1.0	-1.2	9.4
1985	4.5	1.7	0.5	1.3	1.5	1.4	-1.1	9.7
1986	4.5	1.7	0.6	1.2	1.4	1.1	-1.0	9.4
1987	4.4	1.7	0.6	1.2	1.4	0.9	-1.1	9.1
1988	4.3	1.7	0.6	1.1	1.4	0.9	-1.1	8.9
1989	4.3	1.7	0.6	1.1	1.4	1.0	-1.2	9.0
1990	4.3	1.9	0.7	1.2	1.3	1.5	-1.0	9.9
1991	4.5	1.9	0.9	1.5	1.4	1.7	-1.8	10.1
1992	4.6	2.1	1.1	1.8	1.4	0.6	-1.1	10.4
1993	4.6	2.2	1.2	1.8	1.3	0.2	-1.0	10.2
1994	4.6	2.3	1.2	1.7	1.3	0.3	-1.0	10.3
1995	4.5	2.4	1.2	1.6	1.3	0.1	-1.1	10.1
1996	4.5	2.5	1.2	1.6	1.3	0.1	-0.9	10.2
1997	4.4	2.5	1.2	1.5	1.2	0.1	-1.1	9.9
1998	4.4	2.4	1.2	1.4	1.2	0.3	-0.9	10.0
1999	4.2	2.3	1.2	1.4	1.2	0.4	-0.8	9.9
2000	4.2	2.2	1.2	1.4	1.2	0.4	-0.8	9.8
2001	4.3	2.4	1.3	1.4	1.2	0.4	-0.9	10.0
2002	4.4	2.4	1.4	1.7	1.2	0.4	-0.9	10.7
2003	4.4	2.5	1.5	1.8	1.2	0.5	-0.9	10.9
2004	4.3	2.6	1.5	1.7	1.2	0.5	-0.9	10.8
2005	4.2	2.7	1.5	1.6	1.2	0.6	-1.0	10.8
2006	4.2	2.9	1.4	1.5	1.1	0.8	-1.1	10.8
2007	4.3	3.2	1.4	1.5	1.2	0.4	-1.3	10.6

Sources: Congressional Budget Office; Office of Management and Budget.

a. Includes unemployment compensation, Supplemental Security Income, the refundable portion of the earned income and child tax credits, Food Stamps, family support, child nutrition, and foster care.

Table F-11.

Deficits, Surpluses, Debt, and Related Series, 1968 to 2007

	Billions of Dollars			Percentage of Potential GDP			Gross Domestic Product (Billions of dollars)	
	Budget Deficit (-) or Surplus	Standardized-Budget Deficit (-) or Surplus[a]	Debt Held by the Public	Budget Deficit (-) or Surplus	Standardized-Budget Deficit (-) or Surplus[a]	Debt Held by the Public	Actual[b]	Potential
1968	-25	-31	290	-3.0	-3.7	34.5	869	840
1969	3	-3	278	0.4	-0.3	30.4	948	916
1970	-3	2	283	-0.3	0.2	28.2	1,013	1,004
1971	-23	-10	303	-2.1	-0.9	27.8	1,080	1,091
1972	-23	-21	322	-2.0	-1.8	27.3	1,177	1,179
1973	-15	-20	341	-1.2	-1.6	26.8	1,311	1,274
1974	-6	2	344	-0.4	0.2	24.3	1,439	1,416
1975	-53	4	395	-3.3	0.2	24.4	1,561	1,620
1976	-74	-35	477	-4.1	-1.9	26.6	1,739	1,794
1977	-54	-21	549	-2.7	-1.0	27.4	1,974	2,004
1978	-59	-32	607	-2.7	-1.4	27.4	2,218	2,216
1979	-41	-14	640	-1.6	-0.6	25.8	2,502	2,481
1980	-74	-9	712	-2.7	-0.3	25.6	2,725	2,779
1981	-79	-17	789	-2.5	-0.6	25.3	3,059	3,115
1982	-128	-43	925	-3.7	-1.3	27.0	3,226	3,420
1983	-208	-112	1,137	-5.6	-3.0	30.9	3,443	3,679
1984	-185	-143	1,307	-4.7	-3.6	33.3	3,847	3,929
1985	-212	-179	1,507	-5.1	-4.3	36.0	4,149	4,193
1986	-221	-211	1,741	-5.0	-4.7	39.2	4,407	4,436
1987	-150	-157	1,890	-3.2	-3.3	40.2	4,654	4,697
1988	-155	-126	2,052	-3.1	-2.5	41.1	5,012	4,998
1989	-153	-117	2,191	-2.9	-2.2	41.0	5,402	5,348
1990	-221	-120	2,412	-3.9	-2.1	42.2	5,737	5,714
1991	-269	-150	2,689	-4.4	-2.5	44.1	5,934	6,092
1992	-290	-186	3,000	-4.5	-2.9	46.8	6,241	6,403
1993	-255	-192	3,248	-3.8	-2.9	48.4	6,578	6,711
1994	-203	-144	3,433	-2.9	-2.0	48.8	6,964	7,039
1995	-164	-146	3,604	-2.2	-2.0	48.8	7,325	7,389
1996	-107	-93	3,734	-1.4	-1.2	48.2	7,697	7,755
1997	-22	-81	3,772	-0.3	-1.0	46.3	8,187	8,139
1998	69	-38	3,721	0.8	-0.4	43.7	8,626	8,514
1999	126	2	3,632	1.4	*	40.7	9,127	8,935
2000	236	105	3,410	2.5	1.1	36.1	9,708	9,450
2001	128	102	3,320	1.3	1.0	33.1	10,060	10,019
2002	-158	-131	3,540	-1.5	-1.2	33.6	10,378	10,536
2003	-378	-288	3,913	-3.4	-2.6	35.5	10,804	11,039
2004	-413	-294	4,296	-3.6	-2.5	37.0	11,504	11,623
2005	-318	-239	4,592	-2.6	-1.9	37.3	12,245	12,316
2006	-248	-229	4,829	-1.9	-1.8	36.9	13,023	13,073
2007	-163	-167	5,035	-1.2	-1.2	36.5	13,670	13,796

Sources: Congressional Budget Office; Department of Commerce, Bureau of Economic Analysis; Office of Management and Budget.

Note: * = between zero and 0.05 percent.

a. Excludes deposit insurance, receipts from auctions of licenses to use the electromagnetic spectrum, timing adjustments, and contributions from allied nations for Operation Desert Storm (which were received in 1991 and 1992).

b. CBO calculated fiscal year numbers from seasonally adjusted quarterly national income and product account data from the Bureau of Economic Analysis.

Table F-12.

Standardized-Budget Deficit or Surplus and Related Series, 1968 to 2007, in Billions of Dollars

	Budget Deficit (-) or Surplus	− Cyclical Contributions	+ Other Adjustments[a]	= Standardized-Budget Deficit (-) or Surplus	Standardized-Budget Revenues	Standardized-Budget Outlays
1968	-25	11	5	-31	140	171
1969	3	14	8	-3	171	173
1970	-3	5	10	2	186	184
1971	-23	-4	9	-10	187	197
1972	-23	*	2	-21	199	220
1973	-15	14	8	-20	214	234
1974	-6	9	18	2	251	249
1975	-53	-22	35	4	301	297
1976	-74	-25	14	-35	309	344
1977	-54	-13	20	-21	357	378
1978	-59	2	29	-32	390	422
1979	-41	9	35	-14	446	460
1980	-74	-21	43	-9	523	532
1981	-79	-23	38	-17	606	623
1982	-128	-62	23	-43	655	698
1983	-208	-88	7	-112	653	765
1984	-185	-30	12	-143	672	815
1985	-212	-17	17	-179	723	902
1986	-221	-12	-1	-211	748	958
1987	-150	-13	-20	-157	816	972
1988	-155	7	37	-126	869	995
1989	-153	19	55	-117	938	1,055
1990	-221	8	109	-120	993	1,113
1991	-269	-50	70	-150	1,070	1,219
1992	-290	-63	41	-186	1,125	1,311
1993	-255	-52	11	-192	1,166	1,358
1994	-203	-29	30	-144	1,246	1,390
1995	-164	-18	*	-146	1,331	1,477
1996	-107	-20	-6	-93	1,417	1,510
1997	-22	15	-44	-81	1,494	1,575
1998	69	41	-67	-38	1,594	1,633
1999	126	67	-57	2	1,661	1,660
2000	236	94	-38	105	1,820	1,715
2001	128	19	-7	102	1,897	1,795
2002	-158	-62	-35	-131	1,815	1,946
2003	-378	-84	6	-288	1,782	2,070
2004	-413	-46	73	-294	1,871	2,166
2005	-318	-21	58	-239	2,084	2,323
2006	-248	-11	8	-229	2,310	2,540
2007	-163	-31	-35	-167	2,484	2,651

Sources: Congressional Budget Office; Office of Management and Budget.

Note: * = between -$500 million and $500 million.

a. Consists of deposit insurance, receipts from auctions of licenses to use the electromagnetic spectrum, timing adjustments, and contributions from allied nations for Operation Desert Storm (which were received in 1991 and 1992).

Table F-13.

Standardized-Budget Deficit or Surplus and Related Series, 1968 to 2007, as a Percentage of Potential Gross Domestic Product

	Budget Deficit (-) or Surplus	− Cyclical Contributions	+ Other Adjustments[a]	= Standardized-Budget Deficit (-) or Surplus	Standardized-Budget	
					Revenues	Outlays
1968	-3.0	1.3	0.6	-3.7	16.6	20.3
1969	0.4	1.5	0.9	-0.3	18.6	18.9
1970	-0.3	0.5	1.0	0.2	18.5	18.4
1971	-2.1	-0.3	0.9	-0.9	17.1	18.1
1972	-2.0	*	0.2	-1.8	16.9	18.6
1973	-1.2	1.1	0.6	-1.6	16.8	18.4
1974	-0.4	0.7	1.3	0.2	17.8	17.6
1975	-3.3	-1.4	2.1	0.2	18.6	18.4
1976	-4.1	-1.4	0.8	-1.9	17.2	19.2
1977	-2.7	-0.7	1.0	-1.0	17.8	18.9
1978	-2.7	0.1	1.3	-1.4	17.6	19.0
1979	-1.6	0.4	1.4	-0.6	18.0	18.5
1980	-2.7	-0.8	1.6	-0.3	18.8	19.2
1981	-2.5	-0.8	1.2	-0.6	19.4	20.0
1982	-3.7	-1.8	0.7	-1.3	19.1	20.4
1983	-5.6	-2.4	0.2	-3.0	17.7	20.8
1984	-4.7	-0.8	0.3	-3.6	17.1	20.7
1985	-5.1	-0.4	0.4	-4.3	17.3	21.5
1986	-5.0	-0.3	0.0	-4.7	16.9	21.6
1987	-3.2	-0.3	-0.4	-3.3	17.4	20.7
1988	-3.1	0.1	0.7	-2.5	17.4	19.9
1989	-2.9	0.4	1.0	-2.2	17.5	19.7
1990	-3.9	0.1	1.9	-2.1	17.4	19.5
1991	-4.4	-0.8	1.1	-2.5	17.6	20.0
1992	-4.5	-1.0	0.6	-2.9	17.6	20.5
1993	-3.8	-0.8	0.2	-2.9	17.4	20.2
1994	-2.9	-0.4	0.4	-2.0	17.7	19.8
1995	-2.2	-0.2	*	-2.0	18.0	20.0
1996	-1.4	-0.3	-0.1	-1.2	18.3	19.5
1997	-0.3	0.2	-0.5	-1.0	18.4	19.4
1998	0.8	0.5	-0.8	-0.4	18.7	19.2
1999	1.4	0.7	-0.6	*	18.6	18.6
2000	2.5	1.0	-0.4	1.1	19.3	18.2
2001	1.3	0.2	-0.1	1.0	18.9	17.9
2002	-1.5	-0.6	-0.3	-1.2	17.2	18.5
2003	-3.4	-0.8	0.1	-2.6	16.1	18.8
2004	-3.6	-0.4	0.6	-2.5	16.1	18.6
2005	-2.6	-0.2	0.5	-1.9	16.9	18.9
2006	-1.9	-0.1	0.1	-1.8	17.7	19.4
2007	-1.2	-0.2	-0.3	-1.2	18.0	19.2

Sources: Congressional Budget Office; Department of Commerce, Bureau of Economic Analysis; Office of Management and Budget.

Note: * = between -0.05 percent and 0.05 percent.

a. Consists of deposit insurance, receipts from auctions of licenses to use the electromagnetic spectrum, timing adjustments, and contributions from allied nations for Operation Desert Storm (which were received in 1991 and 1992).

Contributors to the Revenue and Spending Projections

T he following Congressional Budget Office analysts prepared the revenue and spending projections in this report:

Revenue Projections

Mark Booth	Individual income taxes
Paul Burnham	Retirement income
Barbara Edwards	Social insurance taxes, Federal Reserve System earnings
Zachary Epstein	Customs duties, miscellaneous receipts
Pamela Greene	Corporate income taxes, estate and gift taxes
Ed Harris	Individual income taxes
Andrew Langan	Excise taxes
Larry Ozanne	Capital gains realizations
Kevin Perese	Tax modeling
Kristy Piccinini	Capital gains realizations
Kurt Seibert	Earned income tax credit, depreciation
David Weiner	Individual income taxes

Spending Projections

Defense, International Affairs, and Veterans' Affairs

Sarah Jennings	Unit Chief
Kent Christensen	Defense
Sunita D'Monte	International affairs (conduct of foreign affairs and information-exchange activities), veterans' health care
Raymond Hall	Defense research and development (stockpile sales, atomic energy)
David Newman	Defense (military construction and family housing, military activities in Iraq and Afghanistan and the war on terrorism), veterans' housing
Michelle Patterson	International affairs (development, security, international financial institutions)

Defense, International Affairs, and Veterans' Affairs (Continued)

Dawn Sauter-Regan	Defense (military personnel, military activities in Iraq and Afghanistan and the war on terrorism)
Matthew Schmit	Military retirement, military health care
Jason Wheelock	Defense (other programs), operations and maintenance, radiation exposure compensation, energy employees' occupational illness compensation
Camille Woodland	Veterans' readjustment benefits, reservists' educational benefits
Dwayne Wright	Veterans' compensation and pensions

Health

Tom Bradley	Unit Chief
Julia Christensen	Federal Employees Health Benefits program, Public Health Service
Jeanne De Sa	Medicaid, State Children's Health Insurance Program
Sarah Evans	Medicare, Public Health Service
Geoffrey Gerhardt	Medicare
Tim Gronniger	Medicare, Public Health Service
Matthew Kapuscinski	Medicare
Lara Robillard	Medicare
Eric Rollins	Medicaid, State Children's Health Insurance Program, Medicare
Robert Stewart	Medicaid, State Children's Health Insurance Program
Shinobu Suzuki	Medicare

Human Resources

Sam Papenfuss	Unit Chief
Christina Hawley Anthony	Unemployment insurance, training programs, Administration on Aging, Smithsonian, arts and humanities, report coordinator
Chad Chirico	Housing assistance
Sheila Dacey	Old-Age and Survivors Insurance, Social Security trust funds
Kathleen FitzGerald	Food Stamps and nutrition programs
Justin Humphrey	Elementary and secondary education, Pell grants, student loans
Deborah Kalcevic	Student loans, higher education
Jonathan Morancy	Child Support Enforcement, Temporary Assistance for Needy Families, foster care, Social Services Block Grant program, child care programs, child and family services
David Rafferty	Disability Insurance, Supplemental Security Income
Jessica Sherry	Low Income Home Energy Assistance Program, refugee assistance
Taylor Tarver	Federal civilian retirement, Pension Benefit Guaranty Corporation, Railroad Retirement

Natural and Physical Resources

Kim Cawley	Unit Chief
Leigh Angres	Science and space exploration, Bureau of Indian Affairs, justice
Megan Carroll	Energy, conservation and land management, air transportation
Mark Grabowicz	Justice, Postal Service
Kathleen Gramp	Spectrum auction receipts, energy, deposit insurance, Outer Continental Shelf receipts
Greg Hitz	Agriculture
Daniel Hoople	Community and regional development, Federal Emergency Management Agency
David Hull	Agriculture
Tyler Kruzich	Water resources, conservation and land management
James Langley	Agriculture
Susanne Mehlman	Pollution control and abatement, Federal Housing Administration and other housing credit programs
Matthew Pickford	General government
Sarah Puro	Highways, Amtrak, mass transit
Deborah Reis	Recreation, water transportation, legislative branch, conservation and land management, other natural resources
Susan Willie	Commerce, Small Business Administration, Universal Service Fund

Other

Janet Airis	Unit Chief, Scorekeeping; legislative branch appropriation bill
Jeffrey Holland	Unit Chief, Projections
Edward Blau	Authorization bills
Barry Blom	Federal pay, monthly Treasury data, report coordinator
Joanna Capps	Appropriation bills (Interior and the environment, Labor–Health and Human Services)
Kenneth Farris	Computer support
Mary Froehlich	Computer support
Amber Marcellino	Other interest, report coordinator
Virginia Myers	Appropriation bills (Commerce–Justice, financial services, general government)
Jennifer Reynolds	Appropriation bills (Agriculture, foreign relations)
Mark Sanford	Appropriation bills (Defense, Homeland Security)
Eric Schatten	Interest on the public debt, report coordinator
Luis Serna	National income and product accounts, report coordinator
Phan Siris	Computer support
Esther Steinbock	Appropriation bills (Transportation–Housing and Urban Development, military construction and veterans' affairs, energy and water)
Patrice Watson	Database system administrator

Glossary

This glossary defines economic and budgetary terms as they apply to *The Budget and Economic Outlook;* it also acts as a general reference for readers. In some cases, the entries sacrifice technical precision for the sake of brevity and clarity. Where appropriate, entries note the sources of data for economic variables as follows:

- (BEA) refers to the Bureau of Economic Analysis in the Department of Commerce,

- (BLS) refers to the Bureau of Labor Statistics in the Department of Labor,

- (CBO) refers to the Congressional Budget Office,

- (FRB) refers to the Federal Reserve Board, and

- (NBER) refers to the National Bureau of Economic Research (a private entity).

Accrual accounting: A system of accounting in which revenues are recorded when they are earned and outlays are recorded when goods are received or services are performed, even though the actual receipt of revenues and payment for goods or services may occur, in whole or in part, at a different time. Compare with **cash accounting.**

adjusted gross income (AGI): All income that is subject to taxation under the individual income tax after "above-the-line" deductions for such things as alimony payments and certain contributions to individual retirement accounts. Personal exemptions and the standard or itemized deductions are subtracted from AGI to determine taxable income.

advance appropriation: Budget authority provided in an appropriation act that is first available for obligation in a fiscal year after the year for which the appropriation was enacted. The amount of the advance appropriation is included in the budget totals for the year in which it will become available. See **appropriation act, budget authority, fiscal year,** and **obligation;** compare with **forward funding, obligation delay,** and **unobligated balances.**

aggregate demand: Total purchases of a country's output of goods and services by consumers, businesses, governments, and foreigners during a given period. (BEA) Compare with **domestic demand.**

AGI: See **adjusted gross income.**

alternative minimum tax (AMT): A tax intended to limit the extent to which higher-income people can reduce their tax liability (the amount they owe) through the use of preferences in the tax code. Taxpayers subject to the AMT are required to recalculate their tax liability on the basis of a more limited set of exemptions, deductions, and tax credits than would normally apply. The amount by which a taxpayer's AMT calculation exceeds his or her regular tax calculation is that person's AMT liability.

appropriation act: A law or legislation under the jurisdiction of the House and Senate Committees on Appropriations that provides authority for federal programs or agencies to incur obligations and make payments from the Treasury. Each year, the Congress considers regular appropriation acts, which fund the operations of the federal government for the upcoming fiscal year. The Congress may also consider supplemental, deficiency, or continuing appropriation acts (joint resolutions that provide budget authority for a fiscal year until the regular appropriation for that year is enacted). See **budget authority, fiscal year,** and **obligation.**

authorization act: A law or legislation under the jurisdiction of a committee *other than* the House and Senate Committees on Appropriations that establishes or continues the operation of a federal program or agency, either indefinitely or for a specified period. An authorization act may suggest a level of budget authority needed to fund the program or agency, which is then provided in a future appropriation act. However, for some programs, the authorization itself may provide the budget authority. See **appropriation act** and **budget authority.**

Balanced Budget and Emergency Deficit Control Act of 1985 (Public Law 99-177): Referred to in CBO's reports as the Deficit Control Act, it also has been known as Gramm-Rudman-Hollings. Among other changes to the budget process, the law established rules that governed the calculation of CBO's baseline. In addition, it set specific deficit targets as well as sequestration procedures to reduce spending if those targets were exceeded. The targets were changed to discretionary spending limits and pay-as-you-go (PAYGO) controls by the Budget Enforcement Act of 1990. However, the discretionary spending limits and the sequestration procedure to enforce them expired on September 30, 2002. PAYGO and its sequestration procedure were rendered ineffective on December 2, 2002, when P.L. 107-312 reduced all PAYGO balances to zero. The remaining provisions, including the rules that govern the calculation of the baseline, expired on September 30, 2006. CBO, however, continues to follow the methodology prescribed in the law for establishing baselines. See **baseline, discretionary spending limits, pay-as-you-go,** and **sequestration.**

baseline: A benchmark for measuring the budgetary effects of proposed changes in federal revenues or spending. As defined in the Deficit Control Act, the baseline is the projection of current-year levels of new budget authority, outlays, revenues, and the deficit or surplus into the budget year and out-years on the basis of current laws and policies, calculated following the rules set forth in section 257 of that law. Section 257 expired in September 2006, but CBO continues to prepare baselines

following the methodology prescribed in the section. Estimates consistent with section 257 are used by the House and Senate Committees on the Budget in implementing the pay-as-you-go rules in each House. See **Balanced Budget and Emergency Deficit Control Act of 1985, budget authority, deficit, fiscal year, outlays, pay-as-you-go, revenues,** and **surplus.**

basis point: One one-hundredth of a percentage point. (For example, the difference between interest rates of 5.5 percent and 5.0 percent is 50 basis points.)

Blue Chip consensus forecast: The average of approximately 50 private-sector economic forecasts compiled and published monthly by Aspen Publishers, Inc.

book depreciation: See **depreciation.**

book profits: Profits calculated using book (or tax) depreciation and standard accounting conventions for inventories. Different from economic profits, book profits are referred to as "profits before tax" in the national income and product accounts. See **depreciation, economic profits,** and **national income and product accounts.**

budget authority: Authority provided by law to incur financial obligations that will result in immediate or future outlays of federal government funds. Budget authority may be provided in an appropriation act or authorization act and may take the form of borrowing authority, contract authority, entitlement authority, or authority to obligate and expend offsetting collections or receipts. Offsetting collections and receipts are classified as negative budget authority. See **appropriation act, authorization act, contract authority, offsetting collections, offsetting receipts,** and **outlays.**

Budget Enforcement Act of 1990: Among other changes to the budget process, this law established discretionary spending limits and pay-as-you-go controls by amending the Balanced Budget and Emergency Deficit Control Act of 1985. See **Balanced Budget and Emergency Deficit Control Act of 1985, discretionary spending limits,** and **pay-as-you-go.**

budget function: One of 20 general-subject categories into which budgetary resources are grouped so that all budget authority and outlays can be presented according to the national interests being addressed. There are 17 broad budget functions, including national defense, international affairs, energy, agriculture, health, income security, and general government. Three other functions—net interest, allowances, and undistributed offsetting receipts—are included to complete the budget. See **budget authority, net interest, offsetting receipts,** and **outlays.**

budget resolution: A concurrent resolution, adopted by both Houses of Congress, that sets forth a Congressional budget plan for the budget year and at least four out-years. The plan consists of targets for spending and revenues; subsequent appropriation acts and authorization acts that affect revenues or direct spending are expected to comply with those targets. The targets are enforced in each House of Congress through procedural mechanisms set forth in law and in the rules of each House. See **appropriation act, authorization act, direct spending, fiscal year,** and **revenues.**

budget year: See **fiscal year.**

budgetary resources: All sources of authority provided to federal agencies that permit them to incur financial obligations, including new budget authority, unobligated balances, direct spending authority, and obligation limitations. See **budget authority, direct spending, obligation limitation,** and **unobligated balances.**

business cycle: Fluctuations in overall business activity accompanied by swings in the unemployment rate, interest rates, and corporate profits. Over a business cycle, real (inflation-adjusted) activity rises to a *peak* (its highest level during the cycle) and then falls until it reaches a *trough* (its lowest level following the peak), whereupon it starts to rise again, defining a new cycle. Business cycles are irregular, varying in frequency, magnitude, and duration. (NBER) See **real** and **unemployment rate.**

business fixed investment: Spending by businesses on structures, equipment, and software. Such investment is labeled "fixed" to distinguish it from investment in inventories. See **inventories.**

Capacity utilization rate: The seasonally adjusted output of the nation's factories, mines, and electric and gas utilities expressed as a percentage of their capacity to produce output. A facility's capacity is the greatest output it can maintain with a normal work pattern. (FRB)

capital: Tangible and intangible resources that can be used or invested to produce a stream of benefits over time. *Physical capital*—also known as *fixed capital* or the *capital stock*—consists of land and the stock of products set aside to support future production and consumption, including business inventories and *capital goods* (residential and nonresidential structures and producers' durable equipment). *Human capital* is the education, training, work experience, and other attributes that enhance the ability of the labor force to produce goods and services. The *capital* of a business is the sum advanced and put at risk by the business's owners: For example, *bank capital* is the sum put at risk by the owners of a bank. In an accounting sense, capital is a firm's net worth or equity—the difference between its assets and liabilities. *Financial capital* is wealth held in the form of financial instruments (stocks, bonds, mortgages, and so forth) rather than held directly in the form of physical capital.

capital gains and losses: The increase or decrease in the value of an asset that comes from the increase or decrease in the asset's market price since it was purchased. A capital gain or loss is "realized" when the asset is sold.

capital income: Income derived from wealth, such as stock dividends, realized capital gains, or the owner's profits from a business. See **capital gains and losses.**

capital services: A measure of how much the stock of physical capital contributes to the flow of production.

cash accounting: A system of accounting in which revenues are recorded when they are actually received and outlays are recorded when payment is made. Compare with **accrual accounting.**

central bank: A government-established agency responsible for conducting monetary policy and overseeing credit conditions. The Federal Reserve System fulfills those functions in the United States. See **Federal Reserve System** and **monetary policy.**

COLA: See **cost-of-living adjustment.**

compensation: All of the income due to an employee for his or her work during a given period. In addition to wages, salaries, bonuses, and stock options, compensation includes fringe benefits and the employer's share of payroll taxes for social insurance programs, such as Social Security. (BEA)

Consolidated Appropriations Act of 2008 (Public Law 110-161): This law and the Department of Defense Appropriations Act of 2008 (Public Law 110-116) provided appropriations for most federal agencies for fiscal year 2008.

constant dollar: A measure of spending or revenues in a given year that has been adjusted for differences in prices (such as inflation) between that year and a base year. See **inflation** and **real**; compare with **current dollar** and **nominal.**

consumer confidence: An index of consumer optimism that is based on surveys of consumers' attitudes about current and future economic conditions. One such measure, the index of consumer sentiment, is constructed by the University of Michigan's Survey Research Center. The Conference Board constructs a similar measure, the consumer confidence index.

consumer price index (CPI): An index of the cost of living commonly used to measure inflation. The Bureau of Labor Statistics publishes the CPI-U, an index of consumer prices based on the typical market basket of goods and services consumed by all urban consumers, and the CPI-W, an index of consumer prices based on the typical market basket of goods and services consumed by urban wage earners and clerical workers. (BLS) See **inflation.**

consumer sentiment index: See **consumer confidence.**

consumption: In principle, the value of goods and services purchased and used up during a given period by households and governments. In practice, the Bureau of Economic Analysis counts purchases of many long-lasting goods (such as cars and clothes) as consumption

even though the goods are not used up. Consumption by households alone is also called consumer spending. See **national income and product accounts.**

contract authority: Authority provided by law to enter into contracts or incur other obligations in advance of, or in excess of, funds available for that purpose. Although it is a form of budget authority, contract authority does not provide the funds to make payments. Those funds must be provided later, usually in a subsequent appropriation act (called a liquidating appropriation). Contract authority differs from a federal agency's inherent authority to enter into contracts, which may be exercised only within the limits of available appropriations. See **appropriation act, budget authority,** and **obligation**.

core inflation: A measure of the rate of inflation that excludes changes in the prices of food and energy. See **consumer price index, inflation,** and **personal consumption expenditure price index.**

cost-of-living adjustment (COLA): An annual increase in payments to reflect price inflation.

CPI: See **consumer price index.**

credit reform: A system of budgeting and accounting for federal credit activities that focuses on the cost of subsidies conveyed in federal credit assistance. The system was established by the Federal Credit Reform Act of 1990 and took effect at the beginning of fiscal year 1992. See **credit subsidy, financing account, liquidating account,** and **program account.**

credit subsidy: The estimated long-term cost to the federal government of a direct loan or loan guarantee. That cost is calculated on the basis of net present value, excluding federal administrative costs and any incidental effects on revenues or outlays. For direct loans, the subsidy cost is the net present value of loan disbursements minus repayments of interest and principal, adjusted for estimated defaults, prepayments, fees, penalties, and other recoveries. For loan guarantees, the subsidy cost is the net present value of estimated payments by the government to cover defaults and delinquencies, interest subsidies, or other payments, offset by any payments to the government, including origination and other fees, penalties, and recoveries. See **outlays** and **present value.**

current-account balance: A summary measure of a country's current transactions with the rest of the world, including net exports, net unilateral transfers, and net factor income (primarily the capital income from foreign property received by residents of a country offset by the capital income from property in that country flowing to residents of foreign countries). (BEA) See **net exports** and **unilateral transfers.**

current dollar: A measure of spending or revenues in a given year that has not been adjusted for differences in prices (such as inflation) between that year and a base year. See **inflation** and **nominal;** compare with **constant dollar** and **real.**

current year: The fiscal year in progress. See **fiscal year.**

cyclical deficit or surplus: The part of the federal budget deficit or surplus that results from the business cycle. The cyclical component reflects the way in which the deficit or surplus automatically increases or decreases during economic expansions or recessions. (CBO) See **business cycle, deficit, expansion, recession,** and **surplus;** compare with **cyclically adjusted budget deficit or surplus.**

cyclically adjusted budget deficit or surplus: The level of the federal budget deficit or surplus that would occur under current law if the influence of the business cycle was removed—that is, if the economy operated at potential gross domestic product (GDP). (CBO) See **business cycle, deficit, potential gross domestic product,** and **surplus;** compare with **cyclical deficit or surplus.**

Debt: In the case of the federal government, the total value of outstanding bills, notes, bonds, and other debt instruments issued by the Treasury and other federal agencies. That debt is referred to as *federal debt* or *gross debt.* It has two components: *debt held by the public* (federal debt held by nonfederal investors, including the Federal Reserve System) and *debt held by government accounts* (federal debt held by federal government trust funds, deposit insurance funds, and other federal accounts). *Debt subject to limit* is federal debt that is subject to a statutory limit on the total amount issued. The limit applies to gross federal debt except for a small portion of the debt issued by the Treasury and all of the

small amount of debt issued by other federal agencies (primarily the Tennessee Valley Authority and the Postal Service).

debt service: Payment of scheduled interest obligations on outstanding debt. As used in *The Budget and Economic Outlook,* debt service refers to a change in interest payments resulting from a change in estimates of the deficit or surplus. See **deficit, net interest,** and **surplus.**

deficit: The amount by which the federal government's total outlays exceed its total revenues in a given period, typically a fiscal year. The *primary deficit* is that total deficit excluding net interest. See **fiscal year, net interest, outlays,** and **revenues;** compare with **surplus.**

Deficit Control Act: See **Balanced Budget and Emergency Deficit Control Act of 1985.**

deflation: A drop in price levels that is so broadly based that general indexes of prices, such as the consumer price index, register continuing declines. Deflation is usually caused by a collapse in aggregate demand. See **aggregate demand** and **consumer price index.**

demand: See **aggregate demand** and **domestic demand.**

deposit insurance: The guarantee by a federal agency that an individual depositor at a participating depository institution will receive the full amount of the deposit (up to $100,000) if the institution becomes insolvent.

depreciation: A decline in the value of a currency, financial asset, or capital good. When applied to a capital good, depreciation usually refers to loss of value because of obsolescence, wear, or destruction (as by fire or flood) and is also called *consumption of fixed capital. Book depreciation* (also known as *tax depreciation*) is the depreciation that the tax code allows businesses to deduct when they calculate their taxable profits. It typically occurs at a faster rate than *economic depreciation,* which is the actual decline in the value of an asset. Both measures of depreciation appear as part of the national income and product accounts. See **book profits** and **national income and product accounts.**

devaluation: The act of a government to lower the fixed exchange rate of its currency. The government implements a devaluation by announcing that it will no longer maintain the existing rate by buying and selling its currency at that rate. See **exchange rate.**

direct spending: Synonymous with *mandatory spending,* direct spending is the budget authority provided by laws other than appropriation acts and the outlays that result from that budget authority. (As used in *The Budget and Economic Outlook,* direct spending refers only to the outlays that result from budget authority provided in laws other than appropriation acts.) See **appropriation act, budget authority,** and **outlays;** compare with **discretionary spending** and **entitlement.**

discount rate: The interest rate that the Federal Reserve System charges on a loan it makes to a bank. Such loans, when allowed, enable a bank to meet its reserve requirements without reducing its lending. Alternatively, the discount rate is the interest rate used to compute the present value of future payments (such as for pension plans). See **Federal Reserve System** and **present value.**

discouraged workers: Jobless people who are available for work but not actively seeking it because they think they have poor prospects of finding a job. Discouraged workers are not included in measures of the labor force or the unemployment rate. (BLS) See **labor force** and **unemployment rate.**

discretionary spending: The budget authority that is provided and controlled by appropriation acts and the outlays that result from that budget authority. See **appropriation act, budget authority,** and **outlays;** compare with **direct spending.**

discretionary spending limits (or caps): Statutory ceilings imposed on the amount of budget authority provided in appropriation acts in a fiscal year and on the outlays that are made in that year. The limits originally were established in the Budget Enforcement Act of 1990. Under that law, if the estimated budget authority provided in all appropriation acts for a fiscal year (or the outlays resulting from that budget authority) exceeded the spending limit for that year, a sequestration—a cancellation of budget authority provided for programs funded by appropriation acts—would be triggered. All discretionary spending limits and the sequestration procedure to enforce them expired on September 30, 2002.

See **appropriation act, Balanced Budget and Emergency Deficit Control Act of 1985, budget authority, Budget Enforcement Act of 1990, discretionary spending, fiscal year, outlays,** and **sequestration.**

disposable personal income: Personal income—the income that individuals receive, including transfer payments—minus the taxes and fees that individuals pay to governments. (BEA) See **transfer payments.**

domestic demand: Total purchases of goods and services, regardless of their origin, by U.S. consumers, businesses, and governments during a given period. Domestic demand equals gross domestic product minus net exports. (BEA) See **gross domestic product** and **net exports;** compare with **aggregate demand.**

ECI: See **employment cost index.**

Economic Growth and Tax Relief Reconciliation Act of 2001 (Public Law 107-16): This law, also known as EGTRRA, significantly reduced tax liabilities (the amount of tax owed) over the 2001–2010 period by cutting individual income tax rates, increasing the child tax credit, repealing estate taxes, raising deductions for married couples who file joint returns, increasing tax benefits for pensions and individual retirement accounts, and creating additional tax benefits for education. The law phased in many of those changes over time, including some that are not fully effective until 2010. Although some of the law's provisions have been made permanent, most are scheduled to expire on or before December 31, 2010. For legislation that modified provisions of EGTRRA, see **Jobs and Growth Tax Relief Reconciliation Act of 2003.**

economic profits: Corporations' profits, adjusted to remove distortions in depreciation allowances caused by tax rules and to exclude the effect of inflation on the value of inventories. Economic profits are a better measure of profits from current production than are the book profits reported by corporations. Economic profits are referred to as "corporate profits with inventory valuation and capital consumption adjustments" in the national income and product accounts. (BEA) See **book profits,**

depreciation, inflation, inventories, and **national income and product accounts.**

effective tax rate: The ratio of taxes paid to a given tax base. For individual income taxes, the effective tax rate is typically expressed as the ratio of taxes paid to adjusted gross income. For corporate income taxes, it is the ratio of taxes paid to book profits. For some purposes—such as calculating an overall tax rate on all income—an effective tax rate is computed on a base that includes the untaxed portion of Social Security benefits, interest on tax-exempt bonds, and similar items. It can also be computed on a base of personal income as measured by the national income and product accounts. The effective tax rate is a useful measure because the tax code's various exemptions, credits, deductions, and tax rates make actual ratios of taxes paid to income very different from statutory tax rates. See **adjusted gross income** and **book profits;** compare with **marginal tax rate** and **statutory tax rate.**

EGTRRA: See **Economic Growth and Tax Relief Reconciliation Act of 2001.**

employment: Work performed or services rendered in exchange for compensation. Two estimates of employment are commonly used. One comes from the so-called establishment survey of employers (the Department of Labor's Current Employment Statistics Survey), which measures employment as the estimated number of non-farm wage and salary jobs. (Thus, a person with more than one job may be counted more than once.) The other estimate comes from the so-called household survey (the Census Bureau's Current Population Survey), which measures employment as the estimated number of people employed. (Thus, someone with more than one job is counted only once.) The household survey is based on a smaller sample than the establishment survey and therefore yields a more volatile estimate of employment. See **compensation** and **unemployment rate.**

employment cost index (ECI): An index of the weighted-average cost of an hour of labor—comprising the cost to the employer of wage and salary payments, employee benefits, and payroll taxes for social insurance programs, such as Social Security. The ECI is structured so that it is not affected by changes in the mix of occupations in the labor force or the mix of employment by industry. (BLS)

entitlement: A legal obligation of the federal government to make payments to a person, group of people, business, unit of government, or similar entity that meets the eligibility criteria set in law and for which the budget authority is not provided in advance in an appropriation act. Spending for entitlement programs is controlled through those programs' eligibility criteria and benefit or payment rules. The best-known entitlements are the government's major benefit programs, such as Social Security and Medicare. See **appropriation act** and **budget authority;** compare with **direct spending.**

establishment survey: See **employment.**

exchange rate: The number of units of a foreign currency that can be bought with one unit of the domestic currency, or vice versa.

excise tax: A tax levied on the purchase of a specific type of good or service, such as tobacco products or air transportation services.

expansion: A phase of the business cycle that begins when gross domestic product exceeds its previous peak and extends until gross domestic product reaches its next peak. (NBER) See **business cycle** and **gross domestic product;** compare with **recession** and **recovery.**

expenditure account: An account established within federal funds and trust funds to record appropriations, obligations, and outlays (as well as offsetting collections) that are usually financed from an associated receipt account. See **federal funds, obligation, outlays,** and **trust funds;** compare with **receipt account.**

fan chart: A graphic representation of CBO's baseline projection of the budget deficit or surplus that includes not only a single line representing the outcome expected under the baseline's economic assumptions but also the various possible outcomes surrounding that line, based on the reasonable expectations of error in the underlying economic and technical assumptions. (CBO calculates those reasonable expectations of error on the basis of the accuracy of its own past projections, adjusted for differences in legislation.) See **deficit** and **surplus.**

federal funds: In the federal accounting structure, all accounts through which collections of money and expenditures are recorded, except those classified by law as trust funds. Federal funds include several types of funds, one of which is the general fund. See **general fund;** compare with **trust funds.**

federal funds rate: The interest rate that financial institutions charge each other for overnight loans of their monetary reserves. A rise in the federal funds rate (compared with other short-term interest rates) suggests a tightening of monetary policy, whereas a fall suggests an easing. (FRB) See **monetary policy** and **short-term interest rate.**

Federal Open Market Committee: The group within the Federal Reserve System that determines the stance of monetary policy. The open-market desk at the Federal Reserve Bank of New York implements that policy with open-market operations (the purchase or sale of government securities), which influence short-term interest rates—especially the federal funds rate—and the growth of the money supply. The committee is composed of 12 members, including the 7 members of the Board of Governors of the Federal Reserve System, the president of the Federal Reserve Bank of New York, and a rotating group of 4 of the other 11 presidents of the regional Federal Reserve Banks. See **federal funds rate, Federal Reserve System, monetary policy,** and **short-term interest rate.**

Federal Reserve System: The central bank of the United States. The Federal Reserve is responsible for setting the nation's monetary policy and overseeing credit conditions. See **central bank** and **monetary policy.**

financing account: A nonbudgetary account required for a credit program (by the Federal Credit Reform Act of 1990) that holds balances, receives credit subsidy payments from the program account, and records all cash flows with the public that result from obligations or commitments made under the program since October 1, 1991. The cash flow in each financing account for a fiscal year is shown in the federal budget as an "other means of financing." See **credit reform, credit subsidy, means of financing,** and **program account;** compare with **liquidating account.**

fiscal policy: The government's tax and spending policies, which influence the amount and maturity of government debt as well as the level, composition, and distribution of national output and income. See **debt.**

fiscal year: A yearly accounting period. The federal government's fiscal year begins October 1 and ends September 30. Fiscal years are designated by the calendar years in which they end—for example, fiscal year 2009 will begin on October 1, 2008, and end on September 30, 2009. The *budget year* is the fiscal year for which the budget is being considered; in relation to a session of Congress, it is the fiscal year that starts on October 1 of the calendar year in which that session of Congress began. See **out-year.**

foreign direct investment: Financial investment by which a person or an entity acquires a lasting interest in, and a degree of influence over the management of, a business enterprise in a foreign country. (BEA)

forward funding: The provision of budget authority that becomes available for obligation in the last quarter of a fiscal year and remains available during the following fiscal year. This form of funding typically finances ongoing education grant programs. See **budget authority, fiscal year,** and **obligation;** compare with **advance appropriation, obligation delay,** and **unobligated balances.**

G

GDI: See **gross domestic income.**

GDP: See **gross domestic product.**

GDP gap: The difference between potential and actual gross domestic product, expressed as a percentage of potential GDP. See **gross domestic product** and **potential gross domestic product.**

GDP price index: A summary measure of the prices of all goods and services that make up gross domestic product. The change in the GDP price index is used as a measure of inflation in the overall economy. See **gross domestic product** and **inflation.**

general fund: One category of federal funds in the government's accounting structure. The general fund records all revenues and offsetting receipts not earmarked by law for a specific purpose and all spending financed by those revenues and receipts. See **federal funds, offsetting receipts,** and **revenues;** compare with **trust funds.**

GNP: See **gross national product.**

grants: Transfer payments from the federal government to state and local governments or other recipients to help fund projects or activities that do not involve substantial federal participation. See **transfer payments.**

grants-in-aid: Grants from the federal government to state and local governments to help provide for programs of assistance or service to the public.

gross debt: See **debt.**

gross domestic income (GDI): The sum of all income earned in the domestic production of goods and services. In theory, GDI should equal gross domestic product, but measurement difficulties leave a statistical discrepancy between the two. (BEA) See **gross domestic product.**

gross domestic product (GDP): The total market value of goods and services produced domestically during a given period. That value is conceptually equal to gross domestic income, but measurement difficulties result in a statistical discrepancy between the two. The components of GDP are consumption (both household and government), gross investment (both private and government), and net exports. (BEA) See **consumption, gross investment,** and **net exports.**

gross investment: A measure of additions to the capital stock that does not subtract depreciation of existing capital. See **capital** and **depreciation.**

gross national product (GNP): The total market value of goods and services produced during a given period by labor and capital supplied by residents of a country, regardless of where the labor and capital are located. That value is conceptually equal to the total income accruing to residents of the country during that period (national income). GNP differs from gross domestic product primarily by including the capital income that residents earn from investments abroad and excluding the capital income that nonresidents earn from domestic investment. See **gross domestic product** and **national income.**

Home equity: The value that an owner has in a home, calculated by subtracting from the home's current market value the value of any outstanding mortgage (or other loan) secured by the home.

household survey: See **employment.**

Inflation: Growth in a general measure of prices, usually expressed as an annual rate of change. See **consumer price index, core inflation, GDP price index,** and **personal consumption expenditure price index.**

inventories: Stocks of goods held by businesses for further processing or for sale. (BEA)

investment: *Physical investment* is the current product set aside during a given period to be used for future production—in other words, an addition to the capital stock. As measured by the national income and product accounts, *private domestic investment* consists of investment in residential and nonresidential structures, producers' durable equipment, and the change in business inventories. *Financial investment* is the purchase of a financial security, such as a stock, bond, or mortgage. *Investment in human capital* is spending on education, training, health services, and other activities that increase the productivity of the workforce. Investment in human capital is not treated as investment by the national income and product accounts. See **capital, inventories, national income and product accounts,** and **productivity.**

JCWAA: See **Job Creation and Worker Assistance Act of 2002.**

JGTRRA: See **Jobs and Growth Tax Relief Reconciliation Act of 2003.**

Job Creation and Worker Assistance Act of 2002 (Public Law 107-147): This law reduced business taxes by allowing businesses to immediately deduct a portion of the cost of purchases of capital goods, increasing and extending certain other deductions and exemptions, and expanding the ability of unprofitable corporations to receive refunds of past taxes paid. Those provisions expire on various dates. The law also provided tax benefits for areas of New York City damaged on September 11, 2001, and additional weeks of unemployment benefits to recipients who exhausted their eligibility for regular state benefits. Most of the law's provisions have expired or have been extended in subsequent legislation. See **Jobs and Growth Tax Relief Reconciliation Act of 2003.**

Jobs and Growth Tax Relief Reconciliation Act of 2003 (Public Law 108-27): This law reduced taxes by advancing to 2003 the effective date of several tax reductions previously enacted in EGTRRA. It also increased the exemption amount for the individual alternative minimum tax, reduced the tax rates for income from dividends and capital gains, and expanded the portion of capital purchases that businesses could immediately deduct under JCWAA. Those provisions expire on various dates. The law also provided an estimated $20 billion for fiscal relief to states. See **capital gains and losses, Economic Growth and Tax Relief Reconciliation Act of 2001,** and **Job Creation and Worker Assistance Act of 2002.**

Labor force: The number of people age 16 or older in the civilian noninstitutional population who have jobs or who are available for work and are actively seeking jobs. (The civilian noninstitutional population excludes members of the armed forces on active duty and people in penal or mental institutions or in homes for the elderly or infirm.) The *labor force participation rate* is the labor force as a percentage of the civilian noninstitutional population age 16 or older. (BLS) See **potential labor force.**

labor productivity: See **productivity.**

liquidating account: A budgetary account associated with a credit program that records all cash flows resulting from direct loan obligations and loan guarantee commitments made under that program before October 1, 1991. See **credit reform;** compare with **financing account** and **program account.**

liquidity: The ease with which an asset can be sold for cash. An asset is highly liquid if it comes in standard units that are traded daily in large amounts by many buyers and sellers. Among the most liquid of assets are U.S. Treasury securities.

long-term interest rate: The interest rate earned by a note or bond that matures in 10 or more years.

Mandatory spending: See **direct spending.**

marginal tax rate: The tax rate that would apply to an additional dollar of a taxpayer's income. Compare with **effective tax rate** and **statutory tax rate.**

MBSs: See **mortgaged-backed securities.**

means of financing: Means by which a budget deficit is financed or a surplus is used. Means of financing are not included in the budget totals. The primary means of financing is borrowing from the public. In general, the cumulative amount borrowed from the public (debt held by the public) will increase if there is a deficit and decrease if there is a surplus, although other factors can affect the amount that the government must borrow. Those factors, known as *other means of financing,* include reductions (or increases) in the government's cash balances, seigniorage, changes in outstanding checks, changes in accrued interest costs included in the budget but not yet paid, and cash flows reflected in credit financing accounts. See **debt, deficit, financing account, seigniorage,** and **surplus.**

monetary policy: The strategy of influencing changes in the money supply and interest rates to affect output and inflation. An "easy" monetary policy suggests faster growth of the money supply and initially lower short-term interest rates intended to increase aggregate demand, but it may lead to higher inflation. A "tight" monetary policy suggests slower growth of the money supply and higher interest rates in the near term in an attempt to reduce inflationary pressure by lowering aggregate demand. The Federal Reserve System sets monetary policy in the United States. See **aggregate demand, Federal Reserve System, inflation,** and **short-term interest rate.**

mortgage-backed securities (MBSs): Securities issued by financial institutions to investors with the payments of interest and principal backed by the payments on a package of mortgages. MBSs are structured by their sponsors to create multiple classes of claims, or *tranches,* of different seniority, based on the cash flows from the underlying mortgages. Investors holding securities in the safest, or most senior, tranche stand first in line to receive payments from borrowers and require the lowest contractual interest rate of all the tranches. Investors holding the least senior securities stand last in line to receive payments, after all more senior claims have been paid. Hence, they are first in line to absorb losses on the underlying mortgages. In return for assuming that risk, holders of the least senior tranche require the highest contractual interest rate of all the tranches.

National income: Total income earned by U.S. residents from all sources, including employees' compensation (wages, salaries, benefits, and employers' share of payroll taxes for social insurance programs), corporate profits, net interest, rental income, and proprietors' income. See **gross national product.**

national income and product accounts (NIPAs): Official U.S. accounts that track the level and composition of gross domestic product, the prices of its components, and the way in which the costs of production are distributed as income. (BEA) See **gross domestic product.**

national saving: Total saving by all sectors of the economy: personal saving, business saving (corporate after-tax profits not paid as dividends), and government saving (budget surpluses). National saving represents all income not consumed, publicly or privately, during a given period. (BEA) See **national income, net national saving, personal saving,** and **surplus.**

natural rate of unemployment: The rate of unemployment arising from all sources except fluctuations in aggregate demand. Those sources include *frictional unemployment,* which is associated with normal turnover of jobs, and *structural unemployment,* which includes unemployment caused by mismatches between the skills of available workers and the skills necessary to fill vacant positions and unemployment caused when wages exceed their market-clearing levels because of institutional factors, such as legal minimum wages, the presence of unions, social conventions, or employer wage-setting practices intended to increase workers' morale and effort. See **aggregate demand** and **unemployment rate.**

net exports: The exports of goods and services produced in a country minus the country's imports of goods and services produced elsewhere; also referred to as the *trade balance.*

net federal government saving: A term used in the national income and product accounts to identify the difference between federal current receipts and federal current expenditures (including consumption of fixed capital). When receipts exceed expenditures, net federal government saving is positive (formerly identified in the national income and product accounts as a federal government surplus); when expenditures exceed receipts, net federal government saving is negative (formerly identified in the national income and product accounts as a federal government deficit). See **capital** and **national income and product accounts.**

net interest: In the federal budget, net interest comprises the government's interest payments on debt held by the public (as recorded in budget function 900), offset by interest income that the government receives on loans and cash balances and by earnings of the National Railroad Retirement Investment Trust. See **budget function** and **debt.**

net national saving: National saving minus depreciation of physical capital. See **capital, depreciation,** and **national saving.**

NIPAs: See **national income and product accounts.**

nominal: A measure based on current-dollar value. The *nominal* level of income or spending is measured in current dollars. The *nominal interest rate* on debt selling at par is the ratio of the current-dollar interest paid in any year to the current-dollar value of the debt when it was issued. The nominal interest rate on debt initially issued or now selling at a discount includes as a payment the estimated yearly equivalent of the difference between the redemption price and the discounted price. The *nominal exchange rate* is the rate at which a unit of one currency trades for a unit of another currency. See **current dollar;** compare with **real.**

Obligation: A legally binding commitment by the federal government that will result in outlays, immediately or in the future. See **outlays.**

obligation delay: Legislation that precludes the obligation of an amount of budget authority provided in an appropriation act or in some other law until some time after the first day on which that budget authority would normally be available. For example, language in an appropriation act for fiscal year 2009 that precludes obligation of an amount until March 1 is an obligation delay; without that language, the amount would have been available for obligation on October 1, 2008 (the first day of fiscal year 2009). See **appropriation act, budget authority, fiscal year,** and **obligation;** compare with **advance appropriation, forward funding,** and **unobligated balances.**

obligation limitation: A provision of a law or legislation that restricts or reduces the availability of budget authority that would have become available under another law. Typically, an obligation limitation is included in an appropriation act. The limitation may affect budget authority provided in that act, but more often, it affects direct spending that has been provided in an authorization act. Generally, when an appropriation act routinely places an obligation limitation on direct spending, the limitation is treated as a discretionary resource and the associated outlays are treated as discretionary spending. See **appropriation act, authorization act, budget authority, direct spending, discretionary spending,** and **outlays.**

off-budget: Spending or revenues sometimes excluded from the budget totals by law. The revenues and outlays of the two Social Security trust funds (the Old-Age and Survivors Insurance Trust Fund and the Disability Insurance Trust Fund) and the transactions of the Postal Service are off-budget. See **outlays, revenues,** and **trust funds.**

offsetting collections: Funds collected by government agencies from other government accounts or from the public in business-like or market-oriented transactions that are required by law to be credited directly to an expenditure account. Offsetting collections, which are treated as negative budget authority and outlays, are credits against the budget authority and outlays (either direct or discretionary spending) of the account to which they are credited. Collections that result from the government's exercise of its sovereign or governmental powers are ordinarily classified as revenues, although they are classified as offsetting collections when the law requires it. See **budget authority, direct spending, discretionary spending, expenditure account,** and **outlays;** compare with **offsetting receipts** and **revenues.**

offsetting receipts: Funds collected by government agencies from other government accounts or from the public in business-like or market-oriented transactions that are credited to a receipt account. Offsetting receipts, which are treated as negative budget authority and outlays, offset gross budget authority and outlays in calculations of total direct spending. Collections that result from the government's exercise of its sovereign or governmental powers are ordinarily classified as revenues, although they are classified as offsetting receipts when the law requires it. See **budget authority, direct spending, outlays,** and **receipt account;** compare with **offsetting collections** and **revenues.**

other means of financing: See **means of financing.**

outlays: Spending to pay a federal obligation. Outlays may pay for obligations incurred in a prior fiscal year or in the current year; hence, they flow partly from unexpended balances of prior-year budget authority and partly from budget authority provided for the current year. For most categories of spending, outlays are recorded on a cash accounting basis. However, outlays for interest on debt held by the public are recorded on an accrual accounting basis, and outlays for direct loans and loan guarantees (since credit reform) reflect estimated subsidy costs instead of cash transactions. See **accrual**

accounting, budget authority, cash accounting, credit reform, debt, fiscal year, and obligation.

out-year: A fiscal year following the budget year. See **fiscal year.**

Pay-as-you-go (PAYGO): Procedures established in the Budget Enforcement Act of 1990 (statutory PAYGO) and in House and Senate rules that are intended to ensure that all laws that affect direct spending or revenues are budget neutral. Under statutory PAYGO, the budgetary effect of each such law was estimated for a five-year period and entered on the PAYGO scorecard. If, in any budget year, the deficit increased as a result of the total budgetary effects of laws on that scorecard, a PAYGO sequestration—a cancellation of budgetary resources available for direct spending programs—would be triggered. Statutory PAYGO and its sequestration procedure were rendered ineffective on December 2, 2002, when Public Law 107-312 reduced all PAYGO balances to zero. In addition, the House and Senate each have a PAYGO rule enforced by a point of order. Since 1993, the Senate has had a rule against considering legislation affecting direct spending or revenues that is expected to increase (or cause) an on-budget deficit. That rule was adopted in its current form in the budget resolution for 2008 (H. Con. Res. 21, 110th Congress). The House rule (established by H. Res. 6, 110th Congress) applies to legislation affecting direct spending or revenues that has the net effect of increasing the deficit or decreasing the surplus. Unlike the Senate rule, the House rule applies on a bill-by-bill basis without reference to cumulative effects. See **Balanced Budget and Emergency Deficit Control Act of 1985, Budget Enforcement Act of 1990, deficit, direct spending, fiscal year, point of order, revenues, sequestration,** and **surplus.**

PCE price index: See **personal consumption expenditure price index.**

personal consumption expenditure price index: A summary measure of the prices of all goods and services that make up personal consumption expenditures and an alternative to the consumer price index as a measure of inflation. See **consumption, consumer price index,** and **inflation.**

personal income: See **disposable personal income.**

personal saving: Saving by households. Personal saving equals disposable personal income minus spending for consumption and interest payments. The *personal saving rate* is personal saving as a percentage of disposable personal income. (BEA) See **consumption** and **disposable personal income;** compare with **private saving.**

point of order: The procedure by which a member of a legislature (or similar body) questions an action that is being taken, or that is proposed to be taken, as contrary to that body's rules, practices, or precedents.

potential gross domestic product: The level of real gross domestic product that corresponds to a high level of resource (labor and capital) use. (Procedures for calculating potential GDP are described in *CBO's Method for Estimating Potential Output: An Update,* August 2001.) See **gross domestic product, potential output,** and **real.**

potential labor force: The labor force adjusted for movements in the business cycle. See **business cycle** and **labor force.**

potential output: The level of production that corresponds to a high level of resource (labor and capital) use. Potential output for the national economy is also referred to as *potential gross domestic product.* (Procedures for calculating potential output are described in *CBO's Method for Estimating Potential Output: An Update,* August 2001.) See **potential gross domestic product.**

present value: A single number that expresses a flow of current and future income (or payments) in terms of an equivalent lump sum received (or paid) today. The present value depends on the rate of interest used (the discount rate). For example, if $100 is invested on January 1 at an annual interest rate of 5 percent, it will grow to $105 by January 1 of the next year. Hence, at an annual 5 percent interest rate, the present value of $105 payable a year from today is $100.

primary deficit: See **deficit.**

private saving: Saving by households and businesses. Private saving is equal to personal saving plus after-tax corporate profits minus dividends paid. (BEA) Compare with **personal saving.**

productivity: Average real output per unit of input. *Labor productivity* is average real output per hour of labor. The growth of labor productivity is defined as the growth of real output that is not explained by the growth of labor input alone. *Total factor productivity* is average real output per unit of combined labor and capital services. The growth of total factor productivity is defined as the growth of real output that is not explained by the growth of labor and capital. Labor productivity and total factor productivity differ in that increases in capital per worker raise labor productivity but not total factor productivity. (BLS) See **capital services** and **real.**

program account: A budgetary account associated with a credit program that receives an appropriation of the subsidy cost of that program's loan obligations or commitments, as well as (in most cases) the program's administrative expenses. From the program account, the subsidy cost is disbursed to the applicable financing account. See **credit subsidy** and **financing account;** compare with **liquidating account.**

Real: Adjusted to remove the effects of inflation. *Real output* represents the quantity, rather than the dollar value, of goods and services produced. *Real income* represents the power to purchase real output. *Real data* at the finest level of disaggregation are constructed by dividing the corresponding nominal data, such as spending or wage rates, by a price index. *Real aggregates,* such as real gross domestic product, are constructed by a procedure that allows the real growth of the aggregate to reflect the real growth of its components, appropriately weighted by the importance of the components. A *real interest rate* is a nominal interest rate adjusted for expected inflation; it is often approximated by subtracting an estimate of the expected inflation rate from the nominal interest rate. See **inflation;** compare with **current dollar** and **nominal.**

real trade-weighted value of the dollar: See **trade-weighted value of the dollar.**

receipt account: An account established within federal funds and trust funds to record offsetting receipts or revenues credited to that fund. The receipt account typically finances the obligations and outlays from an associated expenditure account. See **federal funds, outlays,** and **trust funds;** compare with **expenditure account.**

recession: A phase of the business cycle that extends from a peak to the next trough and that is characterized by a substantial decline in overall business activity—output, income, employment, and trade—for at least several months. As a rule of thumb, though not an official measure, recessions are often identified by a decline in real gross domestic product for at least two consecutive quarters. (NBER) See **business cycle, gross domestic product,** and **real;** compare with **expansion.**

reconciliation: A special Congressional procedure often used to implement the revenue and spending targets established in the budget resolution. The budget resolution may contain *reconciliation instructions,* which direct Congressional committees to make changes in laws under their jurisdictions that affect revenues or direct spending to achieve a specified budgetary result. The legislation to implement those instructions is usually combined into a comprehensive *reconciliation bill,* which is considered under special rules. Reconciliation affects revenues, direct spending, and offsetting receipts but usually not discretionary spending. See **budget resolution, direct spending, discretionary spending, offsetting receipts,** and **revenues.**

recovery: A phase of the business cycle that lasts from a trough until overall economic activity returns to the level it reached at the previous peak. (NBER) See **business cycle.**

rescission: The withdrawal of authority to incur financial obligations that was previously provided by law and has not yet expired. See **budget authority** and **obligation.**

revenues: Funds collected from the public that arise from the government's exercise of its sovereign or governmental powers. Federal revenues come from a variety of sources, including individual and corporate income taxes, excise taxes, customs duties, estate and gift taxes, fees and fines, payroll taxes for social insurance programs, and miscellaneous receipts (such as earnings of the Federal Reserve System, donations, and bequests). Federal revenues are also known as federal governmental receipts. Compare with **offsetting collections** and **offsetting receipts.**

risk premium: The additional return that investors require to hold assets whose returns are more variable than those of riskless assets. The risk can arise from many sources, such as the possibility of default (in the case of corporate or municipal debt) or the volatility of interest rates or earnings (in the case of corporate stocks).

S corporation: A domestically owned corporation with no more than 100 owners who have elected to pay taxes under Subchapter S of the Internal Revenue Code. An S corporation is taxed like a partnership: It is exempt from the corporate income tax, but its owners pay individual income taxes on all of the firm's income, even if some of the earnings are retained by the firm.

saving rate: See **national saving** and **personal saving.**

savings bond: A nontransferable, registered security issued by the Treasury at a discount and in denominations from $50 to $10,000. The interest earned on savings bonds is exempt from state and local taxation; it is also exempt from federal taxation until the bonds are redeemed or reach maturity.

seigniorage: The gain to the government from the difference between the face value of minted coins put into circulation and the cost of producing them (including the cost of the metal used in the coins). Seigniorage is considered a means of financing and is not included in the budget totals. See **means of financing.**

sequestration: An enforcement mechanism established in the Balanced Budget and Emergency Deficit Control Act of 1985 that would result in the cancellation of budgetary resources available for a fiscal year. The mechanism enforced the discretionary spending limits and pay-as-you-go (PAYGO) procedures of that law, as amended. A sequestration of discretionary budget authority would occur in a fiscal year if the budget authority or outlays provided in appropriation acts exceeded the applicable discretionary spending limit for that year. A PAYGO sequestration would occur in a fiscal year if the total budgetary impact of laws affecting direct spending and revenues was not deficit neutral in that year. The discretionary spending limits and the sequestration procedure to enforce them expired on September 30, 2002. PAYGO and its sequestration procedure were rendered ineffective on December 2, 2002, when Public Law 107-312 reduced all PAYGO balances to zero. See **appropriation act, Balanced Budget and Emergency Deficit Control Act of 1985, budget authority, direct spending, discretionary spending limits, fiscal year, outlays, pay-as-you-go,** and **revenues.**

short-term interest rate: The interest rate earned by a debt instrument (such as a Treasury bill) that will mature within one year.

state and local government security (SLGS): A time deposit sold by the Treasury to issuers of state and local government tax-exempt debt to facilitate compliance with the Internal Revenue Code's *arbitrage provisions,* which restrict state and local governments from earning profits by investing bond proceeds in higher yielding investments.

statutory tax rate: A tax rate specified by law. In some cases, such as with individual and corporate income taxes, the statutory tax rate varies with the amount of taxable income. (For example, under the federal corporate income tax, the statutory tax rate for companies with taxable income below $50,000 is 15 percent, whereas the rate for corporations with taxable income greater than $18.3 million is 35 percent.) In other cases, the statutory tax rate is uniform. (For instance, the statutory federal tax rate on gasoline is 18.4 cents per gallon for all taxpayers.) Compare with **effective tax rate** and **marginal tax rate.**

Subchapter S corporation: See **S corporation.**

subsidy cost: See **credit subsidy.**

surplus: The amount by which the federal government's total revenues exceed its total outlays in a given period, typically a fiscal year. See **fiscal year, outlays,** and **revenues;** compare with **deficit.**

Tax Increase Prevention Act of 2007 (Public Law 110-166): This law provided relief from the individual alternative minimum tax for the tax year that ended December 31, 2007. See **alternative minimum tax.**

Treasury bill: A security issued by the Treasury with a maturity of 28, 91, or 182 days. Interest on a Treasury bill is calculated as the difference between the purchase price and the value paid at redemption.

Treasury bond: A fixed-rate, interest-bearing security issued by the Treasury that matures in 30 years.

Treasury inflation-protected security (TIPS): A marketable security with a maturity of 5, 10, or 20 years issued by the Treasury that is designed to protect investors from inflation. The principal of a TIPS is linked to the consumer price index, and at maturity, the security pays the greater of the original or the adjusted principal. The security makes semiannual interest payments based on a fixed rate of interest and the adjusted principal amount.

Treasury note: A fixed-rate, interest-bearing security issued by the Treasury with a maturity of 2, 5, or 10 years.

total factor productivity: See **productivity.**

trade balance: See **net exports.**

trade-weighted value of the dollar: The value of the U.S. dollar relative to the currencies of U.S. trading partners, with the weight of each country's currency equal to that country's share of U.S. trade. The *real trade-weighted value of the dollar* is an index of the trade-weighted value of the dollar whose movement is adjusted for the difference between U.S. inflation and inflation among U.S. trading partners. An increase in the real trade-weighted value of the dollar means that the price of U.S.-produced goods and services has increased relative to the price of foreign-produced goods and services. See **inflation.**

transfer payments: Payments made to a person or organization for which no current or future goods or services are required in return. Federal transfer payments include Social Security and unemployment benefits. (BEA)

trust funds: In the federal accounting structure, accounts designated by law as trust funds (regardless of any other meaning of that term). Trust funds record the revenues, offsetting receipts, or offsetting collections earmarked for the purpose of the fund, as well as budget authority and

outlays of the fund that are financed by those revenues or receipts. The federal government has more than 200 trust funds. The largest and best known finance major benefit programs (including Social Security and Medicare) and infrastructure spending (such as the Highway Trust Fund and the Airport and Airway Trust Fund). See **budget authority, offsetting collections, offsetting receipts, outlays,** and **revenues;** compare with **federal funds.**

U

nemployment rate: The number of jobless people who are available for work and are actively seeking jobs, expressed as a percentage of the labor force. (BLS) See **discouraged workers** and **labor force.**

unified budget: The entire federal budget, which consolidates all on-budget and off-budget outlays and revenues. See **off-budget, outlays,** and **revenues.**

unilateral transfers: Payments from sources within the United States to sources abroad (and vice versa) that are not made in exchange for goods or services. Examples include a private gift sent abroad, a pension payment from a U.S. employer to an eligible retiree living in a foreign country, or taxes paid to the United States by people living overseas.

unobligated balances: The portion of budget authority that has not yet been obligated. When budget authority is provided for one fiscal year, any unobligated balances at the end of that year expire and are no longer available for obligation. When budget authority is provided for a specific number of years, any unobligated balances are carried forward and are available for obligation during the years specified. When budget authority is provided for an unspecified number of years, the unobligated balances are carried forward indefinitely, until one of the following occurs: the balances are expended or rescinded, the purpose for which they were provided is accomplished, or no disbursements have been made for two consecutive years. See **budget authority, fiscal year,** and **obligation;** compare with **advance appropriation, forward funding,** and **obligation delay.**

user fee: Money that the federal government charges for services or for the sale or use of federal goods or resources that generally provide benefits to the recipients beyond those that may accrue to the general public. The amount of the fee is typically related to the cost of the service provided or the value of the good or resource used. In the federal budget, user fees can be classified as offsetting collections, offsetting receipts, or revenues. See **offsetting collections, offsetting receipts,** and **revenues.**

Yield: The average annual rate of return on an investment held over a period of time. For a fixed-income security, such as a bond, the yield is determined by several factors, including the security's interest rate, face value, and purchase price and the length of time that the security is held. The *yield to maturity* is the effective interest rate earned on a fixed-income security if it is held until the date on which it comes due for payment.

yield curve: The relationship formed by plotting the yields of otherwise comparable fixed-income securities against their terms to maturity. Typically, yields increase as maturities lengthen. The rate of that increase determines the "steepness" or "flatness" of the yield curve. Ordinarily, a steepening (or flattening) of the yield curve is taken to suggest that short-term interest rates are expected to rise (or fall). See **short-term interest rate** and **yield.**